Cultures of Globalization

Much has been written about the economic and political implications of the contemporary process of globalization. Much less has been written about the specific cultural implications. This book seeks to add to our knowledge of these latter by bringing together researchers from different disciplines with the common goal of exploring the emerging cultural relations among groups and individuals in terms of coherence and hybridity, identity and allegiance, and cooperation and conflict. As the world's peoples increasingly travel, work, trade, recreate, and otherwise communicate with each other, relative cultural isolation (and isolationism) is becoming less and less possible. What does this mean for cultural coherence, stability and identity across the planet? What have been the cultural implications of, and reactions to, this increasing global interdependence among peoples? From more global and theoretical perspectives to more empirical and case-specific approaches, the various authors attempt to come to terms with the ever evolving and complex cultural content of contemporary globalization.

This book was previously published as a special issue of *Globalizations*

Kevin Archer is Associate Chair of the Department of Geography at the University of South Florida. He received his Ph.D. degree from The Johns Hopkins University.

M. Martin Bosman is Associate Professor in the Department of Geography at the University of South Florida. He received his Ph.D. (Geography) from the University of Kentucky in 1999.

M. Mark Amen is Academic Programs Director for the Kiran C. Patel Center for Global Solutions at the University of South Florida and has been a member of the faculty in the Department of Government and International Affairs since 1982.

Ella Schmidt is Assistant Professor in the Interdisciplinary Social Sciences Program at USF St. Petersburg. She received her Ph.D. from the University of California at Davis.

Rethinking Globalizations

Edited by Barry Gills, University of Newcastle, UK

This series is designed to break new ground in the literature on globalization and its academic and popular understanding. Rather than perpetuating or simply reacting to the economic understanding of globalization, this series seeks to capture the term and broaden its meaning to encompass a wide range of issues and disciplines and convey a sense of alternative possibilities for the future.

1. Whither Globalization?
The Vortex of Knowledge and Globalization
James H. Mittelman

2. Globalization and Global History
Edited by Barry K. Gills, William R. Thompson

3. Rethinking Civilization
Communication and terror in the global village
Majid Tehranian

4. Globalization and Contestation
The New Great Counter-Movement
Ronaldo Munck

5. Global Activism
Ruth Reitan

6. Globalization, the City and Civil Society in Pacific Asia
Edited by Mike Douglass, K.C. Ho and Giok Ling Ooi

7. Challenging Euro-America's Politics of Identity
The Return of the Native
Jorge Luis Andrade Fernandes

8. The Global Politics of Globalization
"Empire" vs "Cosmopolis"
Barry K Gills

9. The Globalization of Environmental Crisis
Jan Oosthoek

10. Globalization as Evolutionary Process
Modeling Global Change
Edited by Geroge Modelski, Tessaleno Devezas and William R. Thompson

Cultures of Globalization

Coherence, Hybridity, Contestation

Edited by Kevin Archer, M. Martin Bosman, M. Mark Amen
and Ella Schmidt

Routledge
Taylor & Francis Group

LONDON AND NEW YORK

First published 2008 by Routledge
2 Park Square, Milton Park, Abingdon, Oxon, OX14 4RN

Simultaneously published in the USA and Canada
by Routledge
270 Madison Ave, New York NY 10016

Routledge is an imprint of the Taylor & Francis Group, an informa business

Transferred to Digital Printing 2009

© 2008 Kevin Archer, M. Martin Bosman, M. Mark Amen and Ella Schmidt

Typeset in Times Roman by Techset Composition, Salisbury, UK

British Library Cataloguing in Publication Data
A catalogue record for this book is available from the British Library

ISBN 10: 0-415-43970-1 (hbk)
ISBN 10: 0-415-49568-7 (pbk)

ISBN 13: 978-0-415-43970-1 (hbk)
ISBN 13: 978-0-415-49568-4 (pbk)

Contents

Locating Globalizations and Cultures

KEVIN ARCHER, M. MARTIN BOSMAN, M. MARK AMEN &
ELLA SCHMIDT

The investigation of globalization and culture is by no means a novel phenomenon on the agenda of the social sciences and humanities. What is new is the renewed and sustained intensity with which research has been rejoined and conducted on both sides of what others consider to be the globalization–culture dialectic. Our initial impetus to write about the relationship between globalization and culture was our realization that divergent positions in the literature stem from the faulty premise that we all know and understand, more or less, what we mean by the twin concepts of 'globalization' and 'culture'. Moreover, the latent assumption seems to have been that as scholars we, more or less, share similar if not the same views when we deploy these concepts. However, this is not only far from the case on both counts, it is also a deeply problematic assumption. Raymond Williams (1979, p. 154) famously admitted to the editors of the *New Left Review* about 'the number of times I've wished that I had never heard of the damn word [culture]. I have become more aware of its difficulties, not less, as I have gone on' (also see Williams, 1983, p. 87). As for defining globalization, consider Ulrich Beck's (2001, p. 19) recent frustration that 'globalization . . . is one of the most rarely defined, the most nebulous and misunderstood, as well as the most politically effective' terms in any language.

Indeed, we have known for some time now that culture is an extremely difficult concept to define. There is little if any consensus on a definition, as A. L. Kroeber and C. Kluckhorn (1952) found in their cataloguing of 164 different definitions of culture. More than 50 years hence, nothing has changed to improve this unsettled state of affairs, except that the number of definitions has increased to 305 (Baldwin *et al.*, 2006). While we have not counted the number of different definitions of globalization in the scholarly literature, we are convinced that it is as numerous (and still growing) as for culture in an area of scholarship that has only been a part of the social sciences for a few decades (Scholte, 2006). And yet, despite or perhaps because of these difficulties, social sciences and humanities scholars continue to rely heavily on discipline-specific uses and, in doing so, are effectively engaging in a dialogue of the deaf. As far as both concepts are concerned, we regard this problem of multiple definitions and multivalent meanings as hindering rather than illuminating further understanding of the relationship between globalization and culture.

We believe that the critical arena where knowledge advances can occur in the foreseeable future is in efforts to define and clarify the considerable and complicated nexus between these two keywords. Toward this end, in April 2006 we hosted two days of intense discussions in Tampa, Florida, with the scholars whose work on globalization and culture appears in this volume. Each of these researchers sent drafts of their work to all conference participants before our meetings. Discussants were invited to engage in a critical dialogue with one another about their draft papers. In light of these debates, the authors wrote second drafts for review and then finalized their work as it appears here.

The research in this volume can be placed in the context of a larger body of literature on globalizations and cultures. Arguably, Frederic Jameson's (1984) now canonical text, 'Postmodernism; or, the Cultural Logic of Late Capitalism', broke ground for what is now a vast amount of published work on this topic. According to Jameson, the relative autonomy of culture, presumably because of the erstwhile hegemony of the nation state, was 'destroyed by the logic of late capitalism' with the result that 'everything in our social life—from economic value and state power . . .— can be said to have become "cultural" in some original and as yet untheorized way' (p. 87). This hypothesis about what was happening both at the commanding heights of the economy and amongst the cultures of everyday life set off a vigorous and at times rancorous debate (Miyoshi, 1995) within the social sciences from which essentially two distinct approaches emerged: 'culture-of-globalization' (i.e., the cultural turn) and the 'globalization-of-culture' (i.e., the global turn). Those in the first group believe that the globalization of culture is merely an instrument of a revamped system of flexible capitalism, or what some now call 'cultural capitalism' (Moore, 2004), whereas the second group believes that globalization is marked by the hollowing out of national cultural spaces either consequent upon the retrenchment of the nation state or because culture continues to be a relatively autonomous sphere.

The 'Cultural Turn' in Globalization Studies

Perhaps one of the most enthusiastic endorsements for the 'cultural turn' in globalization studies has come from the sociologist Malcolm Waters (1995, pp. 9–10), who writes: 'We can expect the economy and the polity to be globalized to the extent that they are culturalized, that is to the extent that the exchanges that take place within them are accomplished symbolically. We would also expect that the degree of globalization is greater in the cultural arena than either of the other two.'

The cultural approach is by now prominent in several of the social sciences, including in economic geography which over the last two decades has carved out a rather impressive body of literature on the growing instrumentalization of urbanized cultures under the redefined parameters of late capitalism. For instance, according to Allen Scott (1997, p. 323):

> capitalism itself is moving into a phase in which the cultural forms and meanings of its output become critical if not dominating elements of productive strategy, and in which the realm of human culture as a whole is increasingly subject to commodification, i.e., supplied through profit-making institutions in decentralized markets. In other words, an ever-widening range of economic activity is concerned with producing and marketing goods and services that are infused in one way or another with broadly aesthetic or semiotic attributes.

This area of study has been called the 'new economic geography' of transnational capitalism because it highlights the constitutive role of culture in economic development and the myriad ways in which capital accumulation strategies are culturally encoded (Ley, 1996; Lee and Wills, 1997).

Others believe that the constitutive role of culture is critical for grasping the continued hegemony of capitalism in the form of globalization (Harvey, 1989, 1990). Culture, they assert, is increasingly being co-opted and deployed as a new accumulation strategy to broaden and deepen the frontiers of capitalism and to displace its inherent crisis tendencies. Some of the more recent empirical evidence for this claim is the incursion of the World Trade Organization (WTO) into cultural matters via the General Agreement on Trade in Services (GATS). This move is being contested by many governments and several non-governmental organizations (NGOs) through the invocation of the so-called *exception culturelle* in the areas of audio-visual products, food sovereignty, forests and ecosystem diversity, water and land rights and indigenous knowledges against GATS (Shiva, 1997).

Since the mid-1990s, the application of GATS has slowly but surely led to a redefinition of culture primarily if not exclusively within the parameters of neo-liberal capitalism. The presumption is that flourishing cultures go hand-in-glove with flourishing capitalism (Harrison and Huntington, 2000). As we mentioned earlier, this strategic articulation and subordination of culture to the requirements of capitalism is what has been called 'cultural capitalism' (Moore, 2004). This line of thinking is best exemplified by David Harvey (1989, 1990) and to a lesser extent by Fredric Jameson (1984, 1991) himself. These theorists have launched an unrelenting critique of cultural capitalism as a 'carnival for the elite' which enables politicians and policymakers to conceal growing socio-spatial inequalities, polarizations, and distributional conflicts between the haves and the have-nots. This critique is further underscored by their dismissal of culture as nothing more than a tool for economic regeneration through the 'mobilization of the spectacle' (Harvey, 1989), because the tourist and entertainment city requires the urban spectacle to reinforce place-marketing and residential development. Revathi Krishnaswamy (2002, p. 108) notes that neo-liberal globalization is 'thriving precisely by emptying out the subversive potential in culture and by incorporating various oppositional and alternative forms of cultural expression across the globe'. In short, for this group, culture is just another commodity available for consumption in the world's supermarkets. A related, more historical critique is that capitalism has always flourished because of its appetite for polymorphous, even postnational or diasporic cultures as a means for sustained growth and crisis displacement.

Others ascribe the cultural turn in globalization studies to more diverse areas of study. For instance, Giles Gunn (2001, p. 36) offers yet another explanation for the cultural turn in globalization studies. He asserts that the shift 'entails a recognition of the reciprocal relations between the economic and the cultural spheres, a recognition that cultures are exchanged along with commodities'.

Finally, scholars such as Vincent Tucker (1999, p. 12), writing from the perspective of the Third World, assert that major political and theoretical interventions there, including dependency and underdevelopment theory and import-substitution economic development strategies, failed partly because of the obsessive focus on economic and political forms of domination and exploitation at the expense of adequately accounting for 'the cultural dimensions of domination'. This oversight, according to Tucker, proved fatal because 'cultural analysis is central to any understanding of power and to any strategy of resistance or dependency reversal' (ibid.). There is indeed a lot to be said for this view. The writings of Franz Fanon (1965, 1967) and Ashis Nandy (1983), which prefigure the postcolonial and postnational critique of western capitalist modernity, align Tucker's position with their claim that to overcome debilitating conditions such as colonialism and imperialism required not only conventional methods of economic organization and political agitation, but also a battery of cultural weapons to decolonize the hearts and minds of the victims of historical oppression and exploitation. Over the years, this view has gained wider acceptance beyond the Third World. For instance, many now believe that the hegemonic power of late capitalism can no longer be viewed primarily as economic or military might, but as cultural hegemony (Tomlinson, 1991). This is what Joseph Nye (1990, 2002, 2004), writing about the decline of US hegemony, has referred to as 'soft power'. Accordingly, political resistance or social autonomy is also a matter of organizing counter-hegemonic cultural strategies and habits (Klein, 2005).

The 'Global Turn' in Cultural Studies

Stuart Hall (1992) and John Tomlinson (1999) were among the first to herald a 'global turn' in the study of culture. It was Tomlinson (1999, p. 1) who argued that 'globalization lies at the heart of modern culture; cultural practices lie at the heart of globalization'. One reason for the global turn in cultural studies is that scholars in this school of thought have typically studied mass-mediated forms of culture, including music, television, film and advertisements, fast foods and fashion—cultural forms that are relatively easily produced, circulated, adopted, recoded and recontextualized in multiple locations—as evidence and examples of the globalization of culture. According to Paul Jay (2001, p. 37), it is this focus on mass-mediated forms of symbolic and semiotic production and circulation that fostered the intersection of globalization theory and cultural studies. Suffice it to say for now that the 'cultural' and the 'global' have risen to new prominence in the social science scholarship of the present and the future (Robertson, 1990).

   According to Simon Gikandi (2000), the link between cultural and globalization studies is partly related to the dissolution of the nation state, hence, as Kevathi Krishnaswamy (2002, p. 107) put it, 'the notion, so central to the narrative of modernity, that cultures are naturally national'. This view underlies the analysis of David Held *et al.* (1999, p. 328), who claim that: 'Cultural globalization is transforming the *context* in which and the *means* through which national cultures are produced and reproduced, but its partial impact on the nature and efficacy of national cultures—on the hold and influence of these messages, values and content—is, as yet, harder to decipher.'

   For the 'globalization-as-culture' group, however, culture is not that easily enjoined due to its inherent counter-hegemonic properties vis-à-vis neo-liberal globalization. Rather, for this group, which is perhaps best exemplified by Arjun Appadurai (1990, 1996; also see Friedman, 1999; Nederveen Pieterse, 2001; Waters, 1995), contemporary globalization is not merely economic, but a system of multiple cultural articulations which are shaped by disjunctive space–time coordinates. In other words, globalization is as much if not more the product of inexorable and accelerated migratory cultural flows and electronic mass mediations beyond the space–time envelopes of the nation-state system and the successive socio-spatial fixes of global capitalism. Appadurai (1996) describes the production of new cultural landscapes or 'ethnoscapes' within which the nation-state system is decentered through the proliferation of global flows and disjunctures in a transnational or deterritorialized fashion. The result, according to Appadurai (1996, p. 33) is that a growing number of societies are now living in 'imagined worlds' instead of 'imagined (national) communities' *pace* Benedict Anderson (1983). On this understanding, globalization has effectively 'provincialized' national space, to borrow from Dipesh Chakrabarty (2001), particularly in the domain of cultural production. This is what Appadurai (1996, p. 4) refers to as the emergence of a new social 'imaginary'.

> Electronic mediation and mass migration mark the world of the present not as technically new forces, but as ones that seem to impel the work of the imagination ... This mobile and unforeseeable relationship between mass mediated and migratory audiences defines the core of the link between globalization and the modern ... [T]he work of the imagination, viewed in this context, is neither purely emancipatory nor entirely disciplined, but is a space of contestation in which individuals and groups seek to annex the global into their own practices of the modern.

In this context, the disjunctive power of culture has the potential to become a formidable political resource against the rapacity of neo-liberal globalization. We return to this view and discuss it more fully in the conclusion to this volume.

This understanding of the nexus between globalization and culture shares a great deal with and is indeed prefigured in the work of some of the pioneers of postcolonial theory such as Homi Bhabha (1994) and Edward Said (1993). Bhabha views the globalization of social and economic spaces as the production of 'unsatisfaction', a position similar to what Said (1999) calls the condition of 'homelessness' which, according to Bhabha, becomes the enabling condition of possibility for 'a global or transnational imaginary and its "cosmopolitan subjectivities"'(Bhabha, 1994, p. 204). Abdul JanMohamed's description (1992, p. 110) of Said's sense of 'homelessness' consequent upon globalization is particularly instructive in this context as well, partly because it moderates some of the 'alternate positivity, whether in the guise of truth or in the interest of alternative group "interests"'(ibid., p. 105) which lurks in the work of Appadurai. Said defines the condition of homelessness as:

> an enabling concept via Raymond Williams's articulation of Gramsci, with the civil and political space that hegemony cannot suture, a space in which 'alternative acts and alternative intentions which are not yet articulated as a social institution or even project' can survive. 'Homelessness', then, is a situation wherein utopian potentiality can endure. (JanMohamed, 1992, p. 105)

Hence, in concert with Bhabha and Said, Appadurai rejects the notion that globalization is a synonym for cultural imperialism or cultural capitalism (Petras, 1993; Ritzer, 1993, 2002). Appadurai insists that 'different societies appropriate the materials of modernity differently' (1996, p. 17) and he argues that 'images of the media are quickly moved into local repertoires of irony, anger, humor, and resistance'. Thus, Appadurai believes that globalization is in many respects the condition of possibility for 'resistance, irony, selectivity, and in general, *agency*' (1996, p. 7).

This view of globalization as active and agential cultural production and consumption more than as passive and coerced state of affairs under the hegemonic terms of a reconfigured Ameri-centric cultural capitalism is also endorsed by John Tomlinson (1999). The mono-cultural capitalist theorization of globalization by David Harvey (1989) and Fredric Jameson (1984, 1998a, 1998b, 1991), among others, according to Tomlinson (1999, p. 171), 'ignores the hermeneutic appropriation which is an essential part of the circulation of symbolic forms'. In other words, cultural production and consumption under the conditions of late capitalism do not travel in a unilinear, top-down manner from the rich to the poor worlds because the flows between geographical areas and across spatial scales always necessitate translation, interpretation, mutations, and adaptation—processes which are captured by Appadurai (1996) and the Center for Transcultural Studies' conceptions of 'vernacularization' and 'social imaginaries' (see Gaonkar and Lee, 2002).

This veritable 'globalization from the grassroots' approach foregrounds the 'impacted' or 'receiving' populations and countries which always already bring their own cultural resources and 'horizons of expectations' to bear in a fully dialectical and often unexpected way upon the imported goods and images of cultural capitalism. In other words, to reduce globalization to merely the cultural logic of global capitalism is far too simplistic because all goods and services are susceptible to recoding and rescripting by so-called 'impact' societies. From this perspective, the cultural impacts of neo-liberal capitalism cannot simply be read off from their goods and services. The meanings of goods and services are never self-formulated; consumers must act upon them in order to produce meaning. The paraphernalia of cultural capitalism contains 'blanks' which only its consumers can fill. And it is an act of vernacular interpretation that is ultimately required to fill the unavoidable cultural blanks in neo-liberal globalization.

This is of course not to suggest that the intercourse between the metropolitan centers of cultural capitalism and the (still) peripheral markets of developing societies are somehow equal in extent, intensity and scale. Globalization as 'vernacularization' (Appadurai, 1996) without an appreciation for the inherited and still considerable 'power geometries' (Massey, 1999) which structure virtually all cultural exchanges would be foolhardy to say the least. To talk about 'vernacularization' is, however, to temper notions of disempowerment and helplessness which often dominate conventional understandings of globalization. But, we fully agree with Revathi Krishnaswamy's (2002, p. 117) admonition that vernacularization 'does not make for a great big dialogic carnival'. Rather, and here the critics of Appadurai have a point, 'the desire of every culture or civilization to complete itself in/through the Other is clearly not played out on an even field' (ibid.). The combined and uneven power geometries of cultural capitalism as it relates to globalization are fairly clearly spelled out by R. Radhakrishnan (2001, p. 329):

> In a world structured hierarchically between East and West, developing and developed nations, is the longing of the West for completion from the East somehow considered not as drastic as the longing of the East for completion by the West? ... Let us say, [to use] fairly stereotypical characterizations just to make a point, the West is looking to the East for spiritual enhancement and enrichment and the East is looking to the West for technological enhancement. Which of the two needs for completion would be considered more dire? In a world-historical situation where materialism and technology are valorized more than spirituality and matters 'interior', it is inevitable that oriental dependency would position itself in a weaker position within the global structure.

We are fully aware that not all scholars on the culture side of the globalization–culture dialectic believe that globalization signals the end of the power of nationalized space and the rise of the multitudes through the production of a disjunctive world overflowing with autonomous and insurgent cultural desires *pace* Hardt and Negri (2000). And yet, because of the disproportionate weight of the argument on the economic side of the globalization–culture dialectic, we believe that it is worth reminding ourselves that 'hegemony is not prepackaged in Los Angeles, shipped out to the global village, and unwrapped in innocent minds' (O'Brien and Szeman, 2001, p. xi).

Gayatri Spivak (1998) for one has pointed out that we should not make light of influential new power geometries, including the financialization (Arrighi, 1994; Harvey, 2003; Martin, 2003) and mediatization of capitalism (Chomsky, 1988; McChesney, 1999) which have imposed formidable limits on the subaltern potentialities of strategic concepts such as cultural 'hybridization' (García Canclini, 1995; Nederveen Pieterse, 1995, 2001; Kraidy, 1999; Bhabha, 1994), 'indigenization' (Tobin, 1992; Ger, 1999; Tomlinson, 1999), 'creolization' (Hannerz, 1987, 1992) and 'vernacularization' (Appadurai, 1996; Hall, 2000). Premature affirmations of subaltern cultural agency and resistance which ignore the worsening socio-economic conditions within which specific translations and hybridizations must take place will only lead to more doom and gloom. As Stuart Hall (2000, p. 216) notes:

Strategies of difference are not able to inaugurate totally different forms of life (they do not work with the notion of a totalizing dialectical 'overcoming'). They cannot conserve older, traditional ways of life intact. ... However, difference does prevent any system from stabilizing itself as a fully sutured totality. It arises in the gaps and aporias which constitute potential sites of resistance, intervention and translation. Within these interstices lies the possibility of a disseminated set of vernacular modernities. Culturally, these cannot frontally stem the tide of westernizing techno-modernity. However, they continue to inflect, deflect and 'translate' its imperatives from below.

This view espoused by Hall, however, begs the following question: if vernacular globalizations, everyday globalizations from below (Brecher *et al.*, 2000), can somehow inflect, deflect or translate neo-liberal cultural capitalism just by 'culture jamming' (Klein, 2005) its strategies in unintended and unpredictable ways, why should the agents of the vernacular bother to produce their own weaponry (epistemological, symbolic or material)? After all, if we accept that what developing and subalternized populations and countries most desire is some form of modernization *sans* neo-colonialism and neo-imperialism, but consistent with the broader logic of the Enlightenment, as Simon Gikandi (2000) suggests, is not the deterritorialization of the nation state and the globalization of cultural flows providing them with what they desire, namely, 'strategies for entering and leaving modernity' (García Canclini, 1995) and, as Hall (2000) notes, 'to some extent on their own terms'? The more pertinent question, from the perspective of economic and cultural justice (Fraser, 1997), is whether such a cultural 'infrapolitics of subordinate groups' (Scott, 2005b) against neo-liberal globalization is sufficient to address the abjection of contemporary capitalism (Bauman, 1998). Alternatively, what vision of hope is there in theories of globalization which overwhelmingly portray the vast majority of the world's population as passive and unsuspecting consumers of cultural capitalism and thereby effectively condemn them to structural invisibility and subalternity (Bauman, 2004)?

The Culture–Globalization Dialectic as a Solution?

Fredric Jameson, who in many ways triggered this debate about the nexus between culture and late capitalism, has suggested that the contending visions of globalization which we have outlined may not necessarily be 'logically incompatible' in that they are 'dialectically related, at least on the mode of the unresolvable antinomy' (1998b, p. 57). Jameson's provocative recommendation for how to proceed is worth considering given the current impasse in the literature, namely, not to 'choose between these two very different views of the matter, but rather to intensify their incompatibility and opposition such that we can live this particular contradiction as our own historic form of Hegel's "unhappy consciousness"' (1998b, p. 64).

One option that the cultural and global turns often seem to forget is that the relationship between globalization and culture may be dialectical, if not fully equal. There are some scholars who hold fast to a dialectical view of globalization and culture and resist the temptation to *a priori* assign exclusive causality to either globalization or culture. For instance, in what might be construed as a local rebuttal to Fredric Jameson's (1984) more abstract formulation about the cultural logic of late capitalism, Allen Scott (1997, p. 325) insists on the productive tensions between culture and economy in his theorizations of late capitalism because of, as he puts it, the 'the intensity of the recursive relations between the cultural attributes of place and the logic of the local production system'. Arguing from the other side of the dialectic, others such as Lily Kong (2000, p. 3) believe that: 'while local cultures contribute to the nature of economic activity, economic activity is also a part of the culture-generating and innovation of particular places'.

However, as Krishnaswamy (2002, p. 115) reminds us, the recognition of mutuality between globalization and culture is often fleeting, for, as she notes, 'culture soon becomes privileged in ways that, at best, barely manage to do what Spivak wants, "keep the economic visible under erasure"'. She argues further that differences of opinion over primacy are 'too quickly reconfigured in cultural terms as a quarrel between those who see globalization as yielding the pleasures of cultural hybridity for the swarming multitudes and those who see globalization as a form of cultural imperialism over the wretched of the earth' (ibid.). In other words, some see the enemy as cultural imperialism (Falk, 1999; Harvey, 2003). This position is rather bluntly expressed by Jeremy Seabrook (2004) to the effect that 'globalization is a declaration of war on all other cultures'. Others paint even darker pictures of cultural balkanization accompanied by endless chaos (Kaplan, 2001; Barber, 1995). In other words, on each side of the dialectic enormous political and theoretical pressures are being brought to bear in the battle for hegemonic concept status.

There are moderating voices, however. Krishnaswamy (2002, p. 108) notes that 'the theoretical category culture appears to have become far too overblown and overdetermined to be politically effective in the age of neo-liberal globalization'. She then partly aligns herself with Harvey by expressing her reservations about the subaltern potential of culture. While we are not ready to go that far, we do agree that what needs to be questioned is where and under what conditions cultural hybridity, translation, inflection, deflection, and so on, is inherently destabilizing and disruptive of the cultural powers of the nation state and neo-liberal capitalism. We should not simply accept the utopian claims about the innate insurgent potentialities of interstitiality and unhomeliness and the production of cultural hybridities and heterogeneities as axiomatic. Rather we should ask whose interests are being served by these narratives. Do they represent the experiences of the postnational postgraduate middle to upper middle class experience (Toor, 2000), or do they reflect the conditions of the vast majority of global migrants who are both desperately poor and dangerously vulnerable (Hondagneu-Setolo, 2001; Parrenas, 2001)? In this context, we appreciate Malini Johar Schueller's (2004, p. 173) reservation that, along with many others in the globalization-of-culture school of thought, 'Bhabha presumes that the transnationals and the migrants produce contramodernity'. We also agree with her that, among others, 'Lisa Lowe in *Immigrant Acts* similarly suggests that Asian American cultural practices engage in a disidentification from the dominant culture' (ibid.; see Lowe, 1996).

Thus, we should not shy away from criticizing Appadurai and other postcolonial and postnational theorists for their relative silence on the question of unequal power relations which minimizes questions of structural inequality, systemic oppression and domination, and institutional discrimination (Winant, 2005). Indeed, we take very seriously Aijaz Ahmad's (1992, pp. 68–69) critique of cultural hybridization and its associated cultural politics of globalization. Ahmed argues that this condition has been enabled precisely because of its complicity with the transnational capitalist class which privileges the position of elite migrants, Robert Reich (1991) and Ulf Hannerz's (1996) 'symbolic analysts' or what Leslie Sklair (2001, p. 295) calls the 'globalizing bureaucrats, politicians and professionals'.

Like Bhabha's and to an extent Nederveen Pieterse's hybridization model, Appadurai's view of globalization as disjunctive flows is open to the criticism that on the whole it tends to ignore ongoing and in many cases worsening gender, race, and class exploitations which are generated by neo-liberal capitalism (Bond, 2006). Instead, Appadurai's theorization of globalization, which is more or less typical of postcolonial and postnational, theories has the tendency to slip into an 'optimistic position that merges into a postmodern celebration of difference and differentiation' (Krishnaswamy, 2002, p. 115). In addition to the inclination to affirm 'cosmopolitanism as an expression of the transnational mobility of more affluent groups' (Roudometof, 2005, p. 65) and as 'transnationalism' which is 'typically connected to recent (and poor) immigrant cohorts' (ibid.), the rhetorical celebration of cultural differences in public speech has resulted in a 'sense of falling away of those structures that had condemned whole segments of [the] population to silence and subalternity' (Krishnaswamy, 2002, p. 115).

Krishnaswamy indicts the work of the Mexican scholar, Néstor García Canclini who in her view makes light of the power of neo-liberal capitalism and all too easily associates culture as hybridization with globalization creating enabling conditions for the proliferation of new cultural formations. García Canclini's work, in Krishnaswamy's (2002, p. 115) words, 'gives ample ammunition to utopian visions of an immense global urban intercultural festival with neither a center nor a dominant cultural mode'. In other words, there is little acknowledgement of the continuing role of massive concentrations of economic and political power in the structuring of combined and uneven relations of economic distribution and relations of cultural recognition (Fraser, 1997). Instead, what is called for is a better understanding of the globalization of culture and the culture of globalization as 'a hegemonizing process, in the proper Gramscian sense' (Hall, 2000, p. 210).

As such, we need to resist the temptation of *a priori* assuming that globalization leads to either cultural heterogeneity or homogeneity absent a careful investigation. As Stuart Hall (2000, p. 215) notes, although globalization is 'structured in dominance', it 'cannot control or saturate everything in its orbit. Indeed, it produces as one of its unintended effects subaltern formations and emergent tendencies which it cannot control but must try to "hegemonize" or harness to its wider purposes. It is a system for *con-forming* difference, rather than a convenient synonym for the obliteration of difference'. In other words, as we have already argued, cultural matters are not a mere synonym for cultural capitalism. However, notwithstanding Hall's advice, even he in the end appears to bias heterogeneity and the perdurability of culture in the face of globalization. In other words, Hall joins Appadurai (1996, 2001) in asserting that it is globalization itself which actually produces the 'subaltern proliferation of difference' or creates 'what Homi Bhabha calls "the borderline time" of minorities' (Hall, 2000, p. 216).

Thus, Hall's otherwise careful formulation echoes the radical position of García Canclini as rendered by Krishnaswamy (2002). Consider Hall's (2000, pp. 215–216) argument that because of the polyvalent cultural politics of globalization the 'classical Enlightenment binary between Traditionalism and Modernity is displaced by a disseminated set of vernacular modernities'. In particular, consider his view that this cultural politics empowers subaltern societies to 'enter "modernity", acquire the fruits of its technologies, and yet do so to some extent on their terms' (ibid.). In the end, even a sophisticated theorist like Hall tends to minimize the enormous costs and obstacles associated with the strategic politics of cultural hybridization, however cautious or calculated (Scott, 2005a, b).

And yet we continue to have strong reservations about the heavy-handed economic and cultural determinisms of those who see the production and circulation of global cultural signs and objects only as coercive impositions over and above the heads of subaltern populations which are thereby rendered as unwitting and naïve dupes of cultural capitalism. We are more interested in Ryan Dunch's (2002, p. 304) position that 'establishing the audience perception of and response to a given cultural product is very difficult to do, and it is quite a different problem from analyzing the cultural attributes of the product itself'. In other words, outlining and explaining the economic dynamics and cultural attributes of globalization as cultural capitalism (Jameson, 1984) does not necessarily tell us anything meaningful about the response- or impact-side of globalization; that is to say, how it is actually understood, interpreted, employed, reshaped, resisted, or even rejected by the targeted consumers of its material and symbolic content. The one-sided study of the discourses and practices of globalization from the perspective of the sending countries is considerably different from the study of the cultural experiences of the so-called globalized multitudes themselves.

In Search of a New Direction

Our invitation to the authors whose work follows was motivated by our concern that the cultural and global turns were incomplete and that something more could be said than that they are dialectically related. If indeed some kind of reciprocity, albeit asymmetrical, constitutes the current globalization–culture dialectic, precisely what does that relationship look like? Can we identify a new synthesis or way of explaining this relationship? The papers that follow deal with various dimensions of the nexus between culture and globalization and they do so from a number of distinct disciplinary, geographical, socio-political, and economic contexts. In their diverse approaches to the multiple cultural articulations of globalization and the equally varied global dimensions of culture, these authors represent a wide range of scholarly images of how people are making sense of the globalizing world in which they live.

Peter Marcuse and David Wilson treat globalization as a *force majeure* to which national and local cultural agents conform. Marcuse holds that leaders in the United States promote a regime culture that reinforces the power of the regime at both national and global scales. His analysis of the manner in which the International Freedom Center at the World Trade Center was handled illustrates the underlying economic interests of this regime culture and the detrimental effects this has on the humanist/arts sense of culture, an effect induced by globalization and which Marcuse labels 'instrumentalized'.

Wilson points out that the 'accelerated global-speak' in Cleveland, Ohio, and Indianapolis, Indiana, since 1990 stems from globalization—a planetary discursive trope that is accommodated at the local level by the mayors of these two cities. The result has been a new kind of socio-spatial polarization, induced by government rhetoric for the purpose of allowing capital to transform these cities. As Wilson notes, this kind of political leadership has increased the vagaries of investment, production, and business, making these rust-belt cities more vulnerable to uneven economic development and the further marginalization of low-income African-American communities.

Sallie Marston, Keith Woodward, and John Paul Jones, III view the global not as a macro-cultural force but rather as co-constituted by people in their everyday local lives. Marston *et al.* explicitly adopt this theoretical position in their critique of spatial ontologies they believe underlie various theories of globalization. They propose a 'flat ontology' wherein the site is a material localization and individual sites are connected across distant places. Their case study of popular filmmaking in Lagos, Nigeria (Nollywood) proposes rethinking what globalization entails.

Jan Nederveen Pieterse offers a theoretically informed and empirically rich interpenetration of the 'global' and the 'local' in his assessment of multiculturalism. Nederveen Pieterse supports his claims concerning multiculturalism and identification by referring to the murder of Theo van Gogh and the Danish cartoon episode, both of which illustrate that 'far off conflicts' are part of multiculturalism conflicts. He goes further, however, by claiming that multiculturalism is global, not just national, engagement (e.g., different significations of Muslim women's headscarves) and does not mean consensus (e.g., reactions in Britain about the Iraq war).

Finally, Patricia Price and Ella Schmidt examine how collectivities of people make use of culture and globalization in their daily lives. Price employs the term *Latinidad* as a 'situational coherence of place-specific social relations' in her street study of *Calle Ocho*, that section of Eighth Street that runs through Miami's Little Havana neighborhood. She considers this street a channel that may or may not bring about solidarity among Latinos. It is a place where people are brought together from increasingly disparate places and walks of life. In *Calle Ocho* people express *Latinidad* as a contingent, cultural event that makes globalization a lived experience through their encounters with one another.

Schmidt is interested in understanding how the temporal and spatial compressions of globalization come to bear on the cultures of people 'on the move' across the territorial borders of nation states. She rejects dichotomous models that limit the analysis of cultural reproduction/reinvention in newly created transnational social spaces because they prevent actors from belonging to, and impacting on, more than one cultural system at the same time. Focusing on the Hñähñu of Hidalgo, Mexico, and Clearwater, Florida, Schmidt explains how migrants transcend geopolitical obstacles and manage to recreate and promote traditional practices in their in new cultural spaces.

Together, these papers represent a diversity of scholarly images concerning just how culture and globalization intersect. Some do so from the lived experiences of people in many parts of the world; and others from the broader, if not systemic and global, confines of regimes, flat ontologies, inherited rhetorics, and multiculturalism. Some transcend the place–space parameters of traditional disciplinary scholarship and others are grounded in the everyday realities of life on the streets of Clearwater and Miami. From these cases, we can learn more about the social actors themselves who are actively and reflexively producing new cultural forms in the context of globalization. Of equal value are those analyses that allow us to consider, at a more abstract if no less real level, whether globalization is a potentially unmediated imposition on culture. We return to these studies in the conclusion where, in reflecting on the rich materials that follow, we adopt a 'global imaginary' approach to the cultural implications of globalization—an approach that ties these papers together in a new understanding of how both institutions and people make sense of the world in which they are engaged.

References

Ahmad, A. (1992) *In Theory: Classes, Nations, Literatures* (London: Verso).

Anderson, B. (1983) *Imagined Communities: Reflections on the Origins and Spread of Nationalism* (London: Verso).

Appadurai, A. (1990) Disjuncture and difference in the global cultural economy, *Public Culture*, 7(2), pp. 295–310.

Appadurai, A. (1996) *Modernity at Large: Cultural Dimensions of Globalization* (Minneapolis, MN: University of Minnesota Press).

Appadurai, A. (2001) The globalization of archaeology and heritage: a discussion with Arjun Appadurai, *Journal of Social Archaeology*, 1(1), pp. 35–49.

Arrighi, G. (1994) *The Long Twentieth Century* (New York: Verso).

Baldwin, J. R., Faulkner, S. L., Hecht, M. L. & Lindsley, S. L. (Eds) (2006) *Redefining Culture: Perspectives Across the Discipline* (London: Lawrence Erlbaum Associates, Publishers).

Barber, B. (1995) *Jihad vs. McWorld* (New York: Times Books).

Bauman, Z. (1998) Globalization: the human consequences (Cambridge: Polity Press).

Bauman, Z. (2004) *Wasted Lives: Modernity and Its Outcasts* (Cambridge: Polity Press).

Beck, U. (2001) *What is Globalization?* Trans. P. Camiller (Cambridge: Polity Press).

Bhabha, H. K. (1994) *The Location of Culture* (London: Routledge).

Bond, P. (2006) *Looting Africa: The Economics of Exploitation* (New York: Zed Books).

Brecher, J., Costello, T. & Smith, B. (2000) *Globalization From Below: The Power of Solidarity* (Boston: South End Press).

Chakrabarty, D. (2001) *Provincializing Europe: Postcolonial Thought and Historical Difference* (Delhi: Oxford University Press).

Chomsky, N. (1988) *Manufacturing Consent: The Political Economy of the Mass Media* (New York: Pantheon Books).

Dunch, R. (2002) Beyond cultural imperialism: cultural theory, Christian missions, and global modernity, *History and Theory*, 41 (October), pp. 301–325.

Falk, R. (1999) *Predatory Globalization: A Critique* (Malden, MA: Polity Press).

Fanon, F. (1965) *Studies in a Dying Colonialism* (New York: Monthly Review Press).

Fanon, F. (1967) *Black Skin, White Mask* (New York: Grove Press).

Fraser, N. (1997) From distribution to recognition? Dilemmas of justice in a 'postsocialist age', in: N. Fraser, *Justice Interruptus: Critical Reflections on the 'Post-Socialist' Condition* (New York: Routledge).

Friedman, J. (1999) The hybridization of roots and the abhorrence of the bush, in: M. Featherstone & S. Lash (Eds) *Spaces of Culture: City-Nation-World* (London: Sage), pp. 230–255.

Gaonkar, D. P. & Lee, B. (Eds) (2002) New imaginaries, Special Issue, *Public Culture*, 12(1).

García Canclini, N. (1995) *Hybrid Cultures: Strategies for Entering and Leaving Modernity*, Trans. C. L. Chiappari & S. L. López (Minneapolis, MN and London: University of Minnesota).

Ger, G. (1999) Localizing in the global village: local firms competing in global markets, *California Management Review*, 41(4), pp. 64–83.

Gikandi, S. (2000) Globalization and the claims of postcoloniality, *South Atlantic Quarterly*, 100(3), pp. 627–658.

Gunn, G. (2001) Introduction: special topic: globalizing literary studies, *PMLA*, 116(1), pp. 16–31.

Hall, S. (1992) The question of cultural identity, in S. Hall, D. Held & T. McGrew (Eds) *Modernity and its Futures* (Cambridge: Polity Press), pp. 273–325.

Hall, S. (2000) Conclusion: The Multi-Cultural Question, in: B. Hesse (Ed.) *Un/Settled Multiculturalisms: Diasporas, Entanglements, Transruptions* (London: Zed Books), pp. 209–241.

Hannerz, U. (1987) The world in Creolization, *Africa*, 57(4), pp. 546–559.

Hannerz, U. (1992) *Cultural Complexity: Studies in the Social Organization of Meaning* (New York: Columbia University Press).

Hannerz, U. (1996) *Transnational Connections: Culture, People, Places* (London: Routledge).

Hardt, M. & Negri, A. (2000) *Empire* (Cambridge, MA: Harvard University Press).

Harrison, L. E. & Huntington, S. P. (2000) *Culture Matters: How Values Shape Human Progress* (New York: Basic Books).

Harvey, D. (1989) *The Urban Experience* (Baltimore, MD: Johns Hopkins University Press).

Harvey, D. (1990) *The Condition of Postmodernity: An Inquiry into the Origins of Cultural Change* (Cambridge, MA: Blackwell).

Harvey, D. (2003) *The New Imperialism* (Oxford: Oxford University Press).

Held, D., McGrew, A., Goldblatt, D. & Perraton, J. (1999) *Global Transformations* (Stanford, CA: Stanford University Press).

Hondagneu-Setolo, P. (2001) *Doméstica: Immigrant Workers Cleaning and Caring in the Shadows of Affluence* (Berkeley: University of California Press).

JanMohamed, A. (1992) Worldliness-without-world, homelessness-as-home: toward a definition of the specular border intellectual, in: M. Sprinker (Ed.) *Edward Said: A Critical Reader* (Oxford: Blackwell), pp. 96–120.

Jameson, F. (1984) Postmodernism, or the cultural logic of late capitalism, *New Left Review* 1(146), pp. 53–91.

Jameson, F. (1991) *Postmodernism, or the Cultural Logic of Late Capitalism* (London: Verso).

Jameson, F. (1998a) *The Cultural Turn: Selected Writings on Postmodernism, 1983–1998* (New York: Verso Books).

Jameson, F. (1998b) Notes on globalization as a philosophical issue, in F. Jameson & M. Miyoshi (Eds) *The Cultures of Globalization* (Durham, NC: Duke University Press), pp. 54–77.

Jay, P. (2001) Beyond discipline? Globalization and the future of English, *PMLA*, 116(1), pp. 32–47.

Kaplan, R.D. (2001) *The Coming Anarchy: The Shattering the Dreams of the Post-Cold War* (New York: Vintage).

Klein, N. (2005) Culture jamming: ads under attack, in: L. Amoore (Ed.) *The Global Resistance Reader* (New York: Routledge), pp. 437–444.

Kong, L. (2000) Culture, economy, polity: trends and developments, *Geoforum*, 31(4), pp. 385–390.

Kraidy, M. M. (1999) The global, the local, and the hybrid: a native ethnography of glocalization, *Critical Studies in Mass Communication*, 16, pp. 456–476.

Krishnaswamy, R. (2002) The criticism of culture and the culture of criticism: at the intersection of postcolonialism and globalization theory, *Diacritics*, 32(2), pp. 106–126.

Kroeber, A. L. & Kluckhorn, C. (1952) *Culture: A Critical Review of Concepts and Definitions* (Cambridge, MA: Harvard University Press).

Lee, R. & Wills, J. (Eds) (1997) *Geographies of Economies* (London: Arnold).

Ley, D. (1996) Urban geography and cultural studies, *Urban Geography*, 17(6), pp. 475–477.

Lowe, L. (1996) *Immigrant Acts: On Asian American Cultural Politics* (Durham, NC: Duke University Press).

Martin, R. (2003) Geography financialized, in: S. Aronowitz & H. Gautney (Eds) *Implicating Empire: Globalization and Resistance in the 21st Century World Order* (New York: Basic Books), pp. 211–228.

Massey, D. (1999) Imagining globalization: power-geometries of space-time, in: A. Brah, M. J. Hickman & M. Mac an Ghaill (Eds) *Global Futures: Migration, Environment and Globalization* (London: Macmillan Press).

McChesney, R. W. (1999) *Rich Media, Poor Democracy: Communication Politics in Dubious Times* (Urbana and Chicago: University of Illinois Press).

Miyoshi, M. (1995) Sites of resistance in the global economy, *Boundary*, 22(1), pp. 61–84.

Moore, P. (2004) Rethinking the idea of profit in professional communication and cultural capitalism, *Journal of Business and Technical Communication*, 18(2), pp. 233–246.

Nandy, A. (1983) *The Intimate Enemy: Loss and Recovery of Self Under Colonialism* (Delhi: Oxford University Press).

Nederveen Pieterse, J. (1994) Globalization as hybridization, *International Sociology*, 9(2), pp. 161–184.

Nederveen Pieterse, J. (1995) Globalization as hybridization, in: M. Featherstone, S. Lash & R. Robertson (Eds) *Global Modernities* (London: Sage), pp. 45–68.

Nederveen Pieterse, J. (2001) Hybridity, so what? The anti-hybridity backlash and the riddles of recognition, *Theory, Culture and Society*, 18(2–3), pp. 219–245.

Nye, J. (1990) *Bound to Lead: The Changing Nature of American Power* (New York: Basic Books).

Nye, J. (2002) *The Paradox of American Power* (New York: Oxford University Press).

Nye, J. (2004) *Soft Power: The Means to Success in World Politics* (New York: Public Affairs).

O'Brien, S. & Szeman, A. (Eds) (2001) Special Issue on 'Anglophone Literatures and Global Culture', *South Atlantic Quarterly*, 100(3), pp. –xi.

Parrenas, R. S. (2001) *Servants of Globalization: Women, Migration and Domestic Work* (Stanford, CA: Stanford University Press).

Petras, J. (1993) Cultural imperialism in the late 20th century, *Journal of Contemporary Asia*, 23(2), pp. 139–148.

Radhakrishnan, R. (2001) Globalization, desire, and the politics of representation, *Comparative Literature*, 53(4), pp. 315–332.

Ray, L. J. & Sayer, A. (1999) *Culture and Economy After the Cultural Turn* (London: Sage).

Reich, R. (1991) *The Work of Nations: Preparing Ourselves for 21st Century Capitalism* (New York: Alfred A. Knopf).

Ritzer, G. (1993) *The McDonaldization of Society: An Investigation into the Changing Character of Social Life* (Thousand Oaks, CA: Pine Forge Press).

Ritzer, G. (Ed.) (2002) *McDonaldization: The Reader* (Thousand Oaks, CA: Pine Forge Press).

Robertson, R. (1990) Mapping the global condition: globalization as the central concept, in: M. Featherstone (Ed.) *Global Cultures* (London: Sage Publications), pp. 15–30.

Roudometof, V. (2005) Transnationalism and cosmopolitanism: errors of globalism, in: R. P. Appelbaum & W. I. Robinson (Eds) *Critical Globalization Studies* (New York: Routledge), pp. 65–74.

Said, E. (1993) *Culture and Imperialism* (New York: Vintage).

Said, E. (1999) *Out of Place—A Memoir* (New York: Knopf).

Scholte, J. A. (2006) Globalization studies: past and future: a dialogue of diversity, *Globalizations*, 1(1), pp. 102–110.

Schueller, M. J. (2004) Postcolonial American studies, *American Literary History*, 16(1), pp. 162–175.

Scott, A. (1997) The cultural economy of cities, *International Journal of Urban and Regional Research*, 21(2), pp. 323–339.

Scott, J. C. (2005a) Beyond the war of words: cautious resistance and calculated conformity, in: L. Amoore (Ed.) *The Global Resistance Reader* (New York: Routledge), pp. 392–410.

Scott, J. C. (2005b) The infrapolitics of subordinate groups, in: L. Amoore (Ed.) *The Global Resistance Reader* (New York: Routledge), pp. 65–73.

Seabrook, J. (2004) Localizing cultures, *Korea Herald*, 13 January, posted at the *Global Policy Forum*. Available at http://www.globalpolicy.org/globaliz/cultural/2004/.

Shiva, V. (1997) *Biopiracy: The Plunder of Nature and Knowledge* (Boston: South End Press).

Sklair, L. (2001) *The Transnational Capitalist Class* (Oxford: Blackwell).

Spivak, G. (1998) Cultural talks in the hot peace: revisiting the 'Global Village', in: P. Cheah & B. Robbins (Eds) *Cosmopolitics: Thinking and Feeling Beyond the Nation* (Minneapolis, MN: Minnesota University Press), pp. 329–350.

Tobin, J. J. (1992) *Re-Made in Japan: Everyday Life and Consumer Taste in a Changing Society* (New Haven, CT: Yale University Press).

Tomlinson, J. (1991) *Cultural Imperialism: An Introduction* (Baltimore, MD: Johns Hopkins University).

Tomlinson, J. (1999) *Globalization and Culture* (Chicago: Chicago University Press).

Toor, S. (2000) Indo-chic: the cultural politics of consumption in post-liberalizing India, *SOAS Literary Review*, 2 (July), pp. 1–30.

Tucker, V. (1999) The myth of development: a critique of Eurocentric discourse, in: R. Munck & D. O'Hearn (Eds) *Critical Development Theory: Contributions to a New Paradigm* (London: Zed Books), pp. 1–26.

Waters, M. (1995) *Globalization* (London: Routledge).

Williams, R. (1979) *Politics and Letters: Interviews with New Left Review* (London: New Left Books).

Williams, R. (1983 [1976]) *Keywords*, revised ed. (New York: Oxford University Press).

Winant, H. (2005) Globalization and racism: at home and abroad, in: R. P. Appelbaum & W. I. Robinson (Eds) *Critical Globalization Studies* (New York: Routledge), pp. 121–130.

Kevin Archer is former chair of the Department of Geography at the University of South Florida. He received his Ph.D. degree from The Johns Hopkins University. His research interests include globalizing cities and socio-spatial polarization as well as the production of post-industrial nature. Archer is co-editor of and contributor to *Relocating Global Cities: From the Center to the Margins* (Rowman & Littlefield, 2006).

M. Martin Bosman is Associate Professor in the Department of Geography at the University of South Florida. He received his MA (Geography) from the University of Natal in the Republic of South Africa and his Ph.D. (Geography) from the University of Kentucky in 1999. He has published widely on the geography of the digital divide and his current research is on globalization and newly emerging city regions. Bosman is assistant editor of *Globalizations* and co-editor of and contributor to *Relocating Global Cities: From the Center to the Margins* (Rowman & Littlefield, 2006).

M. Mark Amen is Academic Programs Director for the Kiran C. Patel Center for Global Solutions at the University of South Florida and has been a member of the faculty in the Department of Government and International Affairs since 1982. He received his doctorate in Political Science from the Graduate Institute of International Studies (Geneva, Switzerland) in 1978 and his research interests are in global political economy, theories of the state, and globalizing cities. Amen is Deputy Editor of *Globalizations* and co-editor of and contributor to *Relocating Global Cities: From the Center to the Margins* (Rowman & Littlefield, 2006).

Ella Schmidt is Assistant Professor in the Interdisciplinary Social Sciences Program at USF St. Petersburg. She received her MA in Cultural Anthropology from the Université Paris VII-Jussieu and her Ph.D. from the University of California at Davis. She has done research on Mexican farmworkers in West Central Florida and changes in their construction of identity. Currently her research focuses on transnational Mexican migrants in Clearwater and Valle del Mezquital, Hidalgo, Mexico and the creation of new social formations in both home and host communities.

The Production of Regime Culture and Instrumentalized Art in a Globalizing State

PETER MARCUSE

Generic Culture, Regime Culture, and the Question of Power

Generic Culture

Generic culture, culture as habits of thought and patterns of behavior, is a quite different concept from culture in the humanist sense; generic culture focuses on habits of thought and patterns of behavior, whereas humanist culture is concerned with the arts and humanities in the various aspects. In this paper I want to discuss each in today's world, and conclude with an argument about the impact of globalization on each. To begin with generic culture: the classic discussion is that of A. L. Kroeber and Clyde Kluckhohn (1963), on which a widely accepted formal definition is based: 'all that in human society which is socially rather than biologically transmitted ... a learned complex of knowledge, belief, art, morals, law, and custom ... learned patterns of behaviour, aspects ... that act below conscious levels ... and patterns of thought and perception' (Hoult, 1974, p. 93; Marshall, 1998, pp. 134–140). Anthony King (1991) calls it the 'anthropological view of culture'. Raymond Williams speaks of the 'social' definition of culture, in which culture is a description of a particular way of life, which expresses certain meanings and values not only in art and learning but also in institutions and ordinary behaviour', and points out that most meanings of culture overlap (Miles, forthcoming, p. 3, quoting Williams, 1965, p. 57; Williams, 1984, p. 76 adds: 'culture is one of the most complicated words in the English language').

The term 'culture' might be applied to the culture of a nation, ethnicity, an occupation, an architectural approach, an attitude towards history, the interpretation of a wide variety of symbols, and many other subjects. In each case, there must be the referent to a particular group whose habits of thought and patterns of behavior are under discussion, and a specific topic to which those habits and patterns relate. Let me call it 'generic culture', for want of a better term.

That the term 'culture' in its various aspects can be applied to a wide variety of subjects (group and subject referents) hardly needs demonstration. Examples are plentiful. I am just reading a piece titled 'Cultural Expectations of Homeownership: Explaining changing Legal Definitions of Flat "Ownership" within Britain' (Robertson, 2006). The referent group is the 'popular classes' in Britain; the referent subject is the preference for home ownership. In my field, urban planning, Bishwapriya Sanyal has published a volume called *The Cultures of Planning* (2005), in which he argues that planning professionals in different countries (the referent group) have different conceptions of the scope, aims, and methods of planning.

There are many aspects of culture, and some that change or lose their usefulness but linger on also; culture cannot be limited by a functionalist definition, and changes with time and individual as well as social experience ... It is a different and complex aspect of generic culture, related to but independent of, and perhaps more long-lasting than, regime culture; what one might call life-style cultures. The mix is one with which I have personal experience. I was born in Germany. Our family immigrated in the 1930s and were part of an exiled culture in the US that drew on a nationalistic current that still identified them with Germany, but not in a way that was then functional. Some went back and others didn't. My parents did not go back because they liked completely different aspects of US culture. They liked the freedom and the looseness and the 'you don't wear ties' and 'you don't say Sir and Mr. to your friends,' also an aspect of culture—perhaps the life-style aspect of culture. The German pattern supports a hierarchical approach that can easily support militarism, but it is not necessarily thus related. It refers to the way of life, or life-styles, aspect of culture. So there are ideologies that support particular practices of power, and the habits and cultural patterns that reflect such ideologies I call regime cultures.

But in none of these generic senses or applications is culture something autonomous, without a history and without links to economic, social, and political patterns and events, in other words, without a material basis. More specifically, culture reflects, among other things, a specific distribution of power. For any given event or structure, 'culture' is not the beginning of an explanation, but comes somewhere down the line. Culture can be manipulated in the service of power, sometimes deliberately, sometimes unconsciously, but with the same result. It may be that we would want to call the conscious manipulation of culture in the interests of power the construction of ideology, much in the way that Karl Mannheim (1968) used that term.[1] Others have used the term 'tropes' to convey much the same meaning, for instance, when David Wilson (this volume) speaks of the trope of globalization, he is saying there is a culture of globalization, and I argue in the conclusion to this article that that is a culture using the pressures of really existing globalization to reinforce existing relations of power.

Regime Culture

I want to use the term 'regime culture' for that manipulation of culture, that ideology, that trope, that reinforces the power of presently established regimes, using 'regime' in the sense of the particular constellation of state and private actors, groups, institutions that effectively govern a political unit at any given historical period.[2] It is a level of culture or a definition of culture, a form of culture, which I want to argue reflects the internalization of the ideology of the dominant powers. The divine right of kings is an ideology that was absorbed into the culture of serfdom and induced obedience and a willingness to serve among peasants in the feudal period. Nationalism was an ideology that was absorbed into the generic culture of the modern period after being internalized and absorbed into popular culture in the French Revolution, as part of the resistance to feudalism and to the aristocracy, inclusive centrally to a bourgeois ideology that reflected the rights to power of the bourgeoisie. The need for *Lebensraum* in Germany before the First World War was an ideology that was absorbed into the acquiescence to militarism, the pride in the military power that was fairly characteristic of the regime culture of Germany before the First World War.

But the examples of regime cultures are plentiful. The myth of the betrayal of Germany in the First World War by the Kaiser was absorbed ultimately by the Nazis and became part of an internalized culture which supported the Nazi rule. Similarly, the ideology of the inferiority of blacks was internalized into racism in support of the power of slaveholders. The cultural acceptance of Orientalism, as Edward Said explicates it, is the characterization of Oriental cultures as 'different', as 'the other', and internalized into support for colonialism. And, in globalization, as I read David Wilson's paper in this volume, the culture of globalism is really an internalization of the neo-liberalist ideology that is purveyed by those that profit most from globalization, particularly the transnational corporations and the imperial power which supports them. In the context of United States imperialism today, the chauvinism that one sees with the flying of American flags and the reaction to the World Trade Center attacks and the initial support for the war in Iraq was based on the internalization of a nationalistic ideology. It is a reflection of power relations both internationally and domestically, and becomes part of a regime culture.

There are a few instances where one might also think, symmetrically, of a culture of resistance, the negative of a prevailing culture. Thus, the slogan of liberty, equality, and fraternity became part of the culture of the French Revolution. And of course the liberties embodied in the Bill of Rights attached to the US Constitution have become part of the political culture in this country, often resting uneasily with its current regime culture, as the debate about the Torture Bill, dealing with the legal rights of 'enemy combatants' in CIA custody, reflects (Savage, 2006). As the cultural internalization of the resistance to the power first of the monarchy and then later during the course of the revolution to a limited portion of the bourgeoisie, union solidarity as a cultural phenomenon is to some extent an internalization of the impact of class differences in society and class conflict as a characteristic of society. Union membership, or working class membership, becomes in part the cultural manifestation of that class position.

In the United States today, we have a semi-official regime culture, produced, implemented, and indeed enforced, by the regime in power. George W. Bush is unusually explicit about his goals: 'I got into politics initially because I wanted to help change a culture', he said. He wanted to banish the old 1960s 'if it feels good, do it' culture and 'help usher in an era of personal responsibility'.[3]

And the discourse that is part of this manipulated regime culture is a part of the process of manipulation. Examining the causes of and responses to our two major recent disasters: the attack on the World Trade Center in New York City and the Pentagon in Washington, and the events leading up to and following Katrina in New Orleans, could illustrate the point—in the World Trade Center case, it is the use of the threat of terrorism after the attack of 9/11, used to bolster a political regime otherwise losing popularity; in the Katrina case, it is the description of the events and the reactions of local African-Americans to them that is skewed by a culture of acceptance of racist stereotypes indiscriminately applied. Both have already been described in detail elsewhere (for the security issue after 9/11, see Marcuse, 2005, 2006a; on Katrina, see Marcuse, 2006b). In this paper the case examined is the handling of the International Freedom Center at the World Trade Center site, where the treatment of the arts and humanist culture reflects the same process of cultural manipulation.[4] In such cases the culture has been produced; there is an actor behind it. It is not that 'the United States' is prejudiced, or that 'it' culturally considers rich people worth more than poor people, or that the worship of the free market is somehow a part of a pre-existing 'American culture'. Nor is it the case that the arts are considered for their commercial value and their critical potential is suppressed because that is somehow 'culturally' the way people see things. Such a way of viewing them is specifically advanced by certain groups and interests, over the opposition of others, and supports the established distribution of power and rejects possible challenges to it. Culture, both in the generic and in the humanist sense, is a terrain of conflict, and the cases described below will show those conflicts in some detail. A dominant ideology is spread by a dominant group/ class, having large authority over the media, educational institutions, and state administrative apparatuses, and absorbed into the values promoted by the regime culture.

The Imposition of Regime Culture: The Case of the International Freedom Center

Culture, in the humanist sense discussed below, was an immediate part of planning for reconstruction in lower Manhattan after 9/11. The earliest plans for the site, the master plan by Daniel Libeskind, included a museum and a 'cultural center', and both the rhetoric of the Lower Manhattan Development Corporation and the various successive plans for Ground Zero all included emphasis on a cultural component.[5] Prior to February 2006, the centerpiece of that cultural component was planned to be the International Freedom Center, with the Drawing Center occupying a secondary but important place in the scheme. The story of the International Freedom Center (the IFC) suggests how the regime culture dominated and ultimately destroyed the concept of a cultural center.

The IFC was promoted by a private non-profit group, and was intended to celebrate the ever-expanding history of freedom in the United States, at one point to cap its exhibition with a copy of the text of President George W. Bush's second Inaugural Address. But somewhere along the line the idea cropped up that the history of freedom in the US might need to make reference to some unfreedoms, if only in earlier periods in which patterns such as slavery or the denial of the right to vote to women or McCarthyism prevailed. That caused an uproar among some of the families of the victims of the attack, and was joined by the governor of the state of New York, who declared unequivocally that 'Nothing in this museum will denigrate the patriotic vision of the United States which underlies our reaction to the attack'.[6]

And no controversies should be aired there. History needs to be rewritten to conform to a new cultural vision of the past promulgated and/or endorsed by the state, with some elements of the past suppressed, and others aspects produced in new and revised form, and no uncomfortable questions asked. The danger that such questions might be asked and the rewriting of history not be entirely effective was enough to kill the idea of the IFC. The parallel story of the Drawing Center at the same site is set forth below.

The new production of a culture with a re-interpreted past is manifest in the persistent, indeed overwhelming, linking of the concept of freedom to the events of 9/11. That process involved not simply naming planned buildings the 'Freedom Tower', showing them silhouetted against the backdrop of the Statue of Liberty whose shape they were intended to emulate, or the naming of the aborted International Freedom Center, but interpreting the events of 9/11 as part of an attack on 'Freedom', as the President did in his very first official statement on the attack and has continually and strenuously repeated ever since.[7] The extent to which this component of state-produced culture has been absorbed into the popular consciousness is testified to by the absolute lack of any questioning of this patently absurd interpretation: to label the World Trade Center, the seat of major international financial corporations and their ancillary servants a symbol of freedom, or to label the Pentagon, the seat of the most overwhelming military might on the face of the earth, a symbol of freedom is (whatever substantive arguments might conceivably be made for such an interpretation) not the way in which those two building were seen in the Arab world, indeed in most of the world, and presumably not the way they were seen by Al Qaeda. And to label many of those who died in the attack 'freedom fighters', without a shred of evidence of the concern of most for such an abstract concept or its workings in the day-to-day world, is part of a manufactured culture. While some may indeed have been concerned with civil rights and the freedom of oppressed peoples, nothing suggests that such concerns drew people to the building (we do not speak of police or fire or rescue workers here); rather, they were engaged in currency speculation, trading in pollution credits, international banking, corporate advertising, etc. But that is a question that dare not raise its head, given the strength of the regime culture.

Nor is it any part of current discussions to question the culture of fear that has been generated around the response to terrorism, about which I have written elsewhere (Marcuse, 2005; see also Marcuse, 2004). As this is written, *The New York Times* publishes a column with an only slightly satirical tone: 'Our ports are sitting ducks for terrorists. Chemical plants, too. Let's not even talk about the Indian Point nuclear plant. [New York's evacuation plans are declared inadequate.] The non-stop message is, "Be afraid, be very afraid"' (Haberman, 2006).

Even debate on the meaning of terrorism is out of bounds in the regime culture: the idea that the history of freedom in the United States, to be chronicled in the International Freedom Center proposed for the World Trade Center site, might include reference to the terror of the Ku Klux Klan in the South was rejected with shock as totally inappropriate in a state-sponsored institution. Presumably the producers of such a regime culture do not wish to draw attention to the extent to which that culture is in fact produced, manufactured, in a way that conceals truth and suppresses questions, the exact opposite of what culture, in at least its humanist interpretation, would do.

Why then so much emphasis on a cultural component at Ground Zero and then in lower Manhattan, to begin with? For reasons that have nothing to do with the inherent value of culture or of tradition or of history, but rather as a spur to economic development and the creation of a 'vibrant downtown' for the benefit of its residents. That instrumental view of humanist culture is taken up in the next section.

Humanist Culture, the Arts, and their Instrumentalization

Humanist Culture and the Role of the Arts

Humanist culture includes both high and mass culture.[8] The substance of what one might call high culture can perhaps be best defined as what it is not: it is not activities that are aimed at economic ends, although they may also be marketed to permit their authors to survive. High culture is sometimes confined to the artistic: museum-class painting, opera, drama, literature, poetry. More broadly, humanist culture would also include philosophy, history, and sociology. The natural sciences are close to humanistic culture, but the relation is one that has been subject to much debate, and is not relevant for the discussion below. Raymond Williams (1965, p. 80, quoted in Miles, forthcoming, p. 5) speaks of this sense of the use of the word 'culture' as an 'independent and abstract noun which describes the works and practices of intellectual and especially artistic activity. This seems often now the most widespread use: "culture" is music, literature, painting and sculpture, theatre and film'.

It is not surprising that in a capitalist society the process of commodification should encompass the products of artistic production as well as other forms of production of goods and services.[9] Thus, paintings are sold at auction, often at astronomical prices; drama is a form of entertainment in which investors play a key role; music is a key part of multiple forms of entertainment produced for profit. The arts have never been self-supporting in a material sense, and Aristotle acknowledged a reality in which they were the domain only of the elite in society. Popular culture, folk songs, street theater, only rarely provided support for the livelihood of their practitioners; certainly for high culture what the market does today is not unlike what various Maecenases did in earlier times. We have spoken of the manipulation of generic culture to form a regime culture, sustaining prevailing distributions of power. In an even broader sense humanist culture can be utilized in parallel fashion, sometimes deliberately, usually not, sometimes radically, usually not. Mathew Arnold certainly saw culture as a means to 'social cohesion in a period of religious decline' (quoted in Miles, forthcoming, p. 9). The Bauhaus and the Situationists tried to bend culture to a more revolutionary political turn, possibly even to create a resistance culture. (The changes produced in a period of globalization are discussed at the end of this paper.) When this happens, culture in the form of the arts begins to impact on culture as a way of life, in the interests of a national culture, while cultural institutions displace the everyday cultures of the neighborhoods they re-code as cultural sites. One could not ask for a better formulation of what the IFC was hoped to do.

The Instrumentalization of the Arts: Culture as Economic Development

No bones are made about the reasons culture is often officially supported. Again, developments at the World Trade Center site afford examples. It is the Deputy Mayor for Economic Development that is in charge of planning for and supporting cultural institutions below Houston Street, and study after study is produced to show the economic benefits of funding for culture and the arts and creative activities.[10] And economic benefits certainly included, perhaps even predominantly, benefits for real estate owners and investors in the adjacent areas; a vibrant neighborhood, after all, commands higher rentals than a dead one. That is not to say that spelling out the economic benefits of locating cultural activities in an area is not an honorable task, and may indeed be very helpful to artists, writers, thinkers, who may have a hard time of it without such arguments for public support, and may indeed promote community development in areas much in need of it.

A different line of argument holds that artists, creative people in the humanist sense, can contribute to economic development directly. The Ford Foundation, for instance, recently issued a Request for Proposals (RFP): Partners for Livable Communities and the Ford Foundation are inviting neighborhood-based arts organizations to apply for funding to produce a community development strategy.[11] The purpose of the funding is to determine the role such organizations can take in mixed-income, mixed-race communities, and the role that active public space can play in assisting the transition often associated with dramatic shifts in demographics and market forces. These strategies must recognize the importance of partnerships between diverse stakeholders to strengthen the position of arts organizations as conduits for civic engagement. The European Union agrees to name a single city each year its European City of Culture, and cities compete for the designation. Why? Not because it helps local artists, but because it attracts tourists, and is thus good for the local economy. Likewise, when a city prides itself on being a 'cultural city', e.g. Salzburg, Venice, Prague, Avignon, Florence, Weimar,[12] it is not because so many artists are resident or work there, but because they were there once in the past; it is the touristic/entertainment value of past cultures that is the driving force behind its recall today.

The attribution of such value to the arts is not without its advantages for them. Artists may be poor, but they are productive. Good art is an economic asset, and delivers value for the community in which it is produced. Artists are risk-takers, not bound by convention, seeking communities that are diverse and open, looking for cheap rents and unconventional spaces. They are thus ideal pioneers in the process of reclaiming run-down housing and run-down neighborhoods. Arts centers are excellent uses for abandoned factory buildings; studios and rehearsal spaces are appropriate re-uses for abandoned factories and warehouses. And artists, though often poor, are no danger to their neighbors and rarely a drain on welfare budgets. In a time of budget shortfalls and tax revolts, an economic argument can be much more effective in convincing politicians to support the arts than more esoteric appeals to humanist values. The dangers of the argument, compared to its advantages, may not be a strong enough reason not to make it, and there is much evidence for its truth. Yet the dangers are very real.[13]

The Instrumentalization of the Arts: the 'Creative Class' Fallacy

The idea that artists are merely parts of a 'creative class', and that it is the 'creative class' that is the motor of economic development, has been pushed most prominently by Richard Florida in countless talks at Chambers of Commerce, books and articles, a web site, and media presentations.[14] What is 'creative' is an important question indeed, particularly in a period in which innovation occupies a high place in the pantheon of contributors to economic progress.[15] Much has been written on the sources of creativity, in psychology, education, sociology, and economics. But that literature is not dealt with. Rather, 'creative' is never defined, but simply taken as an attribute of occupations comprising some 30% of the working population; thus, podiatrists, accountants, stock brokers, managers, journalists, teachers, lawyers, sales people, managers, are all creative. Indeed, some are super-creative: librarians, sports figures, social scientists, as well as engineers and artists. It is hard to tell just what 'creative' is supposed to mean as a classification of occupations. Some careful reviews of Florida's data suggest all he means is simply 'college educated' (see e.g. Peck, 2005). The category hardly defines who is creative, nor is it neutral socially and independent of the distribution of power and wealth. Robert Reich's (1991) symbolic manipulators or Erik Olin Wright's (1979) professional-managerial class might serve better as a tool for analyzing changes in the economy; for understanding what is happening, with level of education one factor among many; the structural role or innovation in the economy in any event needs to be brought into focus.

Leaving aside, then, Florida's particularly sloppy sociological definition of the 'creative class', and rescuing what might be a kernel of importance in the concept, is there a new importance to creativity in a globalized world today? Yes, but not in the way that the moral value of the term suggests. To be creative is a good thing, almost anyone would agree. A plumber who can figure out what a newly discovered problem is and devise an appropriate remedy, a shoemaker who can design a shoe to fit a particular foot, an artist who can paint a masterpiece, a cellist who can play a Bach sonata—these all have creativity as a desirable attribute. But beware: Andrew Fasted, of Enron fame, was creative in his accounting schemes also, and the development of new financial instruments with which to speculate in global markets is of a different social value than the composition of a symphony or the staging of a classic play in a new and telling performance, just as the discovery of a vaccine is of a different value than the design of a stealth bomber, writing a poem is different from creating an advertising campaign for a status good. People may of course differ on what is of value (although I will argue below that art inherently is of a value very different from the marketing of a commodity); the point here is primarily that to use the term 'creative' indiscriminately to cover all these activities is to suppress the question of real values entirely.

The kernel of truth in the creativity discussion is related to the changes that accompany globalization in our world. I have suggested that really existing globalization is a combination of the expansion and concentration of power with technological advances, a point developed further in the concluding section of this paper. Those advances are real, and they require creativity for their continuation. There are in fact high returns to education today, to certain kinds of education for certain people, but more returns than in pre-global periods. A globalized economy does indeed demand creativity of a certain kind for economic success. In this sense, the debate about the meaning of creativity is more important today than it has been in the past. And the danger is that, in the conflation of humanist cultural creativity with technical and instrumental creativity, either amoral technical creativity is valorized far above its real value, or cultural creativity is tainted and devalued in its competition with its rival. Putting English majors and business majors in the same boat distorts the contribution of both.

The amoral (in the sense of disregarding humanist values) apotheosis of creativity has another unfortunate consequence. Creativity is associated, in the minds of Richard Florida and his like, with certain cultural characteristics. In *The Rise of the Creative Class* (2001) and in his lectures to audiences around the country, Florida extols the qualities of city life which he considers inextricably linked to creativity, to the attraction of the creative class: cafes, active night life, an 'arts' scene, high culture as well as jazz clubs, casual dress, boutique shopping—characteristics of what is called above the life-style aspect of culture. His advice to mayors is to promote those characteristics of their cities. But these are characteristics that appeal to 'yuppies', to aspiring young professionals, to the professional-managerial class, not to struggling artists, actors or poets—or to poor people generally, or to immigrants, or to most of the elderly. Life-style culture as the *Creative Class* discussion has it is a description of a social and economic class. Recommendations to focus on it lead to an economically biased set of recommendations that relies on the economic value of a distorted definition of creativity to make both a moral and economic justification for subservience to the upper middle class. All creativity is good, and globalization requires high degrees of creativity; therefore give priority to the interests of all creatives, goes the logic. Its result is to polarize and divide.

The Dangers of the Instrumentalization of Humanist Culture

One danger is immediate, the other is longer-term and deeper. Immediately, artists have become pioneers in the process of gentrification, the reoccupation of run-down and cheap housing by new residents, eventually displacing those residents who may still be there and in the long run promoting exclusionary displacement, reducing the amount of housing available to others of low income.[16]

The longer-run danger is more substantive, and harder to document. Art is, by its nature, challenging. It is intended to arouse, to question, to provide new perceptions. Cynthia Freeland (2001, p. 207), in an excellent book, describes its diversities, but finds a common theme (quoting Robert Irwin: Art is 'a continuous examination of our perceptual awareness and a continuous expansion of our awareness of the world around us'). That examination is likely to be unsettling. She gives recent examples, such as the picture of the Virgin Mary spattered with elephant dung shown at a Brooklyn Museum of Art exhibition that enraged Rudolph Giuliani to the point where he threatened to withhold city funds from the well-regarded museum. It is no accident that so much great art has been anti-war, and implicitly critical of the authorities that wage it. Quite non-political art may also be very political in its implications; in fact, the directness of political posturing may be the worst way to communicate politically critical meaning, as in Stalinist sculptures of heroic working class heroes. By contrast, the visions of beauty, of an imagined place, *Là, tout n'est qu'ordre et beauté*,[17] comes as an inevitable contrast to the actual world of disorder, ugliness, unrest, deprivation, attacks on the senses.[18]

That is not the kind of art that political leaders or even foundations want, generally, to support—certainly not leaders of the order of Rudolph Giuliani. The story of the Drawing Center at the World Trade Center site, set forth below, suggests the problem is not confined to a particular politician or a particular setting. Perhaps no harm is done; it simply means one argument for support as economic development fails. But it is also a message to artists: if you want funding, if you want media attention, if you want success, temper your art and move it into less controversial areas. Not always: the dung Virgin, after all, was hung, and Mostly Mozart concerts are very popular. There will always be some within the ranks of those with wealth and power who will be ambivalent about the world they inhabit, and value the challenges that controversial art provides. And visions of beauty can be ornament and entertainment. But also are often deeply moving, and perhaps disturbing, to many. But the risk to the degradation of the meaning of art through its instrumentalization, as always with its commodification, is great. Art may be instrumentalized in the service of power, or in the service of commerce, but in both cases its affirmative character belies its authentic often (necessarily?) critical content (see Marcuse, 1968).

The line between purely authentic culture and commercial culture is not simply the relation to financial success, for 'authentic' artists may also in fact be commercial successes (everything from Shakespeare to Verdi or *Les Enfants de Paradis*). And some great and authentic art has served power well: Velasquez, Corneille, the great Gothic cathedrals. Exploration of the substantive content and quality of art is inescapable if the distinctions are to be clarified, and the line between is not a clear one.

In this constellation, who is it that produces art? Well, of course, immediately, the artist. But the artist is a social being, like all of us, and in a sense even more directly and publicly, because the artist interprets and portrays the world that he or she perceives, and those perceptions are of its social character, which in turn shapes the perception of it. Thus the work of the artist is responsive both to the generic culture in which he or she works, and to the immediate material conditions in which he or she is compelled to work. The response to the generic culture, to the extent influenced by the regime culture of the day, may well be resistance and critique, if at some cost to the artist.[19] But the response to the funders of art and the employers or patrons of art, the producers of art at one remove and those who make it a public rather than merely a private activity, is more immediate, and imposes an additional burden on the artist to remain true to the nature of his or her perceptions and vision. The danger is clear.

Globalization and the Production of Culture

Globalization in the form in which it exists today accentuates both the production of a regime culture as part of generic culture and the instrumentalization of the arts as part of humanist culture. A definition of globalization, a deservedly controversial term, will help clarify the argument made here. It is offered, not to resolve extensive debates about its proper meaning—indeed, that meaning varies with the context and purpose for which it is used—but simply to indicate the way in which it is used in this paper.[20]

'Globalization' is an elastic term, and has been defined in numerous different ways. I would separate the general concept of globalization, the potential for all major human activities to be interconnected on a global scale, from really existing globalization, globalization as we find it about us today. Really existing globalization has two separable components.

'Really Existing Globalization' is an intuitively meaningful and clearly definable term that should be in wider use. It might be defined as: the leap in technological development including major advances in communications and transportation capacities, in turn facilitating international production and exchange; and the concentration of profit-driven ownership and control, on an increasingly international basis, represented by the increased economic and political power of corporations with owners and operations across international borders—both in the context of neo-capitalism in the economic sphere and neo-liberalism in the political sphere; both on an increasingly global scale.

The impact of these developments on culture is manifold. It includes: an increasing threat to local, regional and national cultures, with undesired encroachments of globalization in cultural, economic, and social spheres—the spread of McDonalds and McDonaldization is a surface manifestation of that threat. A renewed regime-sponsored nationalism/patriotism/chauvinism based on the threat of terrorism, although it has engendered a substantial anti-globalization movement, shows the strength of this trend. More broadly, a strengthening of chauvinist national cultures, as nation states seek to support the competitive positions of their own businesses and cultural producers; a global form of culture that is not cosmopolitan or international in the nineteenth century sense, but rather reflects the increasing dominance of the United States as an imperial, post-colonial power, with English becoming a homogenizing language and US cultural production pressing hard for dominance against other national and local cultures.[21] A convergence of class-specific cultures spread globally among the upper classes and in mass culture, e.g. sports, but with a striking difference: upper class culture is unitary, 'global', while mass culture buys the global but retains a strong national linkage, as in the Olympics. A valorization of the 'global' as a good in itself, so that 'world-class' becomes an attribute of quality, with cities wanting to be seen and marketed as 'global cities'.

In the specific cases discussed in this paper, two very immediate impacts of really existing globalization can be traced, in the one case the impact of insecurity and concern about globally based terrorism on the production of regime culture, in the other cases the impact of globally based economic competition on the instrumentalization of the arts.

In the case of the production of regime culture, it is the use of global threats to security that legitimates a defensive patriotism that is intolerant of dissent and suspicious of any criticism that might weaken national self-esteem or under-cut assertions of national superiority. In the case of the production of an instrumentalized humanist culture, it is the use of global competition in the economic sphere that legitimates the imposition of 'positive' values on humanist cultural production and suppresses any critical content potentially disturbing to economic competitiveness and growth. Specifically, the fingerprints of globalization are all over the handling of the International Freedom Center. The World Trade Center was indeed a global trade center; the global reach of the Pentagon is well known. Al Qaeda reached both from bases across the globe. The patriotism which is such an essential ingredient of the present regime culture is one fomented by highlighting the position of the United States in a global world, stressing the dangers from an attack from global sources on that position, emphasizing how different the country is from other countries elsewhere on the globe. The purpose of the International [*sic*] Freedom Center is to show the world how the United States stands for freedom; any content that might question the purity of that history is anathema. The whole rebuilding of lower Manhattan might be further defined in terms relying heavily on belief in the importance of its global position to the health of the rest of the city and the nation: the push for funding, as a response to the attack, of the direct transit link to the international airport; the subsidizing of international firms locating in lower Manhattan; the memorialization of the highly paid international traders and financial workers as freedom fighters; the building up of internationally attractive tourist facilities at ground zero; the support for massive investment in security measures to protect globally related activities—in all these cases, the manipulation of public opinion to produce a regime culture provides the necessary support for measures that, otherwise, would be strongly contested, if only in terms of the priorities of other needs and the celebration of other values.

Likewise, globalization is intimately connected with the instrumentalization of the arts as a force for economic development.[22] The validation of activities labeled 'creative' regardless of their substance, whether fine arts or speculation on the stock market, the emphasis on contributions to the globally competitive position of the economy, based on the contribution of creativity as a generic concept, the use of the arts as a tourist attraction with the reliance on tourism as a growth sector of the economy, particularly international tourism, are all parts of the same pattern. The introduction of culture as a tool of economic development is partly a response to the competition from other cities, and at its apex the desire to become or remain a global city is a reaction to the competition of other global cities, now, given the wonders of communication and transportation technology, in much closer competition with each other. The view that investment in infrastructure in lower Manhattan is necessary for New York City's economy rests on the belief that the global financial activities taking place there are the motors of the entire city's economy. This regime and other regimes have produced official cultures before; the regime culture we witness today, produced by this particular state at this particular time, is heavily reliant on its global context for its effectiveness.

In the process, 'culture' has become a subcategory of entertainment in the amusements sections of daily newspapers.[23] 'Art' has become an industry category of the Bureau of Labor Statistics similar to 'personal services' or 'manufacturing' or 'mining'; 'artists' have become a niche market and a category of players in the real estate market; 'creative' has been applied equally and without irony to accounting practices at Enron and the writing of poetry; and, further in the process, the value of art for humanistic purposes is undercut, and any discordant notes, even in as relatively inconspicuous form as the drawing of uncomfortable scenes or reminders of unhappy events, is suppressed, as the Drawing Center learned to its cost. Really existing globalization has increased this danger, because it has increased the pressure on cities to compete with each other on a global basis, and has emphasized the role of generalized creativity in success in the competition. If high levels of creativity are mandatory for a successful global city, and if artists contribute to creativity as well as to the gentrification needed to attract other 'creatives', then the argument to fund art and humanist culture as an instrument of economic competition is great, but only acceptable art, of course. And in the process of becoming acceptable as an instrument of economic development, art faces a danger to the critical contribution it can make to society.[24]

In the case both of the manipulation of generic culture and the instrumentalization of humanist culture, the urban land use needs of globalizing cities have been advanced (see Marcuse and van Kempen, 1999b). The pressure for security against global and invisible enemies has helped bring about a citadelization of high-income business sections of central cities and the fortification of gated communities, developments strongly desired by professional and managerial and ownership sections of an increasingly polarized population, and the gentrification desired by the up-and-coming professional-managerial class is well served by artists, seen simply as actors in the real estate market, turning areas near inner cities from slums into desirable living quarters (see Smith, 2002).

Globalization, in its really existing form, has been used effectively to spread regime culture and instrumentalize humanist culture in this new century, raising long-existing patterns to new levels of pervasiveness and intensity.

Notes

1 By 'ideology' Mannheim (1968) meant thought systems, and specifically those promulgated by society's ruling groups that preserve their own power and obscure the reality that might challenge it.

2 Not only in the US. The culture of the private economy probably spreads faster than state culture, e.g. an article in *The New York Times*, 26 February 2006, as this is written, is headlined 'In India, Going Global Means Flaunting It', and describes the spread of designer labels and bling bling (diamonds, jewelry and all forms of showy style), was coined by New Orleans rap family Cash Money Millionaires back in the late 1990s to describe the rich of India. But the handling of issues of terrorism, the spread of surveillance, the limitations on speech, are also spreading rapidly. See Graham (2004).

3 Quoted by Dowd (2006). 'Personal responsibility' has become a code word for programs like workfare, intended to discipline the work force.

4 'Ground Zero "Freedom Center" Quashed Phil Hirschkorn', From CNN, 28 September 2005. Available at http://www.cnn.com/2005/US/09/28/wtc.rebuilding/. See http://select.nytimes.com/search/restricted/article?res=FA0611F639540C7A8EDDA00894DD404482 for *The New York Times* account.

5 See http://www.renewnyc.com/plan_des_dev/wtc_site/new_design_plans/Sept 2003_refined_design.asp.

6 See Mahoney and Feider (2005) and Healy (2005). A chronology of the controversy is at: http://www.fepproject.org/commentaries/worldtradecenterchron.html#15.

7 Office of the Press Secretary, 11 September 2001, 'Statement by the President in this Address to the Nation'. Available at: http://www.whitehouse.gov/news/releases/2001/09/20010911-16.html.

8 The line between purely commercial culture and 'authentic' culture is not simply the relation to financial success, for 'authentic' artists may also in fact be commercial successes (everything from Shakespeare to Verdi or *Les Enfants de Paradis*). Exploration of the substantive content and quality of art is inescapable.

9 This is rather an over-simplification. There are different arts, artists differ, and art patrons differ. It requires a much more careful and detailed analysis to be accurate.

10 For instance, Ann Markusen's work (Markusen and Johnson, 2006) or the studies of the Center for an Urban Future (2005) in New York, or the efforts recounted in Nataraj (2006, pp. 55–56).

11 Set forth at http://downsideupthemovie.org/RFP.pdf.

12 For a complete list see http://en.wikipedia.org/wiki/European_Capital_of_Culture#Past_European_Capitals_of_Culture.

13   See the work of Anne Markusen, for instance, or Kleiman *et al.* (2002) (which incidentally uses the terms 'creative' and 'cultural' interchangeably, e.g. in attempting accurately to identify the creative sector, it is the cultural sector that is referred to), or the film *Downside UP*, 'describing how art can change the spirit of a place. What happens when an impoverished working-class town [North Adams, Mass.] decides that its only hope for survival lies within the world of contemporary art?' (New Day Films).

14   For a full account of Florida's arguments and responses, see Peck (2005).

15   The withdrawal of the Drawing Center, one of the cultural institutions planned for the World Trade Center site, because of concerns that some of its exhibitions might present potentially discordant messages, is a recent very public case (see Pogrebin, 2006). Wikipedia summarizes the story succinctly: 'At one point there was a plan for the site to house several cultural organizations and the Freedom Center. Due to objections from victim's families and the New York State Governor, George Pataki, the plans for the site have been reconfigured. The Drawing Center, an arts organization that has a long history of showing a wide spectrum of works, including an exhibition which was critical of the Iraq War, was asked to censor itself in order to be a part of the future reconstruction site. Both the Freedom Center and The Drawing Center, argued that freedom of expression is integral to the institutions and artists involved'. Available at http://en.wikipedia.org/wiki/The_Drawing_Center.

16   See the early work of Damaris Rose (1984), who first pointed to the process and much work thereafter, including particularly that of Neil Smith. For the specific case of New York City, see Zukin (1990).

17   From Baudelaire's 'L'invitation au Voyage.'

18   It is an argument made in detail in Marcuse (1978).

19   See the painting at http://www.blackcommentator.com/175/175_art_richardson_venture_and_freedom.html, in which the image of imprisonment and the desire for physical escape is blurred with the image of mental freedom within the mind. See the discussion at Marcuse (1978).

20   For a fuller discussion, see Marcuse and Van Kempen (1999a, pp. 5, 261–262), and Marcuse (1997, pp. 29–48).

21   And, I believe, in a different way from nineteenth century or earlier conquests, in which the dominant language would become combined with the local, e.g. Creole, Yiddish, and Afrikaans.

22   See note 2 above.

23   *The New York Times*, the paper of record for the United States, heads its section on 'the arts' in its widely read Sunday edition: 'Arts and Entertainment'.

24   Which explains why critical or political art is necessarily often subtle and seemingly esoteric; more in-your-face phenomena would not be tolerated, or at least would not be funded.

References

Center for an Urban Future (2005) *Creative New York*, New York: Center for an Urban Future, December.

Dowd, M. (2006) Awake and scream, *The New York Times*, 16 September.

Florida, R. (2001) *The Rise of the Creative Class* (New York: Basic Books).

Freeland, C. (2001) *But is it Art? An Introduction to Art Theory* (Oxford: Oxford University Press).

Graham, S. (ed.) (2004) *Cities, War, and Terrorism: Towards an Urban Geopolitics* (Malden, MA: Blackwell Publishing).

Haberman, C. (2006) We will bury you in debt, *The New York Times*, 24 March, p. B1.

Healy, P. (2005) Pataki warns cultural groups for museum at Ground Zero, *New York Times*, 25 June.

Hoult, T. F. (1974) *Dictionary of Modern Sociology* (Totowa, NJ: Littlefield, Adams).

King, A. D. (1991) *Urbanism, Colonialism, and the World-Economy: Cultural and Spatial Foundations of the World Urban System* (New York: Routledge).

Kleiman, N. *et al.* (2002) *The Creative Engine* (New York: The Center for an Urban Future, 11 November).

Kroeber, A.L. & Kluckhohn, C. (1963) *Culture: A Critical Review of Concepts and Definitions* (New York: Vintage Books).

Mahoney, J. & Feiden, D. (2005) Zero tolerance at WTC, no US-bashing at site, Pataki says, *Daily News*, 25 June, p. 7.

Mannheim, K. (1968[1936]) *Ideology and Utopia: An Introduction to the Sociology of Knowledge*, Trans. L. Wirth & E. Shils (New York: Harcourt, Brace & World).

Marcuse, H. (1968) The affirmative character of culture, in: *Negations, Essays in Critical Theory* (Boston: Beacon Press).

Marcuse, H. (1978) *The Aesthetic Dimension* (Boston: Beacon Press).

Marcuse, P. (1997) Glossy globalization, in: P. Droege (Ed.) *Intelligent Environments* (Amsterdam: Elsevier Science Publishers), pp. 29–48.

Marcuse, P. (2004) The 'war on terrorism' and life in cities after September 11, 2001, in: S. Graham (Ed.) *Cities, War and Terrorism: Towards an Urban Geopolitics* (Malden, MA: Blackwell Publishing).

Marcuse, P. (2005) The 'threat of terrorism' and the right to the city, *Fordham Urban Law Journal*, XXXII, pp. 767–785.

Marcuse, P. (2006a) The threat of terrorism after 9/11: security or safety in the city, *International Journal of Urban and Regional Research*, 30(2), pp. 919–929.

Marcuse, P. (2006b) Rebuilding a tortured past or creating a model future: the limits and potentials of planning, in: C. Hartman & G. Squires (Eds) *There's No Such Thing as a Natural Disaster* (New York: Routledge).

Marcuse, P. & Van Kempen, R. (Eds) (1999) *Globalizing Cities: A New Spatial Order?* (Oxford: Blackwell).

Marcuse, P. & van Kempen, R. (Eds) (1999) Introduction and conclusion, *Globalizing Cities: A New Spatial Order?* (Oxford: Blackwell).

Markusen, A. & Johnson, A. (2006) *Artists Centers: Evolution and Impact on Artists, Neighbouhoods, and Economies*, University of Minnesota: Humphrey Institute of Public Affairs.

Marshall, G. (1998) *A Dictionary of Sociology*, 2nd ed. (Oxford: Oxford University Press).

Miles, M. (forthcoming) *Cities and Cultures: Critical Introductions to Urbanism and the City* (Oxford: Routledge).

Nataraj, N. (2006) Seeing and remembering, *Color Line* (Spring), pp. 55–56.

Peck, J. (2005) Struggling with the creative class, *International Journal of Urban and Regional Research*, 29(4) (December), pp. 742–770.

Pogrebin, R. (2006) Exiled from Ground Zero, arts center loses leader, *The New York Times*, 18 March.

Reich, R. (1991) *The Work of Nations: Preparing Ourselves for 21st Century Captialism* (New York: Random House).

Robertson, D. (2006) Cultural expectations of homeownership: explaining changing legal definitions of flat 'ownership' within Britain, *Housing Studies*, 21(1) (January), pp. 35–52.

Rose, D. (1984) Rethinking gentrification: beyond the uneven development of Marxist urban theory, *Environment and Planning D: Society and Space*, 2, pp. 47–74.

Said, E. (1979) *Orientalism* (New York: Vintage).

Sanyal, B. (Ed.) (2005) *Comparative Planning Cultures* (London: Routledge).

Savage, C. (2006) Bush could bypass new torture ban: waiver right is reserved, *Boston Globe*, 4 January. Available at: http://www.boston.com/news/nation/articles/2006/01/04/bush_could_bypass_new_torture_ban/.

Smith, N. (2002) 'New globalism, new urbanism': gentrification as global urban strategy, *Antipode*, pp. 427–450.

Williams, R. (1965) *The Long Revolution* (Harmondsworth, Penguin; 1st ed. London: Chatto & Windus, 1961).

Williams, R. (1984) *Keywords* (Fontana Communications Series, New York: Oxford University Press; 1st ed. London: Collins, 1961).

Wright, E. O. (1979) *Class Structure and Income Determination* (New York: Academic Press).

Zukin, S. (1990) *Loft Living: Culture and Capital in Urban Change* (New Brunswick, NJ: Rutgers University Press).

Peter Marcuse is Professor of Urban Planning in the Graduate School of Architecture Planning and Preservation at Columbia University.

City Transformation and the Global Trope: Indianapolis and Cleveland

DAVID WILSON

Introduction

Today, fear and anxiety stalk many US cities. These places purportedly face a new grim and stark reality—of dark and deepening global times—which hovers, waiting to batter and threaten their economic fortunes. The widely accepted script is blunt and ominous: a new hyper-mobility of capital 'annihilative of space by time' looms to eradicate jobs, investment, and manufacturing in these cities (Harvey, 1989; Brenner and Theodore, 2002a). New technologies, new ways of producing goods and services, and an increasingly centralized capital class purportedly connect to impose, in the words of Michael Burawoy (2000), a transformative crisis. A logical outcome has supposedly followed: a desperate city competition for new investment and businesses. In the script, a handful of cities strike out to be 'global centers' for commerce and economy (e.g., Chicago, New York). Other cities, in contrast, are said to struggle to either sustain a 'regional-city' status, to stabilize, or simply to survive.

This paper examines this notion of globalization in another way: as an expedient rhetorical invoking. A focus on two prominent cities, Indianapolis and Cleveland, suggests that globalization, while an undeniable reality, is also a convenient invocation of a powerful realism that assists capital's drive to physically and socially restructure these cities. This invoking, what I call the global trope, is shown to be a complex and elaborate rhetoric that has helped mobilize and put into play one vision of city growth and restructuring that emphasizes the production of affluent play spaces, upmarket residential communities, and conspicuous consumption zones. To partake in this global-speak, it is chronicled, is to deploy power and offer haunting and frightening images that assists growth machine designs and aspirations.[1] This global rhetoric, a perceptual apparatus with potent material consequences, serves up a digestible reality that, following Wagner-Pacific (1994), legitimates redevelopment and restructuring programs by making certain actions thinkable and rational and others not.

Three main points are chronicled.[2] First, neoliberal governance in Indianapolis and Cleveland boldly offers this new global-speak that helps construct a circuitry of understandings that drives current social and physical transformation. Local real-estate capital (a privileged post-war economic coalition in city policy that has always been entangled with local elite dreams for profit, prestige, and civic improvement) is the central driving force. Second, this new global trope is a deceptively sophisticated and coercive rhetorical formation. Its production of an economic and social reality, made the world's truths in uncompromising objectivity, immerses people in an emotively infused and persuasive 'planning and policy predicament'. And, third, this political governance, deftly using the global trope, now generates a new low-income-punishing uneven development across Indianapolis and Cleveland which most decisively sears low-income African-American communities. These neighborhoods, now, suffer from a bolstered functional logic ascribed to them, to warehouse 'contaminants' in the global-compelled city restructuring, which deepens deprivation in these spaces.

To frame this study, two important points. First, I agree that there is truth to a sense of a global unfolding in recent years. Much evidence suggests that the US economy and many city economies became more mobile and far-reaching after 1990. Medium and large-scale capital across America progressively restructured themselves across the late 1970s and 1980s to get to this point (Knox, 1997; Brenner and Theodore, 2002). A punishing six-year recession in the early and mid-1970s led this capital to re-examine and re-form its market strategies and organizational structure. Many corporations consciously downsized or eliminated inefficient plants, spurned high-labor-cost communities, participated in key acquisitions of firms, and aggressively incorporated new technologies (Warf and Holly, 1997; Short, 2004). Larger, more powerful entities formed that today tend to more far-flung operations across regions and countries. Thus, 51 global corporations whose headquarters and facilities dot America's cities today now rank within the 100 largest economies in the world (Anderson and Cavanaugh, 2000). In this context, one-third of US trade today is simply transactions among various units of the same corporation (Anderson and Cavanaugh, 2000).

But there is another side to these proclamations: a new reality of punishing globalization can be more rhetoric than real. Simply put, globalization does not uniformly affect all cities and all economic sectors within them (Pile *et al.*, 1999). US cities have different economic bases and ties to global corporations and investment that make globalization's influence highly uneven. At the same time, even in the most 'global' of cities, economic bases have tended to be heavily place-dependent (Cox, 1993). Chicago, for example, has a more 'footloose—global' economic base than Indianapolis, Kansas City, or St. Louis, i.e., it contains a significant presence of well capitalized, place-resilient producers like Sara Lee, Boeing, and SBC. These companies have the distinctive combination—substantial assets, far-flung operations, minimal dependence on local conditions to produce—that make outmigration an option. Yet, these producers in Chicago are still the exception rather than the rule, and account for a surprisingly low level of total employment: planner M. Fried (2004) estimates this at 18% to 20%.

In the second framing point, this global trope is posited as rooted in a deeper force so far merely hinted at: the continuous production of a strategic uneven development. The form of this uneven development fluctuates over time but always in response to the same central process: local and societal regimes of capital accumulation. Cultivating this unevenness, Neil Smith's (1984) lifeblood for making the city an instrument for accumulation, produces an economically taut landscape that can efficiently service the interests of local growth machines. Thus, during the golden age of the Fordist societal growth dynamic, cities like Chicago, Cleveland, St. Louis, and Detroit built and progressively embellished their trademark feature: large factory districts dominating downtowns ringed by tiers of worker districts (Judd, 1979; Teaford, 1990). One aspect of this city that concerns this paper, Black ghettos, were quickly and efficiently established to aid a small real-estate capital but formed most fundamentally to assist the Fordist industrial economy's need for cheap and prevalent low-wage workers (see Wilson & Grammenos, 2000; Wilson, 2005; Wacquant, 2002a, 2002b).

I suggest that the latest phase of this uneven development features the use of the global trope to drive real-estate accumulation, and has direct roots in post-1970 processes. Local and societal circumstances were changing in this period with the collapse of Fordist economics and the Keynesian-welfarist complex. As flexible production systems, labor-market deregulation, and a retrenched welfare state became the societal adjustment, many large US cities were battered. These cities, desperate to revitalize moribund economies, typically rallied around an 'opportunity structure' provided by the structural economy, potentially lucrative real-estate (see Smith, 2002). Cultivating an existent gentrification, in particular, could generate substantial revenues for real-estate capital and local government (see Smith, 2002; Weber, 2002). In this context, policy fixes have arisen to help revalorize land in key districts: tourism, historic preservation, and cultural upscaling. Currently, desires of growth machines to cultivate a new city-wide differentiation is most manifest in two drives, to build expansive (but fortressed) upmarket spaces and to more deeply isolate the 'contaminating' influence of black ghettos and black bodies.

The Rise and Dynamics of the Global Trope

Since 1990, an accelerated global-speak, spearheaded by a now widely identified unit, neoliberal governance, has resoundingly reverberated across many US cities (Wilson, 2007). Dynamics in Indianapolis and Cleveland reflect this. These neoliberal governances, at their core, adopt and offer a free-market mantra that has been rapidly assimilated into planning and policy circuits. A once starkly utopian intellectual movement, aggressively grounded nationally by Reagan in the 1980s and acquiring its technocratic gloss via the 'Washington Consensus' in the 1990s, now propels these governances forward (Brenner and Theodore, 2002). As we learn in these cities, this mantra as a kind of frame has imposed a new sense of normality on once problematic and contentious policy notions, e.g., killing the welfare state, supplanting a politics of redistribution with a politics of wealth production, and using the police apparatus to hyper-aggressively cordon off poor Black and Latino social spaces.

Yet it is important to distinguish between the appearance and reality of these neoliberal units as they propel city restructuring. At a superficial level, they appear as blunt neoliberal operatives, flagrantly offering a kind of new shock treatment (e.g., necessity of concentrating public and private resources in select spaces, demanding the racial poor to be productive and civically contributory or pay the price). But things are more complex: these governances elaborately craft and stage a presentation of realities to seize the terrain of the rational and progressive (Wilson and Wouters, 2004). These entities thus engage in elaborate cultural projects, i.e., they root themselves in and work through settings of situated meanings and understandings to acquire form and legitimacy. In this, these governances operate within common understandings of the world's processes (e.g., 'globalization', 'proper role of government'), people (e.g., 'immigrants', 'minority youth'), and places (e.g., 'the downtown', 'the ghetto', 'the good neighborhood'). These governances, ultimately, ground their ideas in something crucial, prevailing circuits of fears, hopes, notions of identities, and sense of processes.

But this governance's fervent offering of the global trope has an important context. One key impetus to this has been such declaration at the national scale—in national publications, magazines, presidential addresses, think-tank reports, and 'expert' oratory— which has permeated public thought and contextualizes these offerings. The proof is in the data. For example, mentions of 'globalization or 'global economy' in *Business Week* escalated from 160 in 1990 to over 290 mentions in 2000 (Miller, 2002). A content analysis of 40 newspapers and magazines found 158, 2,035, and 17,638 stories using the term 'globalization' in 1991, 1995, and 2000, respectively (Miller, 2002). To the trusted and authoritative *New York Times* (2001), the reality of globalization is undeniable: it has set in as 'a ... fluid, infinitely expanding and highly organized system that encompasses the world's entire population, but which lacks any privileged position or "places of power"'.

In this setting, key 'talking heads' have assumed dominance. For example, billionaire financial speculator and media guru George Soros (1998), the media's poster boy for globalization, talks frequently in public forums and TV studios about this, comparing it to the dawn of the machine age and age of reason. To Soros, a new hyper-competition for jobs and investment faces America and its places given their ascendant speed, movement, and footlooseness. Producers, to Soros, now seamlessly move in and out of regions, countries and continents. Split-second decisions conveyed by frenetic telecommunications systems instantaneously move jobs and investment and coordinate far-flung operations. To Soros, the world has irreversibly changed: policy has to be responsive and make the country and its cities more competitive.

Local media and politicians in and looking onto Indianapolis and Cleveland have followed suit to also unleash this rhetoric. To US Conference of Mayors Representative Marc Morial (2002), 'every mayor [now] needs to be a player on the global economic scene. Every mayor must recognize that our cities, no matter how big or small, are important to the new global economy'. Morial 'challenge[s] every single mayor to spread th[is] message throughout your city, to your editorial boards, to your Chambers of Commerce, to the pulpits of your places of worship'. Similarly, a communiqué issued by the Transatlantic Mayors Summit in 2000 said: 'mayors ... are no longer the traditional city planners of the past 100 years, but rather ombudsmen and innovative leaders [that] . . . conduct their own foreign policy'. 'For the good of their citizens', stated the communique, 'mayors will increasingly enter the international arena and become global players'.

Without doubt, some of this rhetoric follows from a sense that these cities face changing times. The sense of a pervasive, locally impinging globalism has been, paraphrasing Nigel Thrift (1995), in the air and embedded in normalcy. But these growth machines also recognize this rhetoric as a kind of expedient resource that can help accomplish something desired: to fully shift local politics to a concern with resource attraction and to forging 'entrepreneurially taut' cities. This invoking could thus fully transition policy to a focus on wealth production and the intensifying of land values that had begun in the 1980s (see Jessop, 1990; Cochrane, 1999). For local developers, builders, realtors, speculators, and producers, this thrust promises something intensely desired: tremendous profits in local land and housing markets For these local governments, this thrust could deliver something important to them with shrinking federal aid across the 1990s: more tax revenues.

Content of the Global Trope

The global trope in Indianapolis and Cleveland deftly extends and is framed by neoliberal principles and designs. Imposed webs of meanings, like symbolic cages, build bars around senses of reality that keep gazes within discrete and confining visions. One reality, in rich emotive and provocative detail, is advanced while alternatives are purged. Here is Mikhael Bakhtin's (1981) implicit dialogue with other points of view, the simultaneity of asserting one vision of city and world and annihilating others. In elaborate framing, the trope serves up a supposed frank and blunt package of truths about city realities and needs that can no longer be suppressed. In assertion, its pleas correspond to nothing less than core truths. As this apparatus has resisted and beaten back competitive visions of city and societal realities, even as it is contested and struggled against, it grows stronger in these cities.

At this rhetoric's core, a supposed new hyper-competitive reality makes rust belt cities easily discardable as places of investment, production, and business. These once enclosed and confident containers of the economic, in the rhetoric, have recently become porous and leaky landscapes rife with a potential for a dramatic economic hemorrhaging. Against this supposed reality, cities are portrayed as beset by a kind of accumulation disorder and uncertainty that now haunts them. As City-County Councilor Glen Howard (1991) noted in discussion, 'Indy is just one more city trapped in the new web of new global times . . . we [the city] have to respond, we have no other choice . . . if jobs and plants go, we will suffer a fate akin to a kind of death'. Similarly, Cleveland planner S. Plann (2004), commented in discussion, 'the rise of the global era . . . this thing called globalization . . . makes capital just incredibly mobile . . . more footloose than in the past; it will go where it is wanted and stay where it is well treated'.

This evolving city, in the rhetoric, is a threatened but historically resilient locale that one more time must act ingenuously to survive. The luminously portrayed signs of this ominous potentiality—municipal fiscal depletion, an aging physical infrastructure, the 'reality' of vast decommodified residential, commercial, and production spaces dotting the city—are offered as signifiers of what the future can bring. Without proper action, here is Cleveland State University's (2001) future city with 'population and income growth no longer driv[ing] it . . . [with] the economy . . . not growing'. It would be Indianapolis City-County Councilor Glen Howard's (1991) soon-to-be city of 'major problems and headaches . . . a city lost in the free-fall of being not competitive and attractive'. Through this rhetoric, a proposed shock treatment of re-regulation, privatization, and re-commodification is grounded and rationalized.

But all is not bleak in this global-speak: possibility and hope are also offered. This part of the rhetoric focuses on the politically expedient theme of city survival. These cities, now, must pursue two crucial imperatives to thwart decline: strengthen the city as a taut entrepreneurial space and meticulously contain black ghettos and their populations. In the first imperative, the assertion is forceful: now cities must push to build attractive consumptive complexes, upper-income aesthetic residential spaces, efficient labor pools, and healthy business climates. This post-1990 rhetoric has been at the heart of what Kevin Cox (1993) earlier identified as the supplanting of a 'politics of redistribution' by a 'politics of resource attraction'. Entertainment, culture, sports, and leisure now become crucial civic business. To fail to commodify these, paraphrasing Indianapolis Mayor William Hudnut (1995), is to ignore the new stepped-up competition for investment, jobs, and resources between cities. In the process, an intensified balkanizing of city space by class and race is not merely normalized, it becomes celebrated as utilitarian and put in the service of city survivability.

In the second imperative, black ghettos and populations are to be systematically isolated as tainted and civic-damaging outcasts. These are communicated, either by bold assertion or innuendo, to be culturally problematic things to be feared, reviled, and cordoned off. Note, for example, comments by Indy planner B. Braggs (2004): 'over the past 15 years ... community leaders have recognized that the city can no longer afford ghettos of unproductive citizens ... We [can't advance] in any meaningful way ... this is not the way a 21st century city functions in a global world'. At work is William Wimsett's (1998) notion of the mobilized fear economy, a general trepidation that now expands to more deeply include black ghettos in these two cities. As Wimsett notes, since 1980 US cities like Indianapolis and Cleveland have increasingly had government by fear, policy by fear, and landscapes of fear, all of which are expediently promoted in talk and print media and political oratory. Now, in these cities, fear of black ghettos is more deeply peddled, which is manifested in a continued strategic, powerful invoking of crime, black men, black youth, streets, and ghettos. A spiral of fear, advanced through rich images, now sells black bodies and spaces as potential violators of the collectivity's socio-moral and economic integrity.

A cast of elaborately narrated characters and processes are crucial to this projection of a burdened but resilient city. The cornerstone of this is an aggressively narrated rise of a new heroic rust belt leader, writer Dean Mosiman's (2002) 'new entrepreneurial mayor'. Discussions about these mayors, a strategic politics, identify the civic visionaries who should lead the needed restructuring: They are cast as emboldened and all-seeing neoliberal beings, Michael Bakhtin's (1981) 'eye of reason'. A human form, made both a resonant symbol of and an articulate mouthpiece for best city revitalization values and strategies, positions these mayors as key narrativists and key exemplars. Through them, the public is to see something crucial: a rational, omniscient voice that clarifies municipal ills and best solutions. This voiced hero, reveling in a kind of analytic virtuosity, ultimately collapses an inchoate process ('new global times') into easily understood images of a new civic problem, the solution, and the appropriate leaders to spearhead change.

At one level, the production exudes an elementary operation of power. These city salvationists are communicated as ideal beings to carry out city change: they supposedly know city needs, the realities of local politics, and who has to be stifled as obstructionists to city advancement. This eye of power sees and knows all: they are the anointed makers of city renewal, re-creation, and re-defining. As the Indianapolis Regional Center Plan (2001), a public–private city growth consortium, noted, 'the new breed of big city mayors has welcomed business back into the city, stressed performance and results at city agencies, downplayed divisive racial politics, and cracked down on the symptoms of social disorder'. 'As a consequence', to the Consortium, 'America's ... cities [can] become vital communities once again'. There could be no better agent of change, the consortium notes, for these globally challenged cities.

But this mayoral construct is also sophisticated enough to reflect the more subtle operation of power. At the center of this, a hybrid personality is deftly sculpted to frame assertions of benevolent and city-serving beings. In narrating them, in particular, strategic assertions of a privileged place of birth, kinds of socialization, and immense real-world experience mesh to create a key signifier: a locally grounded, neoliberal being. Seizing the ground of general, commonsense neoliberalism, these mayors are made to bear central notions of prevailing public sentiment: the benevolence and wisdom of 'localness', wariness of politics and politicians, and 'down-to-earth' conservative values. Populated with such meanings, this character is injected with an unshakable populist sensibility that knows neighborhoods, local tastes, and local culture. A kind of grounded, neoliberal guy is forwarded which, as a creative construct, takes the public to a carrier of their own sensibilities.

Media narrations of the 1990s neoliberal political darling, Stephen Goldsmith of Indianapolis, illustrate this. He has been widely depicted, first and foremost, as an attuned, intuitive neoliberalist who knows local life. This Indy 'guy', infused with grass-roots values and aesthetics, purportedly toils to bolster this reality. Bearing the local in his soul, he strikes out to enhance what the sensible Indy community supposedly wants: everyday livability. To local planner B. Braggs (2004), 'Goldsmith is Indy born, raised and educated ... [and] made his mark as a leader who knew what Indy needed and wanted ... he re-energized local spirits and the business community with projects like Circle Centre Mall and Conseco Fieldhouse that gave us pride and national standing'. 'Under the leadership of ... Goldsmith', to the Annie E. Casey Foundation (in Professional Experience, 2003), 'ambitious and innovative reforms have helped revitalize the core of the city [and] cultivated neighborhood empowerment'.

Yet these Super Mayors and media, in the rhetoric, would be irresponsible if they did not identify a dilemma facing these cities: enigmatic black ghettos. The depictions take numerous forms. To Indianapolis Mayor Goldsmith (2003a), too industrial cities like Indianapolis today find themselves in '[a] free fall ... [that] mayors found ... when they came to office during the 1990s'. Mayors, to Goldsmith, are 'fellow foot soldiers in a war that pits us ... openly against poverty and the force of urban decay ... also against our own state and federal governments'. The problem, to Goldsmith, is 'counterproductive welfare programs, public housing initiatives, and a "war on poverty", all of which simply exacerbate the plight'. More blatantly, columnist Nicholas von Hoffman (1991) calls inner city black communities in these cities 'a wasteland wherein children are trained to be muggers and hookers as thoroughly and effectively as white collar children are trained to be accountants'.

These narrations ultimately treat these spaces and people in a curious way: compassion is allocated but to restless and counter-civic beings that seem more wild and wooly than deprived. Notions of context and struggle frequently punctuate presentations, but of a fantastically out-of-control people and place. Inner city fears and fantasies, this way, are adroitly mapped onto this terrain. These spaces, amid detail, remain an abstract phenomenon, what Liam Kennedy (2000) calls a socio-psychological fantasy. Political caricature is smuggled into the 'truth' of faithful reportage which serves to demonize these spaces and curtail a reason for societal involvement in their affairs. Offers of culturally adrift, morally relative places theatricalize 'a people' for their differences, rather than pinpointing their innate sameness that deepens stereotype.

The global trope ultimately projects two important themes as neoliberal instruments. It offers the complementary 'truths' of what circumstances these cities now face and what they must do to survive. This whole, borrowing from Wendy Hollway (1984), offers purportedly progressive positions for subjects to adopt that legitimate potentially contentious actions (e.g., using public funds to subsidize gentrification, more scrupulous policing and monitoring of public spaces, cutting block grant funds to low-income neighborhoods). Yet use of such discourse by growth elites is anything but surprising. These formations, following Norman Fairclaugh (1992), are the modern alternative to flagrant violence and oppression. The now established rule in complex societies, to Fairclaugh, is to make and manage rather than to nakedly repress. Seizing and extending the terrain of logical and progressive via discourse, to Fairclaugh, is potent politics.

The Impacts

The global trope in these cities now drives a new uneven development that exacerbates socio-spatial polarization. Three key processes are fueled by this rhetoric: a concentration of investment in gentrification enclaves and select downtown areas, an intensification of disciplining forms of state intervention that impose market rule across urban space, and policy that explicitly fragments cities into mosaics of 'deserving' and 'undeserving' terrains. New redevelopment zones, i.e., the Circle Center Mall Axis (Indianapolis), the Public Square–Historic Gateway Cluster (Cleveland), and the North–South Gentrification Corridor (Indianapolis), have become hyped revitalization icons for what their cities ostensibly need to build. In contrast, the age-old city demon, the black ghettos of East and West Indianapolis and East Cleveland are to many planners and growth advocates places to be managed and buffered. In these terrains, black bodies are openly stored and isolated as problematic city contaminants.

In post-1990 Cleveland, the 'global-touting' administrations of Michael White and Jane Campbell have driven the city's new uneven development. Each government, populist in thrust, has mirrored the reality of neoliberal policy and project: a rhetoric of small government has barely disguised a profoundly interventionist local state. Their interventions have been fueled by a belief that urban real-estate could be heated up by a mix of physical impositions and spatial banishings. They, focusing on the core, have engaged and regulated people, land, and institutions via offering drastic welfare cuts, rigorously policing the streets (declaring war against beggars and the homeless), extolling and administering Workfare, attacking the public unions, providing more than $50 million after 1990 to 'culturalize' downtown, and offering new zoning codes and variances. These governments in traditionally democratic Cleveland have been, as Plann (2004) suggests, the most active in the city's history.

To drive restructuring, Cleveland has been repetitiously cast in a cautiously optimistic global frame. Reportage and oratory has the city threatened by globalization but historically resilient and capable of acting innovatively to survive. The Civic Task Force on International Cleveland (2003), for example, calls the city a place with 'an ... opportunity to revitalize[;] ... through continued internationalization of ... population and employment opportunities ... economic revitalization [can] occur'. Its black ghettos, alternatively, are repetitively signified as dysfunctional and best marginalized amid new global realities. Thus, strategies to deal with the city's massive Eastside Black ghetto, from popular Mayoral Candidate Robert Triozzi (2005), should involve 'bringing back police ministations ... and put[ting] Cleveland back on the economic development map'. Cuyahoga County Commissioner Jimmy DiMora (2005) notes a solution: 'to build on Cleveland's arts and cultural industry as if our community's future depend[ed] on it'. In the name of city progress and evolution, it is communicated, black ghettos can be marginalized for the broader city's good.

In this context, government resources have obsessively concentrated downtown with one thing privileged: salable culture. Cleveland, long the quintessential blue-collar American city, had pre-1980 experienced social and physical transformation via a traumatic deindustrialization. This deindustrialization was particularly pummeling between 1971 and 1981, with closure of the US Steel plant, General Motors' Coit Road factory, the Westinghouse lightning products plant, and six General Electric plants (Warf and Holly, 1997). To stem this tide, gentrification and upscaling was crafted in select downtown neighborhoods and the core in the mid-1980s. The key places were the Rock and Roll Hall of Fame, the Old City and the Flats gentrification districts, sparkling Gund Arena, and new hotels and clubs. After 1990, the growth machine built on this transformation labored to symbolically bury the image of 'the Mistake by the Lake' under the hype of the Chamber of Commerce's 'Comeback City'.

In the new restructuring, a deeper privatopia of wealth and discerning pleasure-taking has been etched into the city. Its stability and fortification has rested on a social and spatial banishing of heterogeneity. Centerpiece projects—the Flats upgrading, Old City upscaling, sprucing up Public Square, re-making the Warehouse District—have been designed and regulated to systematically exclude particularly poor blacks. In architectural layout, physical design, police monitoring, and zoning specification, the message has been clear: a problem minority', i.e., their class and cultural position, diverges from these space's texture and purpose and are to be repelled. Thus, as casual observation reveals, these areas are now dominated by easily monitored and surveilled cul-de-sacs, local resident surveillance teams assisted by the police, intense police patrol and regulation, and rental and homeownership prices that preclude residency by the non-middle class. Patrols and casual surveillance are seemingly constant, a compelling check and reminder of who is to use this space and who is to be purged from it.

In the shadows of this flurry of upgrading, black ghettos have worsened. East Cleveland, predominantly Black and low- and moderate-income, has been most afflicted by the concerted restructuring effort. Block grant monies once helping this area's poorest Black neighborhoods, Hough, Glenville, and Fairfax, have been substantially diverted to build the new upscale Cleveland. Hough experienced a more than 40% decline in block grant funds received from 1990 to 2000, with a dramatic thinning of subsidized day care provision, the affordable housing construction program, and job creation initiatives (Skrabec, 2004). Centrist City Councilor M. Wallach (2004) calls this withdrawal of resources 'anything but surprising, a response to the new realities that securing funds to help the poor are now extremely difficult ... the cuts really hurt the Hough area ... the poor now have to help themselves ... practice self-uplift ... start to think entrepreneurially ... this is the new rhetoric of a supposedly progressive Cleveland'.

Now poverty is intensified in its three most impoverished black ghettos, Hough, Glenville, and Collinwood. More than 70% of these households unofficially live below the poverty level (Rentgen, 2004). These neighborhoods today have infant mortality rates above 15 per 1,000, a figure that rivals Uruguay's 17 per 1,000 and Mexico's 20 per 1,000 (see CIA World Fact Book, 2003). On 105th Street in Glenville, only 15 minutes from Cleveland's vibrant downtown, almost every storefront is boarded up. In Collinwood, beggars and the homeless multiply across its main thoroughfare, 152nd Street, in a desperate fight to survive. Hough, one of the six poorest urban neighborhoods in America, had more than one in three of its residential parcels tax delinquent in 2001, compared to the city's less than one in ten (Center on Urban Poverty and Social Change, 2001).

Equally devastating, social service agencies that once relied on public funds have severely contracted or disappeared. Indicative of this, the Collinwood Community Services Center, a major community resource decimated by funding cuts, now struggles to provide basic necessities to residents: meals, day care, and housing assistance (see Naymik, 2003). A crushing debt, $300,000, threatens facility closure on top of already severe cutbacks. A critical question in the eyes of the community is the agency's survivability. 'At this point, I don't know [about surviving]', says South Collinwood Councilperson Roosevelt Coats (in Naymik, 2003). Cash is needed to cover basic operating costs: outstanding utility and food bills, salaries, and maintenance. Desperate measures to stay afloat are now routine. 'I offer creditors fifty bucks, whatever they will take, even a dollar', says Executive Director Wallace Floyd. 'I'm honest and tell them that [with cutbacks] we just don't have the money.'

To make matters worse in these neighborhoods, its land and property (like the rest of the city) is more strenuously subjected to market rule. Along with black ghettos floated in public discourse as culturally failing and productively inept, this is a recipe for neglect and abandonment. Neoliberal principles in the ghetto mean something very different than these same tenets outside of it. Market rule disciplines much of Cleveland to revalorize; this same rule deadens land and property worth and its institutional supports in these ghettos. Simply put, the private sector and its legion of investors do not at the moment want to reinvest in housing, jobs, or venture projects here. As planner Chris Jenks (2004) put it, 'as places for profit ... these neighborhoods are barely on the map'. Thus, Cleveland Planner B. Hennepin's (2004) notion of 'the continued black ghetto quandary' and his plea for 'all of Cleveland ... and the ghetto ... to find resuscitation via the market ... which will impose a needed order' casts the die for something predictable: the further abandonment of these spaces by the private sector.

In Indianapolis, the trope of globalization occupies center-stage in the face of especially curious circumstances: stable job and industry growth. The city expanded its number of jobs by 3.7% and industries by 4.0% between 1980 and 1997 (Center For Economic Development, 2004). Indy's economy, moreover, is dominated by light industry and service provision and is hardly global and footloose, which the notion 'global economy' references. Yet aggressive rhetoric about the need to entrepreneurialize city form under Mayors William Hudnut, Stephen Goldsmith, and Bart Peterson have steered government resources from neighborhood development and job creation to 'culturalize' the city, e.g., build a downtown mall (Circle Centre Mall), a professional sports stadium (Conseco Fieldhouse), and acres of gentrification.

Mayors Hudnut, Goldsmith, and Peterson have dramatically chiseled the new post-1990 uneven development into Indianapolis's fabric. These governments, too, have been deceptive and illusory neoliberal projects. Bold oratory of a retrenched government has barely concealed a new forceful local state that, more strictly than before, regulates land, property, the employment base, and social service provision. Like Cleveland, the goal has been to heat up urban real-estate via a mix of physical impositions and spatial banishings. Its post-1990 arsenal has added, in particular, new, stepped up policing methods (Project Saturation, the Zero Tolerance Team), new land-use control devices (e.g., removing the homeless and beggars from downtown streets), Workfare and No Child Left Behind, and the intensified subsidizing of downtown redevelopment (see Grunwald, 1998). A conservative local state, staunchly Republican, keenly inserts itself into local lives and spatial configurations.

In the process, public resources have been massively diverted to build an upscale downtown. Like Cleveland, these projects have been lucrative to real-estate interests (e.g., the Simons, J. Scott Keller) and have not been meaningfully job-creating or economically propulsive (see Wilson, 1996). The rise of Circle Center Mall, Conseco Fieldhouse, White River Park, and new upmarket hotels are its centerpiece. Gentrification has also intensified in its near downtown neighborhoods anchored in two spaces: Lockerbie Square and Fletcher Place. By the end of his second term (1992–1999), Mayor Steven Goldsmith had presided in funneling more than $1.5 billion in new downtown spending (IndyStar.com, 2001). Sports stadia, upscale housing, restaurant rows, and theater blocks have replaced acres of working-class neighborhoods and open spaces. 'Indiana-no-place', in short order, gained national notoriety to become the Republican-hyped model for ideal city redevelopment in America (cf. Goldsmith, 2003a).

But in the process, funds to meet the poor's housing and social needs have been cut and often superficially used. Most notably, block grants for Eastside neighborhoods have declined by more than 40% while the city-wide decline was approximately 25% between 1990 and 2000 (City of Indianapolis, 2003). The once 35 subsidized day-care facilities and eight counseling–drug treatment centers dwindled to eight and four by 2000 (City of Indianapolis, 2003). To make matters worse, neo-liberal forms of intervention have come to dominate in these areas. Funds to 'distressed neighborhoods' have gone mainly to two sources: Community Development Corporations (CDCs) and the National Center for Neighborhood Enterprise (NCNE). The city's seven major CDCs, substantially controlled by a conservative City County Council, have used funds to mainly paint homes, fix up houses, repair torn streets, and enroll residents in entrepreneurial programs (Maher, 2003). They, like other CDCs across Urban America, had become remarkably corporate and de-radicalized by the 1990s (see DeFillipis, 2004). CDCs, operating in ascendant neoliberal times, often function pragmatically as corporate collaborating entities (see Porter, 1997).

The other source of funds in Indianapolis for distressed neighborhoods, NCNE, has been conservative mogul Robert Woodson's national outreach center. His city development model pushes to re-entrepreneurialize social climates and physical spaces by nurturing individual responsibility, business acumen, and supplanting 'bad' culture. Its increased use across inner city America, initially in trials, appeared widely as central government policy across numerous cities in America in the 1990s (it was embraced and widely used by John Norquist in Milwaukee, Rudolph Giuliani in New York, and Stephen Goldsmith in Indianapolis). Its implementation in Indianapolis has emphasized one pillar of this: faith-based programs and church-led social expertise to revitalize neighborhoods. At its core, it has turned more than 15 churches into major providers for social counseling, job expertise, drug control, and micro-enterprise classes (see National Center for Neighborhood Enterprise, 2003). Each operates in the context of proffering faith-based and 'good' cultural values: Indy's black ghettos are to be further established as isolated and compliant labor pockets.

In this setting, new city funding priorities have decimated the predominantly Black East Side: block grants for housing and social projects have been cut by more than 35% in the last three years (Braggs, 2004). Now, more than 60% of Eastside residents are unofficially below the poverty level, with under-employment rampant (see Kelly, 2003). The fall-out is commonly noted by community leaders and residents. To Rev. Byron Alston, a long-term supporter of local black youth in the area, increased crime has followed from worsened living conditions, and 'we are tired of going to funerals' (in Kelly, 2003). To Alston, decent paying jobs have all but disappeared, government is remote and hostile, and too many turn to illicit activities like selling drugs to survive. 'We want to give hope', said the Rev. Donnie Golder of Temple of Praise Assembly, 'but conditions are harder than ever' (in Kelly, 2004). In this context, to writer Fred Kelly (2003), vague interventionist strategies by volunteers (church officials, block groups) are the principal—and a limited—corrective for the community's pressing needs.

And even momentary escape by residents from the grinding poverty is difficult. Random walks outside this Eastside area can easily prove shameful and demeaning, and at its worst, deadly. The Indianapolis Police Department, notorious for its harsh enforcement of social spaces (see Jet, 1995), rigorously polices the downtown area for 'Eastside interlopers'. To writer Fred Goldstein (2001), the police routinely 'harass African American youth and treat them as if they were violent gang members ... the cops have "jump out boys" who jump out of squad cars and swoop down on black youth'. And from our observations, police officers, black or white, move through the Eastside, paraphrasing James Baldwin, 'like occupying sol-dier[s] in a bitterly hostile country'. That is why, following Baldwin, the police ride in cars or walk in twos or threes. Poverty and blackness here, to City Councilperson Glen Howard (1991), translates into a perception of intransigent culture and values. Such 'troublesome' people, supposedly antithetical to cultivating a vibrant consumer and producer center, must be regulated and controlled. Not surprisingly, Indianapolis has experienced two large riots since 1995 over police brutality (see Goldstein, 2001).

These ghettos in Indianapolis ultimately fall prey to a maxim that propels the Indy growth machine: the need for growth leaders to be brutally efficient and partition the city into separate social spheres given new hyper-global times. As one city planner noted in discussion, 'the new [global] times ... the new order of the day ... without blinking an eye, the choice is obvious, we have to re-make the downtown or else ... decay and collapse could prevail'. The result is to further something perverse: the creation of not one city—Indianapolis—but a multiplicity of dis-connected places. What has emerged is an expansive urban terrain simultaneously stable and on the edge, islands of differentiated spaces bonded only by the sense of being in a place called 'Indianapolis'. Downtown celebrated spaces, the new consumptive playgrounds, are forged as places of hard rock stability, but at the expense of purging dissimilar people and spaces around it to create a multitude of disconnected 'cities'.

Neighborhood associations and housing groups in Indianapolis and Cleveland have not totally wilted in the face of this reality: some have operated 'below' CDCs but with depleted funds. As one head of a housing group in Cleveland said, 'it's became much more difficult to help the poor ... the money is no longer there, we get money from the local CDC which is block grant dollars, but priorities of City Hall have changed ... It has become "in" to fix up downtown and its public hotspots, "out" with the needs of the poor'. A similar story comes from the head of a social service agency in Indianapolis. 'The CDCs complain about a steep cut in their budgets from City Hall, but it's us who are bearing the brunt of the turn away from the poor. It's [helping the poor] just no longer popular and seen as important to city improvement ... The City more than ever caters to the needs of builders and developers who want to gentrify ... that's the priority'.

Conclusion

I conclude the discussion with two final points. First, the reality of this global trope refutes the near mantra-like belief that city growth machines and 'globalization' are inherently oppositional forces. In short, it is false to automatically counterpose city growth machines and 'globalization' as always antithetical to each other, a fallacy that too many urban researchers continue to support. This study suggests, alternatively, that these machines, as centers of rhetorical pro-duction and power, can seize the day's concerns and constitute a sense of powerful globalization that help their restructuring ambitions. Globalization, as a deployed construct, can nourish a fervent desire of growth machines: to restructure cities to their specifications. To be sure, these coalitions have not invented this global concept, and it does exist as an elusive, highly uneven process. But in aggressive oratory, they continue to draw on it, magnify it, and caricature it as they take advantage of this ambiguous notion in common thought.

A final point: this global trope should be seen as complex, tension-ridden, and anything but a simple done-deal. At the heart of this difficulty is that a surprisingly elusive abstraction—new global times—is always being simplistically grounded and empiricized. The global trope is an elusive abstraction in two ways. First, it is a barely present reality, an empirical ambiguity (see Cameron and Palen, 2003). It is basically non-visible to people in space, said to lay way beyond the domain of states and regions. It is also absent temporally, with globalization widely invoking the sense of an inexorable, futuristic unfolding as the telos of capitalism. In this context, growth machines toil to 'proof' globalization as something observable, legible, and on the move. In this process, a sense of easy-to-understand local ills is widely served up as irrefutable evidence. In a potentially controversial rendering, manifestations of globalization are projected to be all around the city: in people (e.g., the black poor), places (e.g., industrial districts), and processes (e.g., city crime, declining public revenues).

In sum, the current 'global influence' in these cities can be seen as a rhetoric as well as a reality. Proclamations of new global times transmit a disciplining code of a new ominous world for public consumption. At its core is growth machine desires to command and steer something crucial to them—physical and social change—in evolving capitalist times. In this case, city growth machines find themselves in a new economic circumstance (hyper real-estate accumulation), a new political reality (neoliberal era), and new social setting (vague public notions of an ominous global world). Drawing out this vague global conception—grounding it, empiricizing it, displaying its supposed effects—thus works through an expedient 'opportunity structure'. Tweaking an old adage, if globalization did not exist, humans would have to create it, for much political mileage can be gained from this as a decisive offering. In the end, it is globalization as an image and a fear, as much as a reality, that today activates people and institutions in these cities to take actions that drive a new uneven development.

Notes

1   I use the terms growth machine and neoliberal governance with distinctive meanings in mind. The term growth machine references the nexus of local-based institutions—prominent builders, developers, realtors, the media, and the local state—that unify around a shared vision of city growth and push aggressively to make this a reality (see Logan and Molotch, 1987). The term neoliberal governance, encompassing the local growth machine, privileges the power and influence of the local state as a body that manages and regulates the diverse spheres of city growth, economic development, housing policy, and socio-spatial life of populations.

2   Data was obtained for this research via textual analysis of newspapers and city technical reports, and open-ended discussions with interviewees. Textual analysis deconstructed stories about city growth, city redevelopment, and city restructuring in two local dailies, *Cleveland Plain-Dealer* and *Indianapolis Star*, and stories from the web. Stories and articles using the terms growth, redevelopment, globalization, and ghetto were identified for review. Open-ended discussions were also conducted in the two cities in the early 1990s and in 2004 and 2005. I conversed with local planners, city officials, city program heads and representatives, community activists, residents, and youth in person or by telephone. To obtain credible responses, all interviewees were initially asked if they preferred to have their names withheld from future write-ups of the data. Nearly 90% of the 65 interviewees opted for this. For this reason, comments by discussants frequently fail to carry a name or simply provide a pseudonym.

References

Anderson, S. & Cavanaugh, J. (2000) Top 200: the rise of global corporate power. Technical report, Global Policy Forum, 77 UN Plaza, Suite 3D, New York.

Bakhtin, M. (1981) *The Dialogic Imagination* (Austin: University of Texas).

Braggs, B. (2004) Discussion with planner, Department of Metropolitan Development, City of Indianapolis, 2 August.

Brenner, N. & Theodore, N. (2002) *Spaces of Neoliberalism: Urban Restructuring in North America and Western Europe* (Oxford: Blackwell).

Brenner, N. & Theodore, N. (2002) Cities and the geographies of actually existing neoliberalism, in: N. Brenner & N. Theodore (Eds) *Spaces of Neoliberalism: Urban Restructuring in North America and Western Europe* (Oxford: Blackwell), pp. 1–33.

Burawoy, M. (2000) Introduction: Reaching for the Global, in: M. Burawoy, J. Blum *et al.* (Eds) *Global Ethnography* (Berkeley: University of California), pp. 1–35.

Cameron, A. & Palen, R. (2003) The imagined economy: mapping transformation in the contemporary state, in: N. Brenner, B. Jessop, M. Jones & G. Macleod (Eds) *State/Space: A Reader* (Oxford: Blackwell), pp. 165–184.

Center on Urban Policy and Social Change (2001) The end of welfare as they knew it: what happens when welfare recipients reach their time limits? Technical report, Mandel School of Applied Social Sciences, Case Western Reserve University.

Center for Economic Development (2004) After the boom: joblessness in Milwaukee. Technical report, available from Center, Milwaukee, Wisconsin.

CIA World Fact Book (2003) Technical report, federal government document, Washington DC.

City of Indianapolis (2003) The consolidated plan. Technical report, Division of Community Development, Department of Metropolitan Development, available from City.

Civic Task Force on International Cleveland (2003) Recommendations to the City of Cleveland. Technical report, City of Cleveland, available from City.

Cleveland State University (2001) Urban update: news from the Maxine Goodman Levin College of Urban Affairs (Fall), pp. 1–3.

Cochrane, A. (1999) Redefining urban politics for the twenty-first century, in: A. Jonas & D. Wilson (Eds) *The Urban Growth Machine: Critical Perspectives Two Decades Later* (Albany, NY: SUNY), pp. 109–124.

Cox, K. (1993) The local and the global in the new urban politics: a critical review, *Environment and Planning D: Society and Space*, 11, pp. 433–448.

DeFilippis, J. (2004) *Unmaking Goliath* (London: Routledge).

DiMora, J. (2005) Commissioners poised to boost arts, again! Media release, Cuyahoga County Department of Development, 26 May.

Fairclaugh, N. (1992) *Discourse and Social Change* (New York: Polity).

Fried, M. (2004) Discussion with local planner, City of Chicago, 11 August.

Goldsmith, S. (2003a) Putting faith in neighborhoods: making cities work through grassroots citizenship. Technical report, Indianapolis, Hudson Institute.

Goldsmith, S. (2003b) Introduction, in: *The Entrepreneurial City: A How-To Handbook For Urban Innovators* (New York: Manhattan Institute For Policy Research), pp. 1–10.

Goldstein, F. (2001) Police brutality—from L.A. to New York, it happens every day, *Workers World*, 22, pp. 11–17.

Grunwald, M. (1998) The myth of the supermayor, *American Prospect*, 40, 1 September, pp. 4–7.

Harvey, D. (1989) *The Postmodern Condition* (Oxford: Blackwell).

Hennepin, B. (2004) Discussion with planner, City of Cleveland, 4 March.

Hollway, W. (1984) Gender difference and the production of subjectivity, in: J. Henriques, W. Hollway *et al.* (Eds) *Changing the Subject: Psychology, Social Regulation, and Subjectivity* (New York: Methuen).

Howard, G. (1991) Discussion with City-County Councilor, City of Indianapolis, 14 May.

Hudnut, W. (1995) *The Hudnut Years in Indianapolis* (Bloomington: Indiana University Press).

Indianapolis Regional Center Plan (2001) Comeback cities: the prospects for a continuing urban renaissance. Technical report, available from City of Indianapolis, Department of Metropolitan Development.

IndyStar.Com (2001) Library fact files, Stephen Goldsmith. Available at http://www.indystar.com.

Jenks, C. (2004) Discussion with planner, City of Cleveland, 10 August.

Jet (1995) Riots, unrest plague three cities after police shootings, allegations of brutality, 21 August, p. 11.

Judd, D. (1979) *The Politics of America's Cities: Private Power and Public Policy* (Glenville, IL: Little & Brown).

Kelly, F. (2003) Ministers to wage anti violence campaign, *Indy News*, 11 October, p. B-1.

Kennedy, L. (2000) *Race and Urban Space in American Culture* (London: Routledge).

Knox, P. (1997) Globalization and urban economic change, *Annals of the American Academy of Political and Social Science*, 551, pp. 17–28.

Logan, J. & Molotch, H. (1987) *Urban Fortunes* (Berkeley, CA: University of California).

Maher, T. (2003) Discussion with professor, University of Indianapolis, 23 June.

Miller, D. (2003) Unspinning the globe, *Red Pepper*, 6–8 June.

Morial, M. (2002) The New World. Speech to the National Urban League, August, transcript available from the Urban League.

Mosimen, D. (2002) Mayors get boost from corporations, *Wisconsin State Journal*, 13 June, p. 1.

National Center for Neighborhood Enterprise (2003) Empowering America's communities. Technical report, available from Center, Washington DC.

Naymik, M. (2003) debt service: financial disaster threatens: a major Eastside community center. Available at http://www.clevescene.com/issues/1990-0.7-08/news.html.

New York Times (2005) In the ring but attached to the cell block, 16 July, p. 1-D.

Peck, J. & Theodore, N. (2000) Contingent Chicago: restructuring the spaces of temporary labor, *International Journal of Urban and Regional Research*, 24, pp. 145–162.

Pile, S., Brook, C. & Mooney, G. (1999) *Unruly Cities?* (London: Routledge).

Plann, S. (2004) Discussion with planner, City of Cleveland, 9 April.

Porter, M. (1997) New strategies for inner-city economic development, *Economic Development Quarterly*, 11, pp. 11–27.

Professional Experience (2003) Technical document. Available at http://www.kig.harvard.edu/virtual/booktour/Old_-Tour_Files/goldsmithbio.htm.

Rentgen, M. (2004) Discussion with planner, City of Cleveland, 12 August.

Short, J. (2004) *Global Metropolitan* (London: Routledge).

Skrabec, J. (2004) Discussion with worker, Department of Community Development, City of Cleveland, 5 June.

Smith, N. (1984) *Uneven Development* (Oxford: Blackwell).

Smith, N. (2002) New globalism, new urbanism: gentrification as global urban strategy, *Antipode*, 34, pp. 212–231.

Soros, G. (1998) *The Crisis of Global Capitalism: Open Society Endangered* (New York: Basic).

Teaford, J. (1990) *The Rough Road to Renaissance: Urban Revitalization in America 1940-1985* (Baltimore, MD: Johns Hopkins University Press).

Thrift, N. (1995) A hyperactive world, in: R. J. Johnston, P. J. Taylor & M. J. Watts (Eds) *Geographies of Global Change* (Oxford: Blackwell), pp. 18–35.

Triozzi, R. (2005) Website 'Triozzi For Mayor'. Available at http://www.blog01.kintera.com/Triozzi/.

Von Hoffman, N. (1991) The real terror is in the streets, *Chicago Tribune*, 14 March, p. 9.

Wacquant, L. (2002a) Deadly symbiosis, *Boston Review* (April/May), 12 pp.

Wacquant, L. (2002b) From slavery to mass incarceration: rethinking the race question in the U.S., *New Left Review*, 13, pp. 41–104.

Wagner-Pacific, R. (1994) *Discourse and Destruction* (Chicago: University of Chicago).

Wallach, M. (2004) Discussion with planner, City of Cleveland, 10 August.

Warf, B. & Holly, B. (1997) The rise and fall and rise of Cleveland, *Annals of the American Academy of Political and Social Science*, 511, pp. 208–221.

Weber, R. (2002) Extracting Value from the city: neoliberalism and urban redevelopment, in: N. Brenner & N. Theodore (Eds) *Spaces of Neoliberalism: Urban Restructuring in North America and Western Europe* (Oxford: Blackwell), pp. 172–194.

Wilson, D. (1996) Metaphors, growth coalitions, and black poverty neighborhoods in a U.S. city, *Antipode*, 28(1), pp. 72–97.

Wilson, D. (2005) *Inventing Black-On-Black Violence: Discourse, Space, Representation* (Syracuse, NY: Syracuse University Press).

Wilson, D. (2007) *Cities and Race: America's New Black Ghettos* (London: Routledge).

Wilson, D. & Grammenos, D. (2000) Spatiality and urban redevelopment movements, *Urban Geography*, 21, pp. 361–371.

Wilson, D. & Wouters, J. (2004) Spatiality and growth discourse: the restructuring of America's rust belt cities, *Journal of Urban Affairs*, 25, pp. 123–139.

Wimsett, W. (1998) The fear economy, *Adbusters Magazine*, 21 (Spring), pp. 10–12.

David Wilson is currently investigating projects pivoting around the political economy of the US city. Specific projects examine the politics of urban growth regimes in Midwest cities, the politics of competing discursive formations that generate gentrified neighborhoods and poor communities, and the racializing of the contemporary urban issues of crime and city growth. At the moment, he serves on the editorial boards of *Urban Geography*, *Professional Geographer*, *Social and Cultural Geography*, Syracuse University Press Society, Space, and Place Book Series, *Inter-Cultural Studies*, and the International Encyclopedia of Human Geography project.

Flattening Ontologies of Globalization: The Nollywood Case

SALLIE A. MARSTON, KEITH WOODWARD & JOHN PAUL JONES, III

Introduction

In this article we examine the intersections between space and globalization. Not the geographies that have been produced by globalization—because for this we have a richly descriptive and detailed atlas of economic, cultural, and political transformations that underwrite a new vocabulary of mobilization, intensification, and hybridization (Appadurai, 1996; Dicken, 2003; Harvey, 1989; Held *et al.*, 2000; Nederveen Pieterse, 2004; Sassen, 1998; cf. Hirst and Thompson, 1999). We focus instead on the spatial imaginaries (Gregory, 1994) researchers bring *to* globalization, concepts that enable them to comprehend, explain, and confront it. We take up this task by drawing from and extending two provocative papers dealing with the spaces of globalization. In the first, J. K. Gibson-Graham (2002) offer critical assessments of the local–global binary that is at the heart of academic and popular conceptualizations of globalization. Noting that the global 'appears as a telos in the ongoing process called "globalization"', they are working to dislodge the opposition from a circumscribed politics in which large scale 'global forces' reign supreme over 'progressive, grassroots, local interventions' (p. 25; also Massey, 1994). In another paper, titled 'Spatialities of Globalization', Ash Amin (2002) is concerned to theorize how globalization should be thought of, geographically speaking. Underlying his work is a fundamental question: how should the local and the global be connected? Contending that 'there is no consensus in social theory about what to say about this spatiality' (p. 385), he goes on to contrast a scalar logic of globalization with a networked one. Both logics are about efforts to find a language for describing how 'territoriality itself is becoming altered by the rise of world-scale processes and transnational connectivity' (p. 387). The Gibson-Graham and Amin papers have prompted us to further consider the conceptual resources available to describe the spatiality of globalization. Here we extend their analyses by asking the following question: what spatial ontologies have been brought to bear on globalization, and how might it appear under an alternative specification? By invoking spatial ontology we signal our attentiveness to the differential relations that drive material compositions and dynamic properties, objects and events, while refusing claims to being or processes that rely upon transcendent spatial categories (Marston *et al.*, 2005).

In the next section we look to Gibson-Graham and Amin to assess some of the understandings of space that have been used to grasp the forces of flux and fixity currently defining globalization. Briefly, if we are to refer to globalization, as Roland Robertson (2004, p. 98) has, as 'the relatively specific path that the world has taken in the direction of becoming singular', then we need to ask what sort of spatiality has been employed to describe and analyze that path. Because globalization implies mobility, transference, and interconnection—a multiplication of linkages among disparate places and peoples and a widening and deepening of their intensities (Dicken, 2003; Giddens, 1990; Held *et al.*, 2000; King, 1997; Nederveen Pieterse, 2004)—its theorists have little choice but to employ a spatial vocabulary in order to understand it (Brenner, 2004). And within that ambit there exists the idea that: (a) globalization rests, at base, on the local–global binary (Gibson-Graham, 2002) and (b) there are two primary candidates for linking the disparate parts of space this binary presumes (Amin, 2002). One concentrates on a set of socially produced, overlapping, and intersecting territorial hierarchies (e.g., neighborhood, city, region, nation); the other focuses attention on spatial extensions of interconnecting flows, networks, and dispersed associations. With Gibson-Graham, we register our complaints with both the theoretical formulation of the local–global binary and the hegemonic force of its political calcifications. We go on, however, to question the ontological status of the global on which conceptions of globalization depend. With Amin, we note our affinities for networks, properly conceived, as the basis for interpreting the objects and events of globalization; unlike him, however, we are prepared to jettison any understanding of globalization that might rely upon scalar imaginaries, no matter how fluid or malleable they are (Marston *et al.*, 2005). In the third section we elaborate a 'flat' site ontology that, we believe, avoids the shortcomings of globalization's spatial ontologies. The significance of the site ontology turns in part on the fact that, in rejecting the local–global optic through which globalization theory is constructed, globalization itself is diminished as an explanatory term.

This article issues a cautionary note against the hegemony of spatial abstractions that circulate within 'globe talk' (Robertson, 1992). To clarify our position, we offer an empirical section that interprets what might otherwise be viewed as an exemplar of globalization, interpreted here through the flat ontology. The case is the film industry known as Nollywood centered in Lagos, Nigeria. Emergent within the past 15 years, it is now reputed to be the largest such industry in the world in terms of numbers of films produced each year. We selected Nollywood because of the ease with which it has been incorporated into globalization's frame, right alongside Mumbai's Bollywood, in aping Los Angeles's Hollywood. We attempt to show that this imitative positioning is itself the product of the spatialities writers have brought *to* globalization, and that a different reading can be marshaled to produce a more culturally and politically attuned understanding of Nigeria's burgeoning film industry. That reading leads us to address in the conclusion a widespread concern of globalization theorists and anti-globalization activists alike: what political tendencies and possibilities reside in the local? We respond by continuing to refuse the premise of the global on which the question is founded, pointing instead to the necessarily site-specific alignment of all politics.

Up and Down and Back and Forth with the Local–Global

Given the conceptual separation of the local and the global in globalization discourse, one of the requisite tasks of globalization theorists has been to find a language for reconnecting them. One starting point is to equate 'the global' with universalism and macro-level structures, while tying 'the local' to particularism and everyday experience. When informed by a dialectical vision, this effort often results in a 'both/and' solution, as when Roland Robertson (1997, p. 73) writes that globalization involves a twofold process of 'interpenetration': the 'universalization of particularism and the particularization of universalism'. On the one hand is the 'dramatic penetration of global forces' (Cvetkovich and Kellner, 1997, p. 3) into everyday life, where the global is understood as 'that matrix of transnational economic, political, and cultural forces that are circulating throughout the globe and producing universal, global conditions, often transversing and even erasing previously formed national and regional boundaries' (Cvetkovich and Kellner, 1997, p. 14). On the other are 'those constellations of conditions that are particular and specific according to country, region, tradition, and other determinants, such as the creation and preservation of local subcultures' (Cvetkovich and Kellner, 1997, p. 15). In describing their combinations, metaphors of interconnection and articulation are often deployed (Cvetkovich and Kellner, 1997; Giddens, 1990; Mamadouh et al., 2004; Nederveen Pieterse 1995; Robertson, 1992, 1997). In most accounts, the local and the global connect across a variety of domains—economic, political, cultural, social—through which the former are differentially mediated in terms that range from accommodation to resistance.

Numerous scholars have noted that power is unevenly embedded in the local and the global (Hardt and Negri, 2000; Harvey, 1996; Massey, 1994, 2005), a point that goes directly to the question of how to theorize opposition to globalization. Gibson-Graham (2002, p. 27) summarizes these geopolitical alignments thus:

> We are all familiar with the denigration of the local as small and relatively powerless, defined and confined by the global: the global is a force, the local is its field of play; the global is penetrating, the local penetrated and transformed. Globalism is synonymous with abstract space, the frictionless movement of money and commodities, the expansiveness and inventiveness of capitalism and the market. But its Other, localism, is coded as place, community, defensiveness, bounded identity, *in situ* labor, noncapitalism, the traditional.

Determined to dislodge the local–global binary from the powerless–powerful one, Gibson-Graham first invoke the commonly acknowledged problems associated with binary opposi- tions, such as their production within a Western epistemology that substitutes multiplicity, permeability, and hybridity with fixity, and their dependence on one another as negated yet productive moments in the constitutive production of the oppositional term (the 'Other'). Concerned that critical resources that might be marshaled against globalization are under- mined when the subordinate term is stripped of its power, Gibson-Graham (2002, p. 31) go on to posit that the local and the global are not 'things in themselves', but interpretive frames, empty of content: 'This move opposes the tendency to objectify both local and global, to perceive "localness" or "globalness" as essential or real qualities of an object'. But instead of carrying these moments of critique forward in ways that might altogether destabilize the binary (pp. 32–33), Gibson-Graham focus their project on reshaping the political 'effectivity of the local' (p. 35) by contrasting global capitalism with diverse, often localized, economies, such as: alternative markets (e.g., community supported agriculture, black market), non-market activities (e.g., barter, gifts), unpaid labor, alternative paid labor (e.g., co-operatives, self-employed), alternative capitalist activities (e.g., socially and ecologi- cally responsible capitalism), and non-capitalist enterprises (e.g., communal). Notwithstand- ing the value of these comparisons—in which, admittedly, the extensiveness of diverse economies is demonstrated—the global is nonetheless untouched by the exercise, a compari- son that redoubles the terms that measure global capitalism's spatial power.

An alternative is to complete Gibson-Graham's (2002, pp. 30–32) unfinished project of deconstruction by undoing the 'structurality of structure' (Derrida, 1966, p. 248) on which the local–global and all other binaries pivot. Proceeding first by questioning the law that governs the desire for an orienting, balancing, and organizing center—logos, essence, presence, origin—we might read 'the global' as one more hallmark of Western science that limits what Derrida called the 'freeplay' of the structure, the otherwise unraveling elements that any struc- ture is said to systematize. Such a reading becomes possible in that moment of recognition when we can begin to think that there might not be a center, 'that the center could not be ... a being- present, that the center [has] no natural locus, that it was not a fixed locus but a function, a sort of non-locus in which an infinite number of sign-substitutions came into play' (Derrida, 1966, p. 249). If 'the global' in globalization discourse (King, 1997, p. 11) cannot bear the weight of transcendence—if it is in fact not a 'being-present'—then in the absence of a locus its only function will be to extend 'the domain and interplay of signification *ad infinitum*' (Derrida, 1966, p. 249).

In so destabilizing 'the global' we find inspiration from John Tagg (1997, p. 157), an art historian who noted that 'concepts of globalism have no status outside of the fields of discourse and practice that constitute them'. As he puts matters, the globe 'would seem to be caught in precisely what the Derridians might think of as a "metaphysics of presence", or the Lacanians as a projection onto the isolated images of the planet of an Imaginary wholeness that represses the multiple and heterogeneous positioning effects of language' (Tagg, 1997, p. 159). This is not to say, as Deutsche (1991) pointedly remarks in defending poststructuralism (also Dixon and Jones, 1998), that the world does not exist, only that it cannot be captured outside of the systems and technologies of representation we bring to bear on it, and that give it its meaning. Thus, that the globe is so large as to be beyond the scope of everyday life (while no doubt true) is not the main point, for experience at any 'level' is never direct, but always mediated through the language and practices that confer upon it reality effects and that organize its resonances and textures (Scott, 1991). The point instead, is that the globe is a transcendent spatial category, an 'impossible object' quite like 'society' in Ernesto Laclau's and Chantal Mouffe's (1985) famous analysis. The 'global' is made possible by the openness and indeterminacy of discourse, qualities enabling it to be stabilized, partially and temporarily, until it is overflowed by a new articulation or representation (Tagg, 1997). In these overcodings, the global signifier is interdependent with other holistic epistemes—such as structure, law, God. As Cosgrove (2001) has shown, unraveling these connective tissues requires genealogical attention to the emergence of specific technologies and techniques of representation, such as those of astronomical measurement and cartographic illustration.

Our second and third criticisms of the spatial ontologies of globalization ensue from this analysis. As Amin (2002) suggests, once the global has been separated from the local, there are a limited number of tropes at our disposal to describe the spaces reconnected by globalization. Most common are those that rely on either scales or networks. Both spatial metaphors work to link together distant phenomena and processes; how they conceive of their displacements is, however, quite different. The scalar approach tends to rely on a hierarchical language of vertically conceived levels to describe globalization's spatial churnings; the network approach employs a horizontal optic, relying on a continuous and often relationally conceived extensivity rather than on a priori territorial demarcations. We look at each of these in turn.

Amin's analysis confirms that the scalar imaginary of globalization theory cannot be disentangled from the history of scale theorizing more generally, especially as it developed in human geography. One of the most important early developments in scale theory was provided by Peter Taylor (1982), whose work not only laid the ground for what is today known as the social construction of scale (Marston, 2000), but which also spatialized world systems theory, an early precursor to contemporary theories of globalization. Typical of a scale-influenced globalization hypothesis is the question of the relative power of the nation state in comparison to the global forces that operate beyond its confines (Taylor, 1982; Tilly, 1984). Whatever one's view of its continuing importance as a key unit in territorialization (compare Brenner, 2004 to Ohmae, 1995 and Strange, 1996), from the vantage point of scale, the nation state sits at a critical juncture between the 'up' of transnational corporations, international monetary and trade blocs, and the magnates of the Western culture industry (Held, 1995), and the 'down' of sub-national, regional, and otherwise local particularisms. For some theorists, globalization is *all about* these scalar imbrications: 'globalization … in both its structural and strategic moments is the creation and/or restructuring of scale as a social relation and as a site of social relations' (Jessop, 2000, p. 341). As Amin (2002, p. 387) summarizes this view:

> Globalisation is seen to multiply and relativise geographical scales of social organization linked to the changing spatial requirements of the latest phase of capitalist development. These are not seen as mutually exclusive or parallel scalar configurations, but as intersecting and overlapping scales, leading to the restructuring of places as territories as they engage in the multiscalar processes and politics.

Amin (2002, p. 388) goes on to sound a cautionary argument against the scalar imaginary, noting that the distinction 'between the "local" and the "global" as separate scalar fields remains problematic'. His concern is not to argue that the global does not exist, but rather that the local is so interpenetrated by outside forces that its ontological status as 'place' in opposition to a globalized 'space' cannot be sustained:

> Surely a key aspect of the transnationalisation of local relations is that we can no longer make an easy distinction between local and global geographies? How localized or global, for example, are the associational politics of worker, immigrant, and NGO . . . groups campaigning for local recognition but relying on international financial and other support networks? (Amin, 2002, p. 388)

In our view, however, the problem is not so much the inseparability of the local and global, but the transcendent imaginary that throws social processes onto higher order spatial registers altogether, whether they are global capitalism *or* global civil society. De-coupling levels of power from this ladder-like imaginary—a project of Amin's as well as Gibson-Graham's—will require ancillary work on a number of binaries, including culture–economy, agency–structure, subjectivity–objectivity, parochialism–cosmopolitanism, static–dynamic, authentic–produced, nostalgic–progressive, and concrete–abstract (Marston *et al.*, 2005). These are all territorializations of a different sort: the reproduction and circulation of any number of small–large imaginaries and their pre-configured hierarchies. Sorting these binaries through the various levels—what processes and at what scales? (e.g., Brenner, 2004)—informs scores if not hundreds of studies on globalization, all of which, by tautology, rely on the transcendent imaginary of the global. Not lastly, from this elevated optic researchers are unwittingly hoisted into the position of detached surveyor. As Gibson-Graham (2002, pp. 34–35) notes, most theorists 'stand outside globalization and "see it as it is"'; is it possible, they ask, 'that the power of globalization . . . has taken over the bodies of its critics?'.

In contrast to the hierarchical approach, some theorists have turned their attention to a different metaphor, one founded on flows and networks (Amin, 2002). Consider first the definition in *Global Transformations*—a classic text in the ever-expanding globalization literature: '*a process (or set of processes) which embodies a transformation in the spatial organization of social relations and transactions—assessed in terms of their extensity, intensity, velocity and impact—generating transcontinental or interregional flows and networks of activity, interaction and the exercise of power* (Held *et al.*, 2000, p. 16, italics original). Drawing directly on the work of Manuel Castells (1996) and his conceptualization of globalization as a 'space of flows', as well as indirectly on actor-network theory (Law and Hassard, 1999), Held *et al.* (2000, p. 16) specify the flows as constituted by 'the movement of physical artifacts, people, symbols, tokens and information across space and time, while networks refer to regularized or patterned interactions between independent agents, nodes of activity, or sites of power'.

Flows are common spatial metaphors to comprehending globalization, but we would be wise to remember that they are just that. As spatial concepts, they rely on the presumption that objects and bodies can become detached from their moorings or nodes and circulate over space, thereby embedding one site into another (Giddens, 1990). One problem with this conceptual optic is the tendency to see aspects of globalization as reducible to horizontally radiating 'out theres' that fly over the materialities of the in-between in order find themselves in the space of the 'in here'. Even more symptomatic is the view that space itself is abolished in a sea of networks and flows. As Schotle (2000) has claimed:

> 'global' relations are social connections in which territorial location, territorial distance and territorial borders do not have a determining influence. In global space 'place' is not territorially fixed, territorial distance is covered in effectively no time, and territorial frontiers present no particular impediment. (quoted in Amin, 2002, p. 386)

As we pointed out earlier (Marston *et al.*, 2005), this view of unfettered flows presents nearly as many problems as the rigid scalar imaginary it promises to overturn. More to our liking is Amin's (2002, p. 389) careful survey of networked space, 'the geographies constituted through the folds, undulations, and overlaps that natural and social practices normally assume, without any a priori assumption of the geographies of relations nested in territorial or geometric space'. What 'grounds' such flows for Amin (2002, p. 391) is a focus on places that are thought of in non-bounded terms, 'as nodes in relational settings, and as [sites] of situated practices'. His analytic emphasis on the 'placement of practices' precludes the 'amorphous and evanescent world geography of incessant fluidity and mobility' (p. 389). Places are, rather, the 'temporary spatiotemporalisation of associational networks of different lengths and duration' (Amin, 2002, p. 391), nodes that embody both actual and virtual forces (Delanda, 2002; Deleuze, 1994; Thrift, 2000). Better than a shifting or reworked territoriality of scales, globalization for Amin (2002, p. 395) is an 'energized network space' marked by 'the intensification of mixture and connectivity as more things become interdependent (in associative links and exclusions)'.

And yet, in the end, Amin (2002, pp. 396–397) is not willing to jettison wholesale the scalar imaginary, and so we find him affirming the continued existence and relevance of 'scalar practices and institutions'. Included in his discussion are a number of processes and institutions that borrow heavily from the local-to-global optic that we have been at pains to critique: a 'global regime of capitalist accumulation', 'downwards' and 'upwards' movements of state activities, autonomous actions attributed to governments at national and local levels, etc. In our view, the deployment of these imaginary geo-units is inconsistent with the main elements of Amin's argument, which we otherwise affirm. They constitute one of the major, if still relatively unacknowledged, differences between ontology informed by hierarchical spatiality and the flat ontology informed by Deleuze, Guattari, and others, to which we now turn.

Ontology without Globalization

Let us first be clear in explaining that, by using the term 'flat', we are not following up one critique of spatial imaginaries with the production of yet another. In particular, our sense of flatness shares no commonalities or affinities with the orgiastic capitalocentrism of Thomas Friedman (2006), who would have us believe that socio-political access and mobility have been flattened (read: equalized) for the entirety of the world's population through a singular and pervasive market blanketing the globe. The exemplary imaginary for such Friedmanesque notions of *culturonomic* flatness is that of the Earth image projected onto the shape of a coin, wherein the totality of the world's relations are made indiscernible from those of the market. 'Flat' in this context can only mean 'reduced to' or 'singularized': the classically capitalist desire for reduction of necessity, distance, and—importantly—difference to the crude, abstract equalizer: money.

In contrast, our conception of *ontological* flatness is an articulation of the world and its workings that resists both the production of formal, typological categories and liberalist fantasies about equalized access through the fluidities of capital-driven flattening. We propose a spatial ontology that recognizes a virtually infinite population of mobile and mutable 'sites' and that is *ontologically flat* by virtue of its affirmation of immanence—or self-organization—as the fundamental process of material actualization. Against the deployment of forms or categories that operate by carving up the world into a delimited set of manageable object-types, we look to the unfolding state of affairs within which situations or sites are constituted as singularities—that is, as a collectivity of bodies or things, orders and events, and doings and sayings that hang together so as to lend distinct consistency to assemblages of dynamic relations. Likewise, rather than proceeding by way of a set of pre-established axiomatics for evaluating what processes are unfolding—a reductive strategy that tends to overlook differences from site to site in favor of roping them together under the banner of equivalence—we argue that investigations must be conditioned by the positional and processual composition of the site to better feel out its speci-ficities. Laid out not as a problem that must be force-fed into the matrix of a preordained solution (scalar 'up theres' or horizontal 'over theres'), but instead as a problematic field that in itself produces the analytic material of its own solvability (Deleuze, 1994, pp. 179–180), the speci-ficity of the site expresses itself in the variety of differences and singularities that lend them-selves to its composition. Approaching the site from this perspective is done in the spirit of retaining the variation and complexity—those elements that scientific reductivism and Fried-manesque capitalocentrism amputate and disregard as noise or accident—that go into making up the deep singularity and specificity of each site. As such, difference—rather than being some-thing that must be controlled or negated in order to arrive at general or reproducible results—becomes fundamentally productive and positive insofar as, without it, a site is stripped of its material situatedness and reduced to being merely another exemplar of a general condition.

A problematic or differential approach to the site—informed by Gilles Deleuze (1994)—articulates ontology as 'pure difference'. Thus, like our assessment of the site, there is an over-lying concern with discovering strategies for thinking and speaking about difference, variation, and complexity that do not at the same time foreclose the possibility of keeping those differences open to further variation and complexity. Deleuze and Guattari explain that analytics approached from the perspective of discussing and retaining difference must be 'anexact yet rig-orous' (1987, p. 483), suggesting that such work must be capable of speaking about difference without reframing a series of differences within orders of stasis and similitude. Elsewhere, Deleuze and Guattari (1994) frame the specificities of philosophy and science in terms of the ways that each distinctly deals with the question of difference and infinite variation. They explain that philosophy creates concepts that endeavor to describe complexity while at the same time keeping open and operating upon the difference that it describes. By contrast, science tends to select out and isolate variables from complex situations in order to establish footholds within complexity so as to better determine the processes of change and variability (Deleuze and Guattari, 1994, p. 202). Our ontological interest in the examination of sites as situ-ated, mutable singularities fosters a theoretical and practical approach to the world that falls somewhere between these accounts of philosophy and science. Specifically, while we take a step back from the abstraction inherent in the creation of concepts, we remain attentive to the need to seek out the articulation of material differences. Likewise, while we resist the scientific tendency to establish still points within a system in order to measure its movements and trans-formations, we do note the importance of seeking out the consistency-producing orders or strata that are *internal* to sites and that contribute to their frequent hangings-together. In this way, there can be said to be a double movement to the site: one trajectory toward continuous variation and differentiation, the other toward repetition and moments of relative stability. This double move-ment is a tendency that generally helps to mark out the horizons of the site. Each, repetition and variation, operates upon the other as a kind of consistency of the site, where the repetitive, inter-active affects of bodies condition trajectories toward situated differentiation.

In the next section, we deploy this understanding to examine one of the most recent victims of global overcoding, the Nigerian film industry popularly known as Nollywood. Its rise in importance as a major industry has drawn countless diminutive comparisons to Hollywood, the latter of which is invoked as a model for the marriage of globalization and film. Against an assumption that, given a certain technology or commodity (all other things being equal), any other system is a 'similar' if inferior copy of an exemplary (Western) one, we argue instead for attention to the specificity of Nollywood as a complex site, and not simply one more instance of globalization.

Nollywood: A Social Site

Our discussion of Nollywood as an example of a flat ontology rests on a small, but excellent collection of scholarly sources; scores of news articles from Nigeria (and a few other African countries), the US, Europe and the UK; Nollywood websites and blogs; our viewing of a set of recent Nollywood films; and our participation in the June 2006 Nollywood Foundation Convention, 'Nollywood, African Cinema and Beyond'—attended by both Nollywood and Hollywood professionals—in Los Angeles, California.[1] The scholarly sources provide detailed insights into the complexities of the video film industry as it is organized in Lagos; the others have helped us to appreciate how actors, directors and producers make the video films and how audiences engage with them.

Here we explore the empirical implications of our site ontology by way of Nollywood, which includes people operating in Surulere, the film industry district in Lagos, Nigeria, as well as in other parts of southern Nigeria, and journalistic and academic commentaries on the industry both within and outside of Nigeria. Whether the label 'Nollywood' was indigenously generated or applied by a US journalist, as has been suggested (Haynes, 2005), matters little to us. What is relevant to our argument is that it operates as a globalizing force, an 'order word' that captures the film-making practices occurring there and inescapably ties them to a distant and, under the imaginary of globalization, a superior other: Hollywood, a spectral refrain that haunts its nominal relatives.

We are, of course, mindful that Hollywood itself is a complex site with connections to other sites of film production around the United States and the world. And we do not mean to imply that Hollywood is somehow unproblematic either as a representation or a set of practices, in contrast to the complexity and difference of Nollywood. Rather, Hollywood too is constituted through a collection of sites of complexity and difference, incorporating a neighborhood of related practices from the prevailing studio system to independent filmmaking, pornography, government and educational media, amateur video production, and YouTube and other internet self-broadcasting video sites. But as an originative site of filmmaking practices, Hollywood has become a powerful coding mechanism such that the label 'Nollywood' makes whatever happens there *like* Hollywood but also *not* Hollywood. Indeed, Nollywood, because of its very name, becomes unavoidably recognized by film professionals as well as non-African audiences as derivative of Hollywood: a less sophisticated, more amateurish rendering of Hollywood comedy, action and thriller movies (Lagos films) or of Bollywood masala movies (Kano films).[2] Calling the site Nollywood territorializes it by way of a non-relational point that operates from beyond it. In this way, Nollywood (and other supposedly imitative sites of film production like Bollywood) appear anchored in place, while Hollywood is transcendent, the trace that standardizes and normativizes the practice of film production. But when we move away from the ordering impulses that comprise globalizing discourses, the practices, doings and sayings that actually constitute filmmaking in Nollywood are distinctly different from those that occur in Hollywood, or Bollywood. Moreover, these video films have very different effects on their audiences. In short, Nollywood is constituted through its own collection of differential relations, and though it certainly does have connections both to Los Angeles and Mumbai—as well as Beijing, New York and London—it assembles a distinct arrangement of entities that possess their own meanings and identities (Chikwendu, 2006; Ojewuyi, 2006; Okwo, 2006).[3]

Practices

Nollywood's video film genres range from action and adventure to historical epics, horror, and morality tales. But the most common description applied to them is melodrama, a genre that has been taken up all over the world from US and Egyptian soap operas to Latin American telenovelas to Indian masala films.[4] As melodramas, the video films routinely rely on particular tensions between the modern and traditional, wealth and poverty, and good and evil. As Haynes (2000, pp. 22–23) writes:

> The videos' extremes of fortune, emotion, and moral character are classic melodramatic elements; their predominantly domestic settings, multiple interwoven plot lines, and emphasis on dialogue rather than action make them resemble soap operas. ... [T]he claim here is not for any particular pure indigenous tradition of melodrama [in Nigeria], but rather for layers of influence and adaptation going back a long way, of which contemporary televised forms are only the most recent.

The centrality of ethnicity in Nigerian life also constitutes a frequent structuring principle in Nollywood video films. Nollywood video films are produced in many of the 250 tribal languages of Nigeria, though Yoruba, Igbo and English are numerically dominant; the advantage of English (65% of the export market) is that it allows for a wide international audience of Africans at home and abroad to appreciate them.[5] As Haynes and Okome (2000, p. 85) note, 'The degree to which video and film production is organized along ethnic lines is quite unusual in Africa— elsewhere films do not carry their ethnicity on their sleeves because production is organized on a national or international basis'.

Technically speaking, Nollywood video films have been characterized as falling somewhere between television and cinema. Unlike Hollywood, video films in Nollywood are made quickly, recorded on video equipment, and marketed directly to the consumer, initially on videocassettes and more recently in digital format. From the moment the camera begins to produce footage, a very different product is being created that possesses a visuality significantly different from more mainstream cinematic products. In addition, the representations of their content, the action and stories they record, derive from a range of video practices that are particular to Nollywood. For example, with an average of ten sequences being shot in a day, the video film is often completed in about two weeks and edited and packaged for sale within another week (Imasuen, 2006). The result is a narrative that is often disjunct, i.e., not rendered as a set of obviously related scenes. The storyline contains any number of subplots that appear, disappear and occasionally reappear, mimicking African oral narrative patterns (Okpewho, 1992) and occurring across any number of apparently tangentially related scenes. A standard two-hour video film is frequently followed by parts two and three released in quick succession—since all three parts are routinely filmed during the same period—so that the full story often sprawls over six hours of viewing. The script is minimal such that the story is produced organically from the interaction between actors as well as whatever intervening opportunities, obstacles and complications might surface while shooting.[6]

Once they are ready for distribution, there are few flashy premiers to hype the video films as there are very few functioning cinemas in Lagos, most of them having been converted to ware-houses or to Christian churches, through the rise of evangelical Protestantism.[7] In addition to which, the films tend to be targeted to, and are particularly popular among, working class people who could not easily afford multiple tickets to such an event (Adesanya, 2000; Haynes, 2000). There are no national tours where stars hawk their new video films. But there are magazines, billboards, radio and television advertisements, as well as Lagos television shows devoted entirely to publicizing the video films and movie posters plastered throughout the city to advertise their upcoming releases. Another method of advertising is through 'touts', individuals paid to generate interest in the video films by hanging out in stores singing high praises of them at the same time that they pretend to be ordinary customers.

Touts are also used to draw people in off the street to theatrical exhibitions of the video films (Ogunleye, 2004).

While some video films do see theatrical release either in the National Theatre or smaller venues, a much larger percentage are delivered for sale each Monday morning by their production agencies (often a coalition of actors; there are no US-type studios, major or minor) to the Idumota electronics market in the central city (Aina, 1995; Alade, 2006; Dibinga, 2006) or to other sites of video film marketing that include Aba, Onitsha and Enugu markets. When a video film is released into a theatre, it is usually its producer(s) who arrange(s) the rental of a venue and the projection equipment, as well as the printing, sale, and collection of tickets (Ogunleye, 2004). If the video films are going straight to the market, established marketers are responsible for 'market research, product design, advertisement, sales promotion, exhibition and distribution' (Ogunleye, 2004, p. 83). About 1,000 titles are released each year, with average sales of about 20,000 to 40,000 per title (less popular video films have estimated sales of about 10,000 per title; the most popular ones sell between 200,000 and 400,000 copies) (Adesyana, 2000; Ayorinde, 1997; Nollywood Foundation, 2006; Ogunleye, 2004).

Most of these video films cost about $US2.50, but many are immediately available through video clubs or more informal networks 'run out of someone's room in a compound with no signboard to advertise their presence' (Haynes and Okome, 2000, p. 73), where pirated copies rent or sell for about a tenth of the price of legal ones (Ogunleye, 2004). In either case, producers receive none of the royalties on these video film rentals.[8] The state, as either a supporter or a regulator of these products, is effectively absent from the scene (Chikwendu, 2006; Nollywood Foundation, 2006).[9] Although regarded by many Nigerian cultural critics as crass (among them, renowned celluloid filmmakers Hubert Ogunde, now deceased, and Adeyemi Afolayan), these video films, popular commercial creations produced largely in the informal sector, are enthusiastically received by a wide audience of Africans (and others) all over the continent as well as abroad.

When the video films leave the market they are usually watched on the millions of TV sets, by way of VCR and CD players, that are possessed by more than 70% of Nigerian urban households. Home viewing is usually preferred to public exhibition attendance for reasons largely due to security, religion, and income. As Foluke Ogunleye (2004) and other Nigerian scholars have written, public spaces are not safe at night in Lagos and, rather than risk armed robbery, many Nigerians have invested in video players in order to watch the videos at home. Religious prohibitions against unaccompanied females on the streets as well as simple poverty keep others at home where many family members are able to view the video films for a price far lower than the cost of one theater ticket. Older releases are often broadcast on television throughout Africa (Haynes, 2006). If the newly released video films have been purchased, and after they have been viewed any number of times—they are played on home sets day and night (Boyer, 2006)—they are passed around among friends and frequently packed into the suitcases of visiting family members who take them and others off to Abidjan, Accra, Lomé, and Cape Town, where they circulate—or, better, to use a site-specific word, are 'passed'—around Africa or travel to London, Paris, New York, Houston and Atlanta. Or they are shipped abroad and made available for purchase by the expatriate African community in video stores and African markets, or through websites. Noting their massive popularity among diasporic Africans, Jonathan Haynes (2005) writes:

> They are what is on television in Namibia and on sale on the streets in Kenya. In Congo, they are broadcast with the soundtrack turned down while an interpreter tells the story in Lingala or other

languages. In New York, Chinese people are buying them. In Holland, Nollywood stars are recognized on the streets by people from Suriname, and in London they are hailed by Jamaicans.

While globalization theorists would argue that the quote above proves the 'globality' of Nollywood, we would contend that it points instead to a series of differentially articulated material connections that link Nollywood to other sites in varying and complex ways. What the quote does not reveal is how the video films are viewed and the impact they have on these differently situated viewers. For instance, Congolese people watching a video film through an interpreter have a very different viewing experience from Igbo or Yoruban Lagosians who watch the same video film in their native language or immigrant Chinese who watch it in New York.[10] To take one simple example, there are particular ethnic rituals and popular practices that occur in the video films that are likely to be meaningless to any viewer who is not acquainted with them (Ekwuazi, 2000; Ogundele, 2000). And what might seem like a silly and inconsequential filmic interlude to some viewers is a key moment for others.

Situated Percepts

We regard the processes of production, consumption, and circulation of Nollywood video film as constituting a series of singularities that contribute to the specificity of Nollywood as a site. We note, however, that the emergence of these specificities does not comprise an exhaustive list of what goes into the composition of the site. Rather, they communicate with other dynamic singularities and, through such interactions, accelerate processes of differentiation. This differentiation plays out most clearly in the examination of the video films that Western critics and audiences tend to reductively view through the improper lens of Hollywood film. Treating them as a bad copy of the Hollywood film, these viewers are inclined to isolate a series of specific elements in the video films that they comprehend as flawed or amateurish imitations; for example, a weak image produced through the use of video rather than celluloid, poor lighting and sound, or technologically transparent representations of the occult or supernatural. We recognize in this moment the ways that Western critics and audiences have been conditioned by the aesthetic spectrum of Hollywood film, treating such situated conditioning as commonsensical when they turn their gaze toward different systems of artistic production.[11]

Against such criticisms, we affirm Flaxman's (2000, p. 12) reading of Deleuze, who suggests that the artistic image inherently concerns the material *production* of sensation:

> the artistic image is neither a representation of an object nor even a visual impression, the first of which connotes mere recognition and the second a limited sensory bandwidth. Rather, the image is a collection of sensations—a 'sensible aggregate', or what Deleuze will ultimately call a 'sign'—that we simply cannot re-cognize and that we encounter, as such, at the very limit of the sensible. Sensations possess the capacity to derange the everyday, to short-circuit the mechanism of common sense, and thus to catalyze a different kind of thinking; indeed, sensations are encountered at a threshold we might call the 'thinkable'.

In short, there is a positive physical force that lends itself to the opening of thought through the image insofar as it runs differentiation and variation across its surface. With regard to Nollywood video film, it is precisely that it does *not* map easily onto an imaginary of the Hollywood film aesthetic that should be acknowledged as the productive moment of artistic creation. Further, it should be noted that the image itself is the result of the dynamic, situated conditions of production that circulate within the milieu where it is created. That is to say, we cannot read into the Nollywood image, which is the product of the materialities of the site, a bastardized version of the Hollywood image, whose production and consumption processes form an entirely different dynamic system and result in an equally different set of images. Nollywood video films constitute a popularized aesthetic that is uniquely *in itself* by virtue of its specific, situated conditions of production and consumption.

Thus, through the specificities and particularities of Nollywood video film production—for example, incorporating fast shooting schedules, small crews, and the use of locations-at-hand—we encounter a *mise-en-scène* unfamiliar to the context of Western cinema. In addition to these production differences, the films contain long sequences with little or no action but extensive, often repetitive dialogue.[12] These sequences can be seen as tedious or mundane. Yet this visual banality, largely absent from Hollywood films, works to bring lived practice and its representation together in ways that make the films deeply accessible and entirely familiar to their audience (Moran, 2005).

For example, interior scenes often appear to be simple apartments (perhaps even a crew member's apartment) rather than the elaborate fantasy spaces of escapism that are the characteristic and clichéd spectacle often encountered in Hollywood films (though conspicuous wealth and deplorable poverty are often dialectical structuring components of Nollywood films). While this practice is no doubt a result of the fast movement (no time to build a set) and small budgets (no money to build a set) of Nollywood video films, there are nonetheless fundamental aesthetics that emerge from the conditions of this system. Specifically, while the climate-controlled Hollywood image often loses itself in ideological fantasy through its fetish for liberalist egalitarianism and bootstrappism, the 'found' aesthetic of Nollywood video film constitutes a fold between the moving image and the scenes in which it is viewed—in the homes and other familiar spaces that constitute the visual landscape of everyday life. This resonance enables the thoughts and percepts corresponding to the video image to share material affinities with those percepts generated through the viewer's own situatedness in an entire series of localized, material landscapes.

But even beyond this, the haste that apparently attends the production of these video films aids in the construction of aesthetic sensibilities far removed from those of the sanitized, homogenized, pasteurized, and generally over-produced aesthetics of Hollywood film.[13] Here, a hallway or a bedroom is converted into an office space through the placement of a desk with a few random books against a wall that remains disconcertingly bare and that fills the screen, becoming the immense key-subject of the shot. Scene after scene is quickly improvised, producing dialogues brimming with awkward stammers and curious pauses, and populated by the uncertain, wild-eyed looks between discussants and eruptions of monologue occasionally diverging into fits of screaming. The relative speed of production renders such apparently strange moments as productive differentiators within video film by virtue of their frequent recurrence. Whether such moments remain accidents or begin to be incorporated into the intended stylistics of Nollywood aesthetics is incidental. What is not incidental is that thought corresponding to such images—the situated and emergently cultural moment resonant with perception of the image—is in part itself conditioned by these filmic ruptures.

In describing the material practices of Nollywood video film production, consumption and circulation, we have intended to show that even as Nollywood Foundation Convention participants talked 'globe talk' in terms of producing a Nollywood 'global brand' or recognizing acclaimed Nollywood actress Genevieve Nnaji as a 'global film star', they were materially connecting with their Hollywood counterparts in an unremarkable conference room in the Omni California Plaza Hotel at 251 South Olive Street in downtown Los Angeles. As a result, it is critically important to appreciate the ontological implications of the news that appeared on 6 August 2006 on the Nollywood.net website that Nigerian director Lancelot Oduwa Imasuen had been awarded a $200,000 non-union Hollywood-financed budget to shoot a film in California and that a Hollywood/Nollywood production deal had been brokered to finance a film to begin shooting in Nigeria in December 2006 (Ajeluorou, 2006). The news, if taken simply as evidence of globalization, wrongly erases the doings and sayings and the physical and sensuous connections that unfolded in and in relation to that conference room and that helped to 'create the enabling environment' (as one of the convention panels was titled) that lies behind the headline.

Conclusion

We have provided a discussion of Nollywood as a material critique of how particular spatial imaginaries of globalization significantly limit our understanding of how the world works. Our primary objective, however, is not simply to expose the analytical limitations of the spatial imaginaries that researchers bring to globalization, but, more importantly, to draw attention to the political limitations that inhere in those imaginaries and the alternatives that are opened up in a flat ontology. Consider, for example, the perspective of the Zapatista revolutionary army's Subcommandante Marcos, a globalization theorist in his own right. In his essay 'How Big is the World?' he specifies a politics grounded not in abstract flows or hierarchies but in material practice (Marcos, 2006). In the essay he is describing a conversation between himself and a colleague, Insurgenta Erika, and later between himself and his imaginary interlocutor, 'Durito'. We quote Marcos at length here because his essay elegantly discloses the underlying politics of our argument. Erika's questions and tentative responses contain a global imaginary—albeit tentative and uncertain—that exists in tension with Marcos's deliberate unfolding of sites as situated, mutable singularities that produce their own politics founded on the central position that the 'world abounds in worlds'. He also makes it clear that those sites are deeply, materially connected to other sites through 'forward', 'backward', and 'sideways' linkages.

Sup—as he calls himself—writes:

> After a day of preparation meetings for the Other Campaign (it was September, it was dawn, there was rain from a far-off cloud), we were heading towards the hut where our things were when we ran into a citizen who all of a sudden came out with: 'Listen Sup, what are the Zapatistas proposing?' Without even stopping, I answered: 'Changing the world'. We reached the hut and began getting things ready in order to leave. Insurgenta Erika waited until I was alone. She approached me and said: 'Listen, Sup, the world is very big', as if she were trying to make me realize what nonsense I was proposing and that I didn't, in reality, know what I was saying when I'd said what I'd said. Following the custom of responding to a question with another question, I came out with: 'How big?'
> She kept looking at me, and she answered almost tenderly: 'Very big'.
> I insisted: 'Yes, but how big?'
> She thought about it for a minute and said: 'Much bigger than Chiapas'.
> …. When we had gotten back … Erika came over to me, carrying a globe, the kind they use in elementary schools. She put it on the ground and told me: 'Look Sup, here, in this little piece, there is Chiapas, and all this is the world', almost caressing the globe with her dark hands as she said it.
> 'Hmm', I said, lighting my pipe in order to gain some time.
> Erika insisted: 'Now you've seen that it's very big?'
> 'Yes, but we're not going to change it all by ourselves, we're going to change it with many compañeros and compañeras from everywhere'.

Later that evening, as he sat alone with his thoughts, Marcos wrote a response to Erika, penned through an irreverent and imaginary compañero, Dorito. His friend dictates to Marcos what he *should* have said to Erika, had he been able to figure out the question about the size of the world and its politics in advance:

> I picked up my pen and notebook. Dorito dictated:
>
> 'If you look at it from above, the world is small and the color green of the dollar. It fits perfectly in the price indexes and the valuations of a stock market, in the profits of a transnational, in the election polls of a country which has suffered the hijacking of its dignity, in the cosmopolitan calculator which adds capital and subtracts lives, mountains, rivers, seas, springs, histories, entire civilizations, in the miniscule brain of George W. Bush, in the shortsightedness of savage capitalism badly dressed up in neoliberal attire. Seen from above, the world is very small because it disregards persons and, in their place, there is a bank account number, with no movement other than that of deposits.
>
> But if you look at it from below, the world stretches so far that one look is not enough to encompass it, instead many looks are necessary in order to complete it. Seen from below, the world abounds in worlds, almost all of them painted with the color of dislocation, poverty, despair, death. The world below grows sideways, especially to the left side, and it has many colors, almost as many as persons and histories. And it grows backwards, to the history which the world below made. And it grows towards itself with the struggles that illuminate it, even though the light from above goes out. And it sounds, even though the silence of above crushes it. And it grows forward, divining in every heart the morrow that will be given birth by those who below are who they are. Seen from below, the world is so big that many worlds fit, and, even so, there is space left over, for example, for a jail.
>
> Or, in summary, seen from above, the world shrinks, and nothing fits in it other than injustice. And, seen from below, the world is so spacious that there is room for joy, music, song, dance, dignified work, justice, everyone's opinions and thoughts, no matter how different they are if below they are what they are'. (Marcos, 2006)

Acknowledgements

We would like to thank Sylvester Okwunodu Ogbechie for inviting us to participate in the Nollywood Foundation Convention 2006; John Holden for research assistance; Tim Finan for providing us with an excellent set of recent Nollywood video films; Micah Boyer for insights on Nollywood video film viewing practices in Lagos; Koren Manning for bringing the Nollywood phenomenon to our attention; and Brian Marks for the Marcos reference. Comments on the paper were generously provided by anonymous reviewers and by Susan Greenbaum, Kevin Grove, Julie Guthman, Gerry Pratt, Susan Roberts, Anna Secor, Matte Sparke and Joel Wainwright; by numerous participants in the 13th Annual Mini-Conference on Critical Geography; and by members of the University of Arizona's Subjectivity, Sexuality and Political Cultures Research Cluster. Finally we would like to thank Mark Amen, Kevin Archer, Martin Bosman, and Ella Schmidt for their invitation to participate in the 'Globalization, Cities, and the Production of Culture' conference and for the opportunity to further develop our thoughts on globalization and a flat ontology.

Notes

1   Foluke Ogunleye (2004) provides a concise history of the emergence and current flourishing of the video film industry in Nigeria, detailing issues of financing, marketing, distribution and advertising as well as providing insights into how some of the industry's problems might be addressed. Also see: Haynes and Okome (2000) and Adesanya (2000).

2   Attendees at the Nollywood Foundation Convention commented that though they would be grateful for the financing as well as the technical capabilities of Hollywood, they see themselves as making a different product as well as catering to a different audience than Hollywood. Former managing director of the Nigerian Film Corporation, Brendan Shehu (1992, pp. 142–145), makes the same point in a collection of essays entitled *No. . . Not Hollywood.*

3   C. Kani Omo, a Nollywood Foundation Convention participant and a Nigerian-American director working in the United States, discussed the distinctiveness of Nollywood video films and the opportunities for marketing them as an African 'global brand'.

4   In a recent article, Jonathan Haynes (2006) has argued that although the dominant genre of Nollywood films is melodrama, the films are not necessarily apolitical or without a social conscience. Video films, especially those made since the end of military rule in Nigeria in 1999, often address forms of politics and popular moralism, particularly around themes of both traditional and modern rule and individual and state political corruption.

5   Video films are also being produced in Kano, in northern Nigeria. There they are made in Hausa, the official language of the north. The Hausa video films are different from those made in Nollywood and there is discussion in the blogsphere about labeling the Kano video film industry 'Kanywood' to distinguish it from Nollywood. For an excellent discussion of Hausa video films see Larkin (1997, 2000) and Johnson (2000).

6   Nigerian attendees at the Nollywood Foundation Convention complained about the problems with shooting in Lagos, especially the incessant hum of generators that litter the landscape of the city because of the unreliability of the public electrical supply. They also described how producers, lacking the finances to pay to cordon off public sites for shooting, had to endure the constant noise and interruption of daily commerce and street activity.

7   Nollywood Foundation Convention participant and screenwriter and producer Michael Ajakwe talked about the arrival of new cinema venues in Lagos consisting of small viewing spaces located near bars and churches. The cost of the ticket is the same as the cost of a Nollywood DVD, about 250 naira (in 2006, 100 naira were roughly equivalent to US$0.80). Articles on Nollywood.net and nigeriaplanet also described the recent opening (date not disclosed) of a multiplex in the Lagos Galleria operated by Silverbird Cinemas. The five cinemas in the multiplex were designed to show celluloid films, but the management also installed DVD projectors to encourage indigenous directors to show their video films, should they meet certain quality standards. The first Nollywood videos shown at the new multiplex had a low turnout. Critics of the multiplex 'expressed fears that it could be another weapon in cultural imperialism' (http://nigeriaplanet.proboards43.com/index.cgi?board=newsachieve&action=print&thread=1126879123 (accessed 30 September 2006)).

8   Said Dibinga, a Nollywood Convention panelist and writer and producer, pointed out that 'piraters'—individuals who copy the original video films and sell them at a far cheaper price through video clubs and other outlets—have formed groups to finance new Nollywood video film productions. Madu Chickwendu, a Nollywood Convention panelist and President of the Producers Guild, reiterated the point that all financing for Nollywood films is in small amounts—there are no large institutional sources of funding—though some of the Christian churches have raised money to fund video films (Oha, 2000).

9   The Chair of the Federal Inland Revenue Service of Nigeria, Ifueko Omoigui, delivered the opening remarks at the Nollywood Foundation Convention. Though her comments were largely directed at the employment possibilities of Nollywood film production—it is estimated that Nollywood currently employs more than 300,000 individuals—she also made reference to the industry's tax revenue potential.

10   It should also be pointed out that even within Nigeria, different ethnic groups view the movies differently. For example, Adesanya (2000) notes that Yorubas watched the video films as a family while Igbo women and children are much more likely to watch them without *pater familia* present.

11   A public reading of this paper accompanied by the viewing of several film clips at a recent academic conference resulted in the audience first laughing and then uncomfortably recoiling from what became almost instantaneously recognized as a colonialist response to the clips. We read in this complex response a jarring moment when the audience, conditioned by a Hollywood aesthetic, is confronted with the new.

12   A common complaint made by Nollywood directors and producers at the Convention was the lack of skilled editors and editing equipment (among other technical skills and equipment). They pointed to these deficiencies as well as time constraints as the reasons for long sequences and dialogic repetitions. One of the major objectives of the convention was to promote the transfer of knowledge, skill and capital from Hollywood to Nollywood in order to address these technical problems. The multinational board of California-based Nollywood Foundation works to promote Nollywood by attracting 'the right investments to improve quality of talent, production and distribution' and bringing it to the attention of investors from around the world.

13   Lancelot Oduwa Imasuen, a Convention panelist and one of Nollywood's best-known and most prolific directors, explained how there are no sets available for shooting in Nigeria so directors use the homes and offices of friends or get permission to use those of the elite. Permission to use these and other spaces such as churches, schools, and other government buildings, has been granted without charge until fairly recently when fees have resulted as crew members have damaged property during filming.

References

Adesanya, A. (2000) From film to video, in: J. Haynes (Ed.) *Nigerian Video Films* (Athens, OH: Ohio University Center for International Studies), pp. 37–50.

Aina, F. (1995) The Idumota connection, *Tempo*, 15 May, p. 15.

Ajeluorou, A. (2006) Lancelot Imasuen goes Hollywood, Nollywood.net, 6 August. Available at http://www.nolly wood.net/Reports/p2_articleid/118 (accessed 30 September 2006).

Alade, M. (2006) Nollywood Foundation Convention panelist.

Amin, A. (2002) Spatialities of globalization, *Environment and Planning A*, 34, pp. 385–399.

Appadurai, A. (1996) *Modernity at Large: Cultural Dimensions of Globalization* (Minneapolis, MN: University of Minnesota Press).

Ayorinde, S. (1997) Booming market for the video, *Guardian*, 1 May, p. 31.

Boyer, Micah (2006) Personal communication.

Brenner, N. (2004) *New State Spaces: Urban Governance and the Rescaling of Statehood* (Oxford: Oxford University Press).

Castells, M. (1996) *The Rise of Network Society* (Oxford: Blackwell).

Chikwendu, M. (2006) Nollywood Foundation Convention panelist.

Cosgrove, D. (2001) *Apollo's Eye: A Cartographic Genealogy of the Earth in the Western Imagination* (Baltimore, MD: Johns Hopkins University Press).

Cvetkovich, A. & Kellner, D. (1997) Introduction: thinking global and local, in: A. Cvetkovich, & D. Kellner (Eds) *Articulating the Global and the Local* (Boulder, CO: Westview Press), pp. 1–32.

Delanda, M. (2002) *Virtual Science, Intensive Philosophy* (New York: Continuum).

Deleuze, G. (1994) *Difference and Repetition*, Trans. P. Patton (New York: Columbia University Press).

Deleuze, G. & Guattari, F. (1987) *A Thousand Plateaus*, Trans. B. Massumi (Minneapolis, MN: University of Minnesota Press).

Deleuze, G. & Guattari, F. (1994) *What is Philosophy?*, Trans. H. Tomlinson & G. Burchell (New York: Columbia University Press).

Derrida, J. (1966) Structure, sign, and play in the discourse of the human sciences, in: R. Macksey & E. Donato (Eds) *The Structuralist Controversy* (Baltimore, MD: Johns Hopkins University Press), pp. 247–272.

Deutsche, R. (1991) Boy's town, *Environment and Planning D: Society and Space*, 9, pp. 13–30.

Dibinga, S. (2006) Nollywood Foundation Convention panelist.

Dicken, P. (2003) *Global Shift: Reshaping the Global Economic Map in the 21st Century*, 4th edition (New York: Guilford).

Dixon, D. & Jones, J. P., III (1998) My dinner with Derrida, or spatial analysis and poststructuralism do lunch, *Environment and Planning A*, 30, pp. 247–260.

Ekwuazi, H. O. (2000) The Igbo video film: a glimpse into the cult of the individual, in: J. Haynes (Ed.) *Nigerian Video Films* (Athens, OH: Ohio University Center for International Studies), pp. 131–147.

Flaxman, G. (2000) Introduction, in: G. Flaxman (Ed.) *The Brain is the Screen: Deleuze and the Philosophy of Cinema* (Minneapolis, MN: University of Minnesota Press), pp. 1–57.

Friedman, T. (2006) *The World is Flat: A Brief History of the 21st Century*, updated ed. (New York: Farrar, Strauss & Giroux).

Gibson-Graham, J. K. (2002) Beyond global vs. local: economic politics outside of the binary frame, in: A. Herod & M. Wright (Eds) *Geographies of Power: Placing Scale* (Oxford: Blackwell), pp. 25–60.

Giddens, A. (1990) *Consequences of Modernity* (Cambridge: Polity Press).

Gregory, D. (1994) *Geographical Imaginations* (Oxford: Blackwell).

Hardt, M. & Negri, A. (2000) *Empire* (Cambridge, MA: Harvard University Press).

Harvey, D. (1989) *The Condition of Postmodernity: An Enquiry into the Origins of Cultural Change* (Oxford: Blackwell).

Harvey, D. (1996) *Justice, Nature and the Geography of Difference* (Oxford: Blackwell).

Haynes, J. (2000) Introduction, in: J. Haynes (Ed.) *Nigerian Video Films* (Athens, OH: Ohio University Center for International Studies), pp. 1–36.

Haynes, J. (2005) Nollywood: what's in a name?, *The Guardian*, 2 July 2005. Available at http://www.odili.net/news/source/2005/jul/3/49.html (accessed 4 September 2006).

Haynes, J. (2006) Political critique in Nigerian video films *African Affairs*, 105(421), pp. 511–533.

Haynes, J. & Okome, O. (2000) Evolving popular media: Nigerian video films, in: J. Haynes (Ed.) *Nigerian Video Films* (Athens, OH: Ohio University Center for International Studies), pp. 51–88.

Held, D. (1995) *Democracy and the Global Order* (London: Polity).

Held, D., McGrew, A., Goldblatt, D. & Perraton, J. (2000) *Global Transformations: Politics, Economics and Culture* (Cambridge: Polity Press).

Hirst, P. & Thompson, G. (1999) *Globalization in Question*, 2nd ed. (Cambridge: Polity).

Imasuen, L. O. (2006) Nollywood Foundation Convention panelist.

Jessop, B. (2000) The crisis of the national spatio-temporal fix and the tendential ecological dominance of globalizing capitalism, *International Journal of Urban and Regional Research*, 24, pp. 323–360.

Johnson, D. (2000) Culture and art in Hausa video films, in: J. Haynes (Ed.) *Nigerian Video Films* (Athens, OH: Ohio University Center for International Studies), pp. 200–208.

King, A. (1997) Introduction: spaces of culture, spaces of knowledge, in: A. King (Ed.) *Culture, Globalization and the World-System* (Minneapolis, MN: University of Minnesota Press), pp. 1–18.

Laclau, E. & Mouffe, C. (1985) *Hegemony and Socialist Strategy: Toward a Radical Democratic Politics* (London: Verso).

Larkin, B. (1997) Indian films and Nigerian lovers: media and the creation of parallel modernities, *Africa*, 67, pp. 406–440.

Larkin, B. (2000) Hausa dramas and the rise of video culture in Nigeria, in: J. Haynes (Ed.) *Nigerian Video Films* (Athens, OH: Ohio University Center for International Studies), pp. 209–241.

Law, J. & Hassard, J. (1999) *Actor Network Theory and After* (Oxford: Blackwell).

Mamadouh, V., Kramsch, O. & van der Velde, M. (2004) Articulating local and global scales, *Tijdschrift vor Economische en Sociale Geografie*, 95, pp. 455–466.

Marcos, S. (2006). How big is the world? *Znet /Latin America*. Available at http://www.zmag.org/content/print_article.cfm?itemID=9789&sectionID = 20 (accessed 3 October 2006).

Marston, S. A. (2000) The social construction of scale, *Progress in Human Geography*, 24, pp. 219–242.

Marston, S. A., Jones, J. P. III & Woodward, K. (2005) Human geography without scale, *Transactions of the Institute of British Geographers*, 30, pp. 416–432.

Massey, D. (1994) *Space, Place and Gender* (Minneapolis, MN: University of Minnesota).

Massey, D. (2005) *For Space* (Newbury Park, CA: Sage).

Moran, J. (2005) *Reading the Everyday* (London and New York: Routledge).

Nederveen Pieterse, J. (1995) Globalization as hybridization, in: M. Featherstone, S. Lash & R. Robertson (Eds) *Global Modernities* (London: Sage), pp. 45–68.

Nederveen Pieterse, J. (2004) *Globalization and Culture: Global Mélange* (Lanham, MD: Rowman & Littlefield).

Nollywood Foundation (2006) *Nollywood: The Nigerian Film Industry* (Press release for the Nollywood Foundation Convention).

Ogundele, W. (2000) From folk opera to soap opera: improvisations and transformations in Yoruba popular theatre, in: J. Haynes (Ed.) *Nigerian Video Films* (Athens, OH: Ohio University Center for International Studies), pp. 89–130.

Ogunleye, F. (2004) A report from the front: the Nigerian videofilm, *Quarterly Review of Film and Video*, 21, pp. 71–88.

Oha, O. (2000) The rhetoric of Nigerian Christian videos: the war paradigm of the *Great Mistake*, in: J. Haynes (Ed.) *Nigerian Video Films* (Athens, OH: Ohio University Center for International Studies), pp. 192–199.

Ohmae, K. (1995) *The End of the Nation State: The Rise of Regional Economies* (New York: Free Press).

Ojewuyi, O. (2006) Nollywood Foundation Convention panelist.

Okpewho, I. (1992) *African Oral Literature: Backgrounds, Character, and Continuity* (Bloomington, IN: Indiana University Press).

Okwo, M. (2006) Nollywood Foundation Convention panelist.

Robertson, R. (1992) *Globalization: Social Theory and Culture* (Newbury Park, CA: Sage).

Robertson, R. (1997) Social theory, cultural relativity and the problem of globality, in: A. King (Ed.) *Culture, Globalization and the World-System* (Minneapolis, MN: University of Minnesota Press), pp. 69–90.

Robertson, R. (2004) Globalization as a problem, in: F. J. Lechner & J. Boli (Eds) *The Globalization Reader*, 2nd ed. (Oxford: Blackwell), pp. 93–99.

Sassen, S. (1998) *Globalization and its Discontents: Essays on the New Mobility of People and Money* (New York: New Press).

Scholte, J. A. (2000) Global civil society, in: N. Woods (Ed.) *The Political Economy of Globalization* (London: Macmillan), pp. 173–201.

Scott, J. (1991) The evidence of experience, *Critical Inquiry*, 17, pp. 773–797.

Shehu, B. (1992) *No ... Not Hollywood: Essays and Speeches of Brendan Shehu*, Ed. E. Hyginus & N. Yacubu (Jos: Nigerian Film Corporation).

Strange, S. (1996) *The Retreat of the State* (New York: Cambridge University Press).

Tagg, J. (1997) Globalization, totalization and the discursive field, in: A. King (Ed.) *Culture, Globalization and the World-System* (Minneapolis, MN: University of Minnesota Press), pp. 155–160.

Taylor, P. (1982) A materialist framework for political geography, *Transactions of the Institute of British Geography*, 7, pp. 15–34.

Thrift, N. (2000) Afterwords, *Environment and Planning D: Society and Space*, 18, pp. 295–322.

Tilly, C. (1984) *Big Structures, Large Processes, Huge Comparisons* (New York: Russell Sage).

Sallie A. Marston is a Professor in the Department of Geography and Regional Development at the University of Arizona. She specializes in cultural and political theory and has written two textbooks on globalization: *Human Geography: Places and Regions in Global Context* and *World Regions: Peoples, Places and Environments*, both with Prentice-Hall.

Keith Woodward is a Lecturer in the Department of Geography at the University of Exeter. He specializes in research on spatial ontology, affect, and politics. He received his PhD from the University of Arizona.

John Paul Jones, III is Professor and Head of the Department of Geography and Regional Development at the University of Arizona. He specializes in spatial theory and methodology. He received his PhD from Ohio State University.

Global Multiculture, Flexible Acculturation

JAN NEDERVEEN PIETERSE

Introduction

Multiculture, said critics, is only different wallpaper and a wider choice in restaurants. But the Danish cartoon episode, the murder of Theo van Gogh in Amsterdam, 7/7 in London and the car burnings in the French *banlieues* show that more is at stake. Multiculture is a global arena. Yet most treatments still conceive of multiculturalism as a national arena. Muslim women's head-scarves from Istanbul and Cairo to Tehran and Lyon display a wide register of meanings, but in the French national assembly have been signified in just one. Multiculturalism means global engagement. To engage with the world is to engage with its conflicts. Multiculturalism is not no man's land. Multiculturalism is not consensus. There is no consensus in Britain about the war in Iraq and there is none among immigrants either. The 'securitization' of cultural difference confirms the interplay between global and multicultural frictions. Multiculturalism is one of the faces of globalization and globalization, at its Sunday best, is human history conscious of itself, which by the way is not always nice.

Multiculturalism in contemporary accelerated globalization is profoundly different from the past. In the past migrants chose between two environments that were often radically different, now communication and travel back and forth is relatively ordinary. In the past migrants had to choose between two overall monocultural settings, now they navigate between two or more multicultural environments. Indians resident in the US can tune in to Indian TV news, alternate with an American show and tune back to Indian satellite programs, while in India foreign broadcasts are more widely available. Immigrant neighborhoods in Germany, the Netherlands and Sweden are fields of satellite dishes. Many Turks abroad lead multicultural lives, tuned to Turkish, German and other European broadcasts. They follow Turkish news, music and shows and choose between Hollywood, Bollywood or Cairo films. Jet travel has made vacations in the home country easier for migrant workers and their families. Retiring and buying a home in the country of origin is now more frequent. Migrant remittances are major revenue flows for the Philippines, Mexico, Pakistan, India, etc. Irish and Scottish politicians canvas expatriates overseas and Mexican politicians campaign among Mexicans living in the US. Transnational relations are no longer simply two-way between country of origin and migration but run across diasporic settlements in multiple continents. Gujarati Indians are continually in touch with family members in the UK, US, Canada, Australia and compare notes about where it is best and most advantageous to study, start a business, find a companion, or enjoy a vacation. Diasporas are linked transnationally and intercontinentally like pearls on a string. Meanwhile in the setting of neoliberal globalization, overall economic inequality is increasing and multiculturalism carries a heavier burden.

Multiculturalism has gone global over time and at a rapid pace particularly since information and communication technology (ICT) and cheaper air travel in the 1990s. Just as ICT revolutionized production (flexible accumulation, offshoring, outsourcing), finance (24/7 global reach), firms (decentralization), it revolutionizes migration and multiculturalism. Migrants can now work in one space and culturally inhabit another. A consequence is that, as Michael Storper (2001) notes, in contemporary globalization the differences *between* localities have lessened and the variety *within* localities has increased.

The nation state is no longer the 'container' of multiculturalism. Yet the multiculturalism literature remains overwhelmingly focused on the relationship between migrants and the host country and national policy options. This is unrealistic. It overlooks that for migrants and their offspring the conversation with the host nation is one among several, a conversation in which participation is optional and partial. The cultural ambience of the host nation is no longer encompassing; e-media tune to many worlds. Second, it underplays the dynamics of the host country—assimilation into what? The 'nation' is a series of vortices of change—local, regional, national, macro-regional, transnational. Asian Muslims in the UK function locally in their workplaces, neighborhoods and cities, regionally, in Yorkshire, etc., nationally, in the context of British policies and culture, move within the European Union on British passports, and relate to their country of origin's culture and transnational Islam or Hinduism. Third, this overlooks the role of rainbow conversations and economies across cultures—such as South African Malays studying Islam in Karachi; Turks selling Belgian carpets to Moroccans in the Netherlands (Nederveen Pieterse, 2003). Fourth, it ignores the emergence of intermediary formations such as 'Euro-Islam' ('a hybrid that attempts to reconcile the principles laid out in the Koran with life in a secular, democratic Europe'; Simons, 2005a), which is neither national nor belongs to another civilization.

Multiculture is global too because several diasporas outnumber the nations. The 73 million people of Irish descent worldwide dwarf the 4 million living in the Irish republic; out of almost 15 million Jewish people worldwide about 5 million live in Israel and similar equations apply to Greeks, Lebanese and Armenians. Multiethnicity exists worldwide and multiculturalism discourse and policy is spreading widely.

Postnationalism may be exaggerated shorthand but surely the national center and space hold much less than they did in the past. Multiculturalism debates suffer from methodological and policy nationalism. Most discussions of multiculturalism are too preoccupied with questions of national policy to cope with issues of multiculturalism that spill over boundaries. The 7/7 bombings in London and the threats of August 2006 created a culture shock (the attackers grew up as British lads) that debate on multiculturalism has not been able to address adequately. It does not work to revisit the customary policy choice of integration or assimilation (Modood, 2005). Global multiculture makes for a complex field that includes engagement with global conflict.

Nations and cultures are no longer 360 degree environments. Conversely this means that Danish cartoons are also seen in Islamabad and Cairo, Illinois and Sarajevo. A joke made by a German commentator is also heard in Istanbul. A speech by President George W. Bush to veterans in Cincinnati plays the following day in Baghdad and on Al Manar TV.

Discussions of globalization and culture are dominated by shorthand such as McDonaldization and the clash of civilizations, which are ideological shortcuts rather than analytics. Second, the approach in terms of general norms—freedom of speech, democracy, human rights—without contextual fine print risks becoming part of institutionalized hypocrisy.

Multiculturalist Conflicts

Some cases may illustrate contemporary dynamics—the Danish cartoons mocking Islam and the murder of Theo van Gogh in the Netherlands. I give brief outlines because the cases have been widely covered in international media and detailed information is readily available.

The Danish cartoons originated in a contest for cartoons mocking Islam issued by one of the country's leading morning newspapers, *Jyllands-Posten*. Twelve cartoons were published on 30 September 2005 alongside this editorial note:

> The modern, secular society is rejected by some Muslims. They demand a special position, insisting on special consideration of their own religious feelings. It is incompatible with contemporary democracy and freedom of speech, where you must be ready to put up with insults, mockery and ridicule. It is certainly not always attractive and nice to look at, and it does not mean that religious feelings should be made fun of at any price, but that is of minor importance in the present context. . . . we are on our way to a slippery slope where no-one can tell how the self-censorship will end. That is why Morgenavisen Jyllands-Posten has invited members of the Danish editorial cartoonists union to draw Muhammad as they see him.[1]

The idea of a cartoon competition came from the newspaper's cultural editor, Flemming Rose. A year earlier he traveled to Philadelphia to visit Daniel Pipes and wrote a positive article about him (Rose, 2004; cf. Bollyn, 2006; Rose, 2006). Daniel Pipes, a fervent neoconservative Zionist who compares militant Islam with fascism (the familiar 'Islamic fascism' idea) and sees total Israeli military victory as the only path to Middle East peace (Pipes, 2001), had been involved in the Danish multiculturalism debate since 2002 when he launched a virulent attack on Muslim immigrants in a newspaper article co-authored with a rightwing Danish journalist and historian

(Pipes and Hedegaard, 2002).[2] The article sparked a debate on multiculturalism with Danish par-liamentarians. By writing about Pipes in 2004 Flemming Rose revisited an attack on Muslims in Denmark that had been in motion for years. This suggests that from their conception the inflam-matory cartoons were part of a transnational arena and reflect an elective affinity with American neoconservative agendas. The way they are framed, using free speech as an intercultural wedge issue, suggests that this is not a happy time to be Muslim in Denmark. The idea of sparking ten-sions with the Islamic world is not far below the surface.

In October Islamic ambassadors sought a meeting with the Danish prime minister, which he declined. In November and December imams from Denmark took the cartoons to meetings with Muslim leaders in the Middle East and the Islamic Organization Conference. Meanwhile the car-toons were being reprinted in 50 countries. What ensued was an orchestrated response of anti-Danish demonstrations and boycotts across virtually the whole Islamic world in early 2006. Thus, a multicultural tussle sparked an almost worldwide conflagration. The fine print, however, indicates that from the outset it was designed to provoke Muslims, to manufacture a 'clash of civilizations' around an artificial arena: free speech versus Muslim rage: 'the exercise was no more benign than commissioning caricatures of African-Americans would have been during the 1960's civil rights struggle' (Smith, 2006). A deliberate provocation met with an organized response. This is multiculturalism as a transnational arena. Discussing this under the heading of the dos and don'ts, pros and cons of free speech is beside the point, or rather frames the issue in the way the provocation sought to achieve. No one now claims that painting swastikas and anti-Semitic slogans is a matter of free speech. They are hate speech and gestures of ethnic cleansing. The cartoons reflect a similar outlook. As Simon Jenkins (2006) notes, 'Speech is free only on a mountain top; all else is editing'.

Until recently Denmark was an exemplary progressive and strongly pro-welfare Nordic country. In the 1990s an anti-tax party had not succeeded in winning votes. An alternative is to keep the social contract but to limit entry by appealing to what Habermas calls the 'chauvin-ism of prosperity'. Using this ladder, rightwing parties have climbed to power by mobilizing anti-immigrant sentiment. Similar frictions run through many European countries—slow growth and welfare states under pressure from neoliberal constituencies who frame globalization in terms of competition. Rightwing parties have used anti-immigrant sentiment in Austria, Belgium, France, the Netherlands and Italy, usually to limited or temporary effect. With the passing of communism, Europe's rightwing parties also face an 'enemy deficit'. This entails various strands of chauvinism—to advance party interests (Haider's FPÖ in Austria, the Front National in France, Vlaams Belang in Flanders, Fortuyn's Leefbaar Nederland), to advance regional interests (Lega Nord in Italy) or to bring a rightwing coalition to power and move econ-omic agendas to the right (Berlusconi's coalition in Italy; the Democratic Liberal Party (DLP) and Japanese nationalism).

In November 2004 the Dutch filmmaker Theo van Gogh was murdered in Amsterdam while riding his bike to work in the morning. In August his latest film was shown on national tele-vision, 'Submission Part I', an 11 minute film that featured semi-naked young women with Arabic Koran texts written on their bare bodies, seen through transparent veils, tokens of their submission to Islam. A play on words because Islam means 'submission'. On his talk show on Amsterdam TV Van Gogh referred to Muslims as 'goat f____'. Van Gogh was stabbed to death by a 26 year old Dutch-born Muslim of Moroccan immigrant parents, Mohammed Bouyeri, who left a five page letter on the body threatening Ayaan Hirsi Ali, and was arrested within hours. A Somali-born woman, Ayaan Hirsi Ali, conceived and co-wrote the film. As a Labor Party policy adviser she had been outspoken for years, described herself as a 'lapsed Muslim' and declared Islam a 'backward religion' and Mohammed 'a pervert and tyrant'. She advised the party policy unit to close all 41 Islamic schools, put a brake on immigration and change article 23 in the Dutch constitution that establishes the rights for setting up separate schools and institutions—a central pillar of the Dutch system and a foundation of multicultural orthodoxy since the 1960s. The party rejected these extreme recommendations. In the wake of 9/11 she published articles arguing that Islam is not capable of integrating into Dutch society. In 2002 she stood as a member of parliament for the free market Liberal Party (VVD) and was elected.

Émigrés who act as cultural mediators, conservatives and progressives, are often granted a privileged status of authenticity. Among the former is V. S. Naipaul, the source of 'Naipaulitis' as shorthand for the émigré from the global South who looks through metropolitan eyes. Among the latter is Edward Said who as a public intellectual consistently spoke up for the South without condescension (Brennan, 1989, 2006). As a character in the multiculturalism drama, Hirsi Ali is closer to Salman Rushdie, a renegade bicultural insider who is taken to speak for 'others'. Some Muslims in the Netherlands accuse her of 'pandering to the Dutch' and many Dutch people tire of her hijacking emancipation agendas for populist polarizing.

The political setting is welfare cuts, health care privatization, 'pension tension', state crackdowns on illegal immigrants and immigrant youth delinquency, restrictive drugs policies and a difficult discussion on multiculturalism that argues that it has failed, largely because of the immigrants' failure to integrate. Pim Fortuyn used anti-immigrant, anti-Muslim sentiment to garner votes: 'There is a tension between the values of modern society and the principles of Islam', 'As far as I'm concerned, no Muslim will ever come in' (Kolbert, 2002, pp. 112, 108). He also took position against Turkey becoming a member of the EU. These figures—Fortuyn ('the right to freely talk crap'), van Gogh ('the Jerry Springer of Dutch social-political discourse'), Hirsi Ali ('no ruckus, no debate')—were (are), in popular parlance, 'attention getters', loud, in your face.[3] Fortuyn, at a time when his political fortunes were rising rapidly, was assassinated by a young animal rights activist; van Gogh was killed by a Muslim of Moroccan descent; Hirsi Ali continued as MP under police protection and left the Netherlands in 2006 to join the neoconservative American Enterprise Institute in Washington DC. Wilders, a rightwing MP and would-be successor to Fortuyn, also known for his anti-Muslim pronouncements, is under police protection too. Ideological murders and MPs under police protection are unprecedented in the Netherlands. In 2006 Hirsi Ali's denaturalization (she lost her passport and status as MP) and then re-naturalization led to the fall of the Dutch government and early elections. Through this episode her influence was reassessed in the media (e.g. Koopmans and Vliegenthart, 2006; Kuper, 2006).

There are further twists to the situation. For years Van Gogh's killer had been an exemplar of integration in Dutch society: employed in a neighborhood youth center, active in local Amsterdam politics, but then he had a falling out with his employers, became alienated and joined Muslim militants. A television documentary gave (unconfirmed) indications that he had been a Dutch intelligence service (AIVD) plant in militant Muslim youth circles, but the service lost control.[4] In the municipal elections of March 2006 the government coalition parties and the Fortuyn-type parties suffered a massive defeat in a landslide swing toward leftwing parties, in large measure due to immigrants voting *en masse* against the anti-immigrant bias of the governing coalition. This is a different kind of multiculturalism backlash.[5] The immigrant vote counts increasingly also in the US, Canada and the UK.

In both episodes in Denmark and the Netherlands, conflict was sparked by deliberate provocations: symbolic violence begat violence. In both episodes the conflicts were about the character of the public sphere, a central arena of multiculturalism. In both cases appeals were made on behalf of 'western values' (free speech, modernity) and involved a politics of tension targeting Islam or Islamism, but in effect marginal immigrants. It seems inappropriate to discuss this in normative terms of free speech or blasphemy; it should be addressed first in political terms: *cui bono*, who benefits from fomenting strife between Muslims and Denmark or Europe? In both cases the target is Islam and the backdrop to these multiculturalist skirmishes is heightened tension in relation to the Middle East. It is appropriate to consider the link between Islam and global multiculture.

The Middle East has long been an arena of geopolitical conflict. Consider the configuration that Tim Mitchell (2002) calls 'McJihad' and Fatima Mernissi (2003) refers to as 'palace fundamentalism': the relationship between western oil companies, the US government, arms sales, the Saudi royal family, wahhabite clergy, and the transnational network of conservative Islam. The nucleus of this configuration goes back to well before World War Two. The conservative Muslim network, sustained by a steady flow of oil dollars, was mobilized in the anti-Soviet war in Afghanistan and by Israel and other governments as counterweights to leftwing forces. In significant measure the conservative Islamic network is a western creation, codependent with modern capitalism, a holdover of anti-communism, and now a source of blowback (Johnson, 2000). What Samuel Huntington calls a clash of civilizations is no clash of civilizations at all but the political ramifications of political interventions in the Middle East going back for over half a century. Political tensions have escalated particularly since 9/11, the war on terror, wars in Afghanistan and Iraq, pressure on Syria and Iran, American expansion in Central Asia with a view to the Caspian basin, and lasting stalemate in Palestine. Conflicts in Bosnia, Chechnya and Kashmir, while not necessarily directly related to wider fault lines, add to the general conflagration involving Islam.

Part of the Middle East stalemate is double-dealing on the part of the United States and other western powers. American support for autocracies and double standards in dealing with Israel continue to alienate and radicalize people in the region. Since political avenues other than Islam are generally closed off, Islam is a major avenue of political articulation. The US claims to seek accommodation in the region through cooperation with moderate governments and moderate Islam by promoting democracy; however its policies (unconditional support for Israel, detention without trial, Abu Ghraib, Guantánamo) alienate the very moderates it claims it wants to cultivate. Since Middle East policies are not under discussion in the US the situation is addressed through ideological repackaging and public diplomacy (Steger, 2005). This targets Islamism as part of a discourse that places Islam on the outskirts of modernity—along the lines of Bernard Lewis, Fouad Ajami, Daniel Pipes, Thomas Friedman, Bassam Tibi, usually in binarisms (tradition–modernity, conservative–progressive, pro–anti-western, etc.). It is difficult to level this diagnosis with the region's decades of global economic integration via the oil industry and decades of political integration under American tutelage, facing Israeli expansion and on the receiving end of the largest arms sales to any part of the world.

How does this affect global multiculture? Recent American policies escalate tensions that reverberate in every circuit. The ongoing stalemate and frustrations felt in the region, the expanding confrontations with the Islamic world, and the diplomacy of bullying have wide ripple effects.

Consider a news item such as this: 'The Bush administration ... proposed Wednesday to spend $85 million to promote political change inside Iran by subsidizing dissident groups, unions, student fellowships and television and radio broadcasts'. According to secretary of state Rice, 'We will use this money to develop support networks for Iranian reformers, political dissidents and human rights activists' (Weisman, 2006). The policy will probably make progressive ideas in Iran suspect and will bolster hardliners, as have past policies such as declaring Iran part of the axis of evil. If hegemonic power strides across borders and adopts regime change from within as policy, then why should migrants be required to integrate in national society rather than integrating, likewise, along cross-border lines?

Flexible Acculturation

Cultural difference as a marker, frontier, vocabulary, vortex, arena of conflict is as old as the hills. Multiculturalism as a manifestation of contemporary globalization is a sequel to multiethnicity, which is as old as the Stone Age when hunter-gatherers, cultivators and pastoralists cohabited and mingled. What is now different by degree is that not just local, domestic differences matter but conflicts that originate elsewhere are also fought out in the arenas of multiculturalism. Different by degree: in the religious wars of sixteenth and seventeenth century Europe translocal differences counted locally too. Contemporary times have been characterized, from a European viewpoint, as neo-medieval in that they show a similar overlap of jurisdictions and loyalties as in the middle ages (Kobrin, 1998). In hindsight the sovereign nation-state era might well appear as an anomalous historical interlude. The idea of nations as insular containers—with a national economy, national market, national firms, national bourgeoisie, national character, national culture, national politics—may seem an interval in a much longer and now resumed experience of cross-border flows that occupy center stage. Historically the translation of cross-border conflicts into local disputes is quite ordinary. In this sense contemporary global multiculturalism is historically normal, more normal than the inward-looking nation-state epoch.

Flexible acculturation is as old as the phenomenon of subcultures that offer variable acculturation, as old as the situation imagined in the song 'By the rivers of Babylon ... we remembered Zion'. What is new is the *scope and degree* of multi-circuit identification. During Nazism in the 1930s some emigrated from Germany while others opted for 'inner migration', taking their thoughts and hopes to imaginary realms. In the US many blacks live on the other side of the tracks in poor housing and receive substandard education and services but participate in alternative circuits—churches, music circuits of blues and hip hop, the sports world in which their stars shine, the Black Entertainment channel, circuits of drugs and crime. These circuits offer belonging, recognition and a sense of feeling at home. Globalization amplifies the sources of the self (Nederveen Pieterse, 2004a) and flexible acculturation is one of the forms this takes. It is cultural agency and picking and choosing cultural affiliation in the setting of global culture.

Asian Muslims in English cities, North African *beurs* in French banlieues and many other migrants and their offspring share experiences of social exclusion and are increasingly ghettoized. 'Asian communities living in several UK cities face social isolation as severe as that experienced in the black ghettoes of divided American cities like Chicago and Miami' (Adam, 2005). UK cities are rising in the world rankings of segregation. 'The idea was that people would assimilate. The danger is that the assimilation process is so slow that for many it is just not possible' (Draper, 2005).

Exclusion in many instances is not occasional but institutionalized. In France *le crise des banlieues* is grounded in urban planning policies that privileged modern high rises à la Le Corbusier, like the high rises in south Chicago and the Bijlmer in Amsterdam Southeast, which combined gigantism and uniformity; city governments in Amsterdam and Rotterdam have razed these housing complexes (Caldwell, 2005b).[6] According to a different view the issue is not the architecture or the housing but the location.[7]

It is not occasional also because multiculturalism often combines with institutionalized amnesia and the refusal to view the country's colonial past in other than a benevolent light. This is a factor notably in France, Belgium, Japan and to a lesser extent the UK. According to article four of a law passed on 23 February 2005,

> it is now compulsory in France to emphasise the positive dimension of the French colonial era in high school history courses and textbooks. When the Socialist party tried to overturn this controversial law recently, it was defeated in the National Assembly by a conservative majority that may have moved further to the right as a result of the recent violence. (Moisi, 2005)

Dominique Moisi comments,

> By imposing political correctness on the teaching of the past, the National Assembly has committed more than a crime. It has made a crucial error. If one of the big challenges confronting France in the global age is that of integrating its minorities, then the imposition of a unilateral reading of history on all French people whatever their origins is not only anachronistic but offensive. Refusal to come to terms with the French imperial past and the Algerian war combines with reluctance to view Algerian immigrants as permanent residents and citizens. (Moisi, 2005)

The French law banning overt religious signs in schools, directed at the wearing of the hijab, fits the same pattern of integration of minorities in terms set by the French elite, in other words monocultural multiculturalism (Vidal, 2004, p. 4; Wieviorka, 2004a). 'France is a multicultural society par excellence still living the Jacobin dream of uniformity' (Wallerstein, 2005).

Exclusion is not occasional also because multiculturalism is under multiple pressures: competitive globalization translates into pressure on welfare states and in view of the securitization of migration (discussed below) immigrants face increasing demands to conform and decreasing resources and incentives to integrate. The welfare state is shrinking precisely when demand for welfare services is expanding. Third, rightwing forces focus on migrants as a soft target and in several countries the political center has moved to the right on multiculturalism.

Global multiculture provides multiple circuits of identification and integration that can make up for social exclusion at least symbolically. Alternative circuits are appealing when mainstream circuits are alienating; in social psychology this two-way traffic is termed interactive acculturation (Bourhis *et al.*, 1997). It takes two to tango: the wider the gap between multiculturalist rhetoric and actual socioeconomic integration the greater the appeal of alternative and symbolic spaces of identification; that seems to be the basic geometry of flexible acculturation. In France, 'the immigrant origin populations turn to Islam, not only out of fidelity to the values and religion of their parents but also because it gives meaning to an existence in a society which tends to despise them, to discredit them or to exclude them ... Here, religion is part of an endeavour to participate in modernity rather than to exclude oneself from it' (Wieviorka, 2004b, p. 284). This may refer to an alternative modernity. Multi-circuit multiculturalism includes tea houses, cyberspace, mosques, 'Muslim by day, disco at night' (Nederveen Pieterse, 1997). Beur youths synchronized their riot actions across Paris quarters and other cities via websites and mobile phones. The easy media terminology of 'riots' underplays their degree of coordination and organization.

For many migrants at the bottom rungs of social experience, multiculturalism is a bogus exercise, a regime of platitudes, a tedious 'race relations industry' that mainly benefits a small elite. The reality of multiculturalism on the ground is often a furnace of discontent where grinding anger results in inner migration into imaginary worlds of cyberspace, subcultures of gangs and petty crime, or desire to strike back and affiliate with hostile forces. This is part of what looms behind the 7/7 and August 2006 episodes in the UK: a backlash against bogus multiculturalism and alienation felt by Muslim youth in UK ghettoes and a response to the belligerent policies of the US and UK in the Middle East, Palestine and Iraq. The appeal of militant Islam is a matter of pull and push. It reflects the nature of conflict in the age of accelerated globalization—conflict is discursive, unfolds through representations, is channeled via media, crosses borders with the speed of light, is no longer spatially sequestered, is subject to multiple interpretations and evokes a wide variety of agency.

A standard response before and after the crisis and a response to 7/7 and the car burnings in France was to blame the victims of social exclusion for their lack of integration. Also in response to 9/11 few bothered to mention the role of American policies in the Middle East. Collective self-reflection is in short supply. At a deeper level this indicates the degree to which power-with-impunity and hypocrisy have been institutionalized.

The structural features that underlie global multiculture and flexible acculturation match those that Robert Cooper, Blair's foreign policy adviser, calls the postmodern state, pertaining in the EU: the fuzzy boundary between domestic and foreign affairs, mutual interference in domestic affairs and mutual surveillance, security based on interdependence and mutual vulnerability (Cooper, 2000; Peters, 2005, p. 110). (In contrast, the US state is characterized by 'defensive modernism'.)

The growing role of 'intermestic' (international–domestic) affairs is a general trend. Global multiculture means engagement with conflicts worldwide. If societies are engaged globally it means that conflicts travel too. Conflicts cannot be contained locally. Multiculturalism and foreign policy cannot be treated separately. This has been part of global experience since the expulsion of the Jews from Spain and Portugal and part of recent European experience for instance in the Kurdish presence in Germany and Sweden. Lines drawn in multiculturalism are often drawn globally, for instance the French foulard affair: 'the French debate has become "global." It has developed both locally and well beyond France, and has considerable diplomatic and geopolitical implications' (Wieviorka, 2004a, p. 72). It reverberates from Turkey to North Africa.

Conflicts in Somalia over the status of women are part of an animal husbanding society and a trading society on the coast, in the throes of change. Folk Islam mixed with patriarchy and neo-patriarchy is party to this change. Dutch society with Somali immigrants also becomes party to this change.

Multiple circuits of integration also mean multi-circuit blowback. The Danish PM not meeting with Muslim ambassadors might score domestic points but loses points in *umma* politics. Koizumi's annual visits to the Yasukuni shrine score with the Japanese right but shrink Japan's standing in the region. President George W. Bush's speeches assuring American audiences that Iraq is on the right track come across differently on Al Jazeera and in living rooms in Basra and Baghdad. The old compartmentalization of audiences and circuits is no more. Multi-circuit multiculturalism is a consequence of what Walt Anderson (1999) calls 'communities in a world of open systems'.

Globalization amplifies the sources of the self and opens multiple organizational avenues, which is not particular to multiculturalism but a general condition. The Zapatistas mobilized in Chiapas and took their cause of democracy and dignity to the nation via savvy media skills and to the world via the internet and international *encuentros* against neoliberalism. Mobile phones played a key part in 'people power' in the Philippines and Thailand, coordinating street action and bypassing mainstream media.

Migrant mobility and connectivity are variable and reflect class and migration history. The Indian diaspora is overall more prosperous and mobile than Pakistani migrants. By comparison to Moroccans, Turks in Europe come from more urban backgrounds (many migrated to urban centers in Turkey before migrating abroad) and have more entrepreneurial experience, and the Turkish economy and diaspora provide greater economic depth.

The account of contemporary globalization as the 'annihilation of distance' (the death of distance, end of geography, etc.) is shallow. What matters is social distance, mediated by cultural affinity. So what is at issue is the arbitrage of distance: distance or exclusion in one circuit is compensated for by integration in another, though not in a linear fashion. Nor are the circuits comparable in the goods they provide. They refer to different sectors—economic, social, cultural, cyberspace, symbolic—and provide diverse benefits.

Flexible accumulation deploys flexible methods (production, product features, location, labor conditions) towards a single purpose (accumulation). *Flexible acculturation* deploys flexible methods (switching and mixing cultural vocabularies and alternating circuits of affiliation) towards the general aim of belonging and being at home in the world. A parallel notion is Aihwa Ong's flexible citizenship.

> I use the term *flexible citizenship* to refer especially to the strategies and effects of mobile managers, technocrats and professionals who seek to both circumvent *and* benefit from different nation-state regimes by selecting different sites for investments, work and family relocation ... They readily submit to the governmentality of capital, while plotting all the while to escape state discipline. (1998, pp. 136, 156–157; and see 1999).

This perspective differs from global multiculture in that the focus is on the Chinese diaspora, mainly on the Pacific Rim, and on elites (many are 'well-heeled Hong Kongers') and their strategies of capitalist opportunism. Global multiculture includes elites but consists mostly of poor and less privileged migrants; it includes diasporas with long histories but also many recent migration chains; it includes economic opportunism but also a wider spectrum of interests. So while Ong's flexible citizenship also refers to diverse cultural politics, its ambit is narrower than flexible acculturation in global multiculture. Another instance of flexibility—spatial, economic, cultural, legal—is Xiangming Chen's work on de-bordering and re-bordering in East Asia's border regions and their 'local cosmopolitanism' (Chen, 2005, p. 40).

Flexible acculturation is multidirectional and exercised by migrants, authorities and other actors. Politicians and governments switch and alternate discourses and policies they apply to migrants and citizens of immigrant origin. Multiculturalism is one register; security and socio-economics are others, including the political economy of the welfare state. As Ong (1998, p. 136) notes, 'nation-states are reworking immigration law to attract capital-bearing subjects while limiting the entry of unskilled labor'. Canada, the US, UK and Australia adopt a 'give us your best and your brightest' brain-drain policy that operates as a tax on poor nations, or foreign aid in reverse (Kapur and McHale, 2005).

A major trend is to reframe migration in security terms. In Europe this goes back to 'Fortress Europe' measures that differentiate between member state and third country nationals and sought to bring migration under control: the Schengen accord, the 1992 European Union Treaty and the Treaty of Amsterdam that brought immigration, asylum and refugee matters under one heading (Waever, 1996). By securitizing issues political elites make these issues 'trump normal democratic processes of debate and negotiation' and trump justice 'since national security takes precedence over justice, and since disloyal minorities have no legitimate claims anyway' (Kymlicka, 2004, p. 157).

The securitization of migration received a boost since 9/11. The United States applied massive security measures, curtailing civil liberties, tightening visa requirements,

eavesdropping, rendition and detentions in Guantánamo, Bagram Airbase as part of the generalized preoccupation with terrorism. According to former national security adviser Richard
Clarke (2005), 7/7 shows the United States the way: 'The British experience this summer has
lessons for us about finding terrorist sleeper cells'. It involves 'infiltrating undercover agents
into the population from which sleepers are recruited' and seeking 'the cooperation of the American Muslim community in identifying possible problem groups and individuals'. European governments participate in the surveillance and security discourse and practices. In Europe
'minority nationalism only becomes securitized when it involves terrorism' (Kymlicka, 2004,
p. 159), but the definition of terrorism has widened.

Global multiculture exemplifies how technological and political changes affect the logics of
globalization and conflict. Borders are not what they used to be, the state no longer holds the
monopoly of the means of violence, technological changes enable the 'democratization' of
lethal weapons (warlords, crime syndicates, gangs) and arenas cross territorial boundaries
(cf. Nederveen Pieterse, 2004b, ch. 6). Gangs from East LA repatriate to El Salvador and
move back again to operate in Louisiana.

Multiculturalism is inherently linked to inequality in the world, as an articulation of global
inequality. Most migration is labor migration. Without steep inequalities people would not
move as much. Secondly, the same processes that reinforce overall global inequality make conditions in many multicultural societies harder. For the world majority neoliberal globalization
creates a world that is harder to live in back home and in the metropolises. Welfare cutbacks
make it harder to get by in multicultural societies while scarce jobs, rising income inequality,
reduced state spending and the privatization of utilities in low-income countries make it harder
to get by there as well. All-round Wal-Mart capitalism does not offer a benevolent script.
This is the dark sea underneath migration and multiculturalism. Multiculturalism going global
affords migrants the opportunity to compare notes on economic dynamics in motion. Global
poverty is part of bogus multiculturalism backlash. But it is not appropriate to reduce the
current tensions to economic deprivation. The imposition of reckless power politics astride
the world unleashes pent up tensions. A further element in the mix is the democratization of
the means of violence.

There is now a strange disjuncture between general abstract principles and real time applications. In March 2006 a group of writers issued a statement warning that Islamism is a
form of totalitarianism which is now the world's main danger: 'After having overcome
fascism, Nazism, and Stalinism, the world now faces a new global threat: Islamism ... We,
writers, journalists, intellectuals, call for resistance to religious totalitarianism and for the
promotion of freedom, equal opportunity and secular values for all.'[8] The writers include
Salman Rushdie, Christopher Hitchens, exiled Bangladeshi writer Taslima Nasreen, Ayaan
Hirsi Ali and Bernard-Henri Lévy. Ideas and ideologies have increasingly become a sphere of
displaced politics (what politics does not want to solve, ideas and moral posturing should
solve), so that in some real-time discursive regimes they seem to mean the opposite of what
they represent.

A pertinent response is the open letter to Prime Minister Blair sent by 38 British Muslim organizations and most Muslim MPs after the airplane bomb threats of August 2006, which accused the
government of adopting policies that expose the nation to terrorist attack (Cowell, 2006). The
upshot is that multiculturalism and foreign policy cannot be treated separately.

A central struggle of multiculturalism concerns access to the public sphere, including public
spaces, institutions, media, symbols and school curricula. The Danish cartoons and in a different
way Hirsi Ali seek to marginalize Muslims in the public sphere. Consider these accounts of

European public spaces in 2006. London in August: 'Terror arrests outside my park; multiethnic peace within' (Goldfarb, 2006); 'Londonistan', according to a conservative British journalist (Philips, 2006) and 'Kasba Holland', a scene of intercultural mixing according to upbeat Dutch writers (Fauwe and van Amerongen, 2006).

Over time, arguably, multicultural sharing of the public sphere and cultural and institutional power sharing is a likely trend in the West and Japan for structural demographic reasons (Tiryakian, 2003). Europe, Japan and the US are graying and ethnic and cultural hegemony is not being reproduced demographically. In this sense multicultural Europe and the 'browning' of America (one in eight Americans is of Hispanic background) are a matter of time. In this light the current skirmishes are rearguard actions that seek to halt what is, for structural economic and demographic reasons, an unstoppable trend.

Global multiculture

According to the Swedish anthropologist Ulf Hannerz (1996, p. 106) there is now a *world culture*, which he gives a supple meaning:

> There is now a world culture, but we had better make sure we understand what this means: not a replication of uniformity but an organization of diversity, an increasing interconnectedness of varied local cultures, as well as a development of cultures without a clear anchorage in any one territory. And to this interconnected diversity people can relate in different ways.

Global multiculture is another way to describe this world culture.

Here multiculturalism has two meanings. Multiethnicity has been the backdrop and infrastructure of global interconnectedness and globalization since time immemorial. It has not been nations that have been globalizing agents (though history books usually present it that way) but rather groups and regions within nations and migrants straddling nations. As mentioned before, several diasporas outnumber the population in the nation of origin, which shows that these trends have been in motion for some time. Growing multiethnicity in recent centuries produces a 'declining congruence between the nation and the state' (Carment, 1994, p. 560). We could interpret this as a changing balance between stationary and roving, sedentary and mobile strands of social life. This is a source of friction and inevitable conflict according to nineteenth century notions of 'hard sovereignty', but twenty-first century trends are towards regional and transnational pooling of sovereignty and soft sovereignty in view of changing technologies, economies, culture and polities.

Contemporary multiculturalism is global because global political economy promotes cross-border traffic. New channels of communication and influence are taking shape. Many pubs in England now follow soccer matches via Al Jazeera Sports Plus, with the volume down, because the subscription charges are much lower than the commercial British sports channels (Carvajal, 2006). New codes and vocabularies come into vogue. Thus, English as a global lingua franca has given rise to 'globish', as a description of global English as a practice and as a movement under the heading 'Don't speak English, parlez Globish'.[9] The new wars are transnational, conflicts and conflict networks straddle boundaries, from the Democratic Republic of Congo's coltan and casserite mines and niche warfare on the borders of Rwanda to the CIA's 'extraordinary rendition' and Guantánamo prison as a transnational site. The saying to fight a network it takes a network, cuts two ways. Cyberspace is global too. NGOs and social movements straddle boundaries. Multiculturalism discourse and policy is spreading globally—under headings such as minority rights, human rights or ethnic coalitions. And for all the attention bestowed on immigration, the other side of the coin is emigration. For instance, 'there are more UK nationals living overseas than there are foreign nationals living in the UK'.[10]

These trends usher in a new geography of global culture and a social formation that represents a new phase of globalization marked by flexible, multi-circuit identification. The conventional discussions of ethnicity and multiculturalism from national viewpoints are incomplete and unreal if they do not take into account the overall global changes. It is as if nation states want to have globalization on their own terms, domesticated and custom fit, picturesque like theme park multiculturalism, but do not concede the many backdoor ways through which they interact with globalization and the agency this involves and evokes.

Acknowledgments

This article is based on a paper presented at conferences at the University of South Florida, Tampa, Utrecht University, the International Sociological Association Congress, Durban and at Stockholm, Gothenburg and Freiburg universities in 2006. I thank participants for comments and in particular Fazal Rizvi, Daniel Beltram, Jan Ekecrantz and Don Kalb. Thanks to Ken Cuno and Lisa Chason for references.

Notes

1   The translation is from *Wikipedia*, under 'Muhammad cartoons controversy'.
2   Also *National Post*, in Danish. Quote: 'For years, Danes lauded multiculturalism and insisted they had no problem with the Muslim customs—until one day they found that they did. Some major issues: Living on the dole: Third-world immigrants—most of them Muslims . . . —constitute 5 percent of the population but consume upwards of 40 percent of the welfare spending. Engaging in crime: Muslims are only 4 percent of Denmark's 5.4 million people but make up a majority of the country's convicted rapists [and] . . . practically all the female victims are non-Muslim. Self-imposed isolation: Over time, as Muslim immigrants increase in numbers, they wish less to mix with the indigenous population. A recent survey finds that only 5 percent of young Muslim immigrants would readily marry a Dane. Importing unacceptable customs: Forced marriages . . . are one problem. Another is threats to kill Muslims who convert out of Islam. . . . Fomenting anti-Semitism: Muslim violence threatens Denmark's approximately 6,000 Jews, who increasingly depend on police protection. . . . Seeking Islamic law: Muslim leaders openly declare their goal of introducing Islamic law once Denmark's Muslim population grows large enough—a not-that-remote prospect. If present trends persist, one sociologist estimates, every third inhabitant of Denmark in 40 years will be Muslim.' The article sparked a debate on multiculturalism with Danish parliamentarians.
3   On Fortuyn, see Broertjes (2002). On van Gogh and Hirsi Ali, see Ali (2004); Bawer (2004); Majid (2004); Cécilia (2005); Simons (2005b); Caldwell (2005a); Linklater (2005).
4   Katja Schuurman, 'Prettig weekend, ondanks alles', 2005. Fauwe and van Amerongen (2006) report on Bouyeri's background.
5   After five years' residence immigrants have the right to vote and stand in municipal but not in national elections, so the left swing has been less marked in the 2006 parliamentary elections.
6   Cf. Hannerz (1992) on high rises and multiculturalism in Amsterdam.
7   'Their physical isolation sustains a sense of alienation, they become dormitory ghettos' (Heathcote, 2005).
8   Other signatories include: Iranian writer Chahla Chafiq, who is exiled in France; French writer Caroline Fourest; Irshad Manji, a Ugandan refugee and writer living in Canada; Mehdi Mozaffari, an Iranian academic exiled in Denmark; Maryam Namazie, an Iranian writer living in Britain; Antoine Sfeir, director of a French review examing the Middle East; Charlie Hebdo director Phillippe Val; and Ibn Warraq, a US academic of Indian and Pakistani origin who wrote a book titled *Why I Am Not a Muslim*. This was widely reported (e.g. 'Writers take aim at Islamic totalitarianism', available at http://www.iol.co.za/index.php?set_id=1&click_id=3&art_id=qw1141148701500B263 (accessed 28 February 2006).
9   See *Wikipedia* under Globish; and Nerrière (2004).
10 As of 2005 4.5 million British passport holders live overseas (Sriskandarajah, 2006).

References

Adam, D. (2005) UK Asians isolated in city enclaves, *The Guardian*, 1 September, p. 12.

Ali, A. H. (2004) Ik bevraag de islam, een religie zonder zelfreflectie, *De Volkskrant*, 30 October, p. 6.

Anderson, W. T. (1999) Communities in a world of open systems, *Futures*, 31(5), pp. 457–463.

Bawer, B. (2004) Tolerant Dutch wrestle with tolerating intolerance, *New York Times*, 4, p. 3.

Benard, C. (2003) *Civil Democratic Islam: Partners, Resources, and Strategies* (Santa Monica, CA: Rand Corporation).

Bollyn, C. (2006) European media provoke Muslims to inflame Zionist 'clash of civilizations', *American Free Press*, 3 February. Available at http://www.rumormillnews.com/cgi-bin/forum.cgi?read=84976.

Bourhis, R. Y., Moïse, L.C., Perreault, S. & Senécal, S. (1997) Toward an interactive acculturation model: a social psychological approach, *International Journal of Psychology*, 32(6), pp. 369–386.

Brennan, T. (1989) *Salman Rushdie and the Third World* (New York: St Martin's).

Brennan, T. (2006) *Wars of Position: The Cultural Politics of Left and Right* (New York: Columbia University Press).

Broertjes, P. I. (Ed.) (2002) *Het fenomeen Fortuyn* (Amsterdam: De Volkskrant, Meulenhoff).

Caldwell, C. (2005a) Daughter of the enlightenment, *New York Times Magazine*, 3 April, pp. 26–31.

Caldwell, C. (2005b) Revolting high rises, *New York Times Magazine*, 27 November, pp. 28–30.

Carment, D. (1994) The ethnic dimension in world politics: theory, policy and early warning, *Third World Quarterly*, 15(4), pp. 551–582.

Carvajal, D. (2006) Al Jazeera on television is causing trouble for British pubs, but it's not political, *New York Times*, 21 August, p. C6.

Cécilia, M.-C. (2005) Netherlands: the pillars are shaken, *Le Monde diplomatique* (March), pp. 4–5.

Chen, X. (2005) *As Borders Bend: Transnational Spaces on the Pacific Rim* (Boulder, CO: Rowman & Littlefield).

Clarke, R.A. (2005) Finding the sleeper cells: the London attackers can show us what to look for, *New York Times Magazine*, 14 August, p. 16.

Cooper, R. (2000) *The Postmodern State and the World Order* (London: Foreign Policy Centre).

Cowell, A. (2006) In open letter, British Muslims throw harsh criticism at Blair and his policies, *New York Times*, 13 August, p. 4.

Draper, I. (2005) Britain: acceptance not integration, *Le Monde diplomatique* (March), p. 5.

Fauwe, L. & van Amerongen, A. (2006) *Kasba Holland* (Amsterdam: Atlas).

Goldfarb, M. (2006) This is London, *New York Times*, 13 August, p. WK11.

Hannerz, U. (1992) *Culture, Cities and the World* (Amsterdam, Centre for Metropolitan Research).

Hannerz, U. (1996) *Transnational Connections: Culture, People, Places* (London: Routledge).

Heathcote, E. (2005) How France's suburbs became dormitory ghettos, *Financial Times*, 19–20 November.

Jenkins, S. (2006) These cartoons don't defend free speech, they threaten it, *Sunday Times*, 5 February.

Johnson, C. (2000) *Blowback: The Costs and Consequences of American Empire* (New York: Henry Holt).

Kapur, D. & McHale, J. (2005) *Give us your Best and Brightest* (Washington, DC: World Bank).

Kobrin, S. J. (1998) Back to the future: neomedievalism and the postmodern digital world economy, *Journal of International Affairs*, 51(2), pp. 361–386.

Kolbert, E. (2002) Letter from Rotterdam: beyond tolerance, *The New Yorker*, 9 September, pp. 106–114.

Koopmans, R. & Vliegenthart, R. (2006) De schijn van heiligheid: onderzoek naar de politieke invloed van Ayaan Hirsi Ali, *NRC Handelsblad*, 2–3 July, p. 35.

Kuper, S. (2006) Holland's crowded house, *Financial Times*, 26–27 August, p. W212.

Kymlicka, W. (2004) Justice and security in the accommodation of minority nationalism, in: S. May, T. Modood & J. Squires (Eds) *Ethnicity, Nationalism and Minority Rights* (Cambridge: Cambridge University Press), pp. 144–175.

Linklater, A. (2005) Danger woman, *Guardian Weekly*, 27 May–2 June, p. 17.

Majid, F. (2004) How Van Gogh provoked Islamists, *Daily Times*, 1 December.

Mernissi, F. (2003) Palace fundamentalism and liberal democracy, in: E. Qureshi & M. A. Sells (Eds) *The New Crusades: Constructing the Muslim Enemy* (New York: Columbia University Press), pp. 58–67.

Mitchell, T. (2002) McJihad: Islam in the U.S. global order, *Social Text*, 20(4), pp. 1–18.

Modood, T. (2005) Remaking multiculturalism after 7/7, *Open Democracy*, 29 September.

Moisi, D. (2005) France is haunted by an inability to confront its past, *Financial Times*, 12 December, p. 15.

Nederveen Pieterse, J. (1997) Traveling Islam: mosques without minarets, in: A. Öncü & P. Weyland (Eds) *Space, Culture and Power* (London: Zed), pp. 177–200.

Nederveen Pieterse, J. (2003) Social capital and migration: beyond ethnic economies, *Ethnicities*, 3(1), pp. 5–34.

Nederveen Pieterse, J. (2004a) *Globalization and Culture: Global Mélange* (Boulder, CO: Rowman & Littlefield).

Nederveen Pieterse, J. (2004b) *Globalization or Empire?* (New York: Routledge).

Nerrière, J. P. (2004) *Don't Speak English, Parlez Globish* (Paris: Eyrolles).

Ong, A. (1998) Flexible citizenship among Chinese cosmopolitans, in: P. Cheah & B. Robbins (Eds) *Cosmopolitics: Thinking and Feeling Beyond the Nation* (Minneapolis, MN: University of Minnesota Press), pp. 143–162.

Ong, A. (1999) *Flexible Citizenship: The Cultural Logics of Transnationalism* (Durham, NC: Duke University Press).

Peters, M. A. (2005) Between empires: rethinking identity and citizenship in the context of globalization, in: P. Hayden & C. el-Ojeili (Eds) *Confronting Globalization: Humanity, Justice and the Renewal of Politics* (London: Palgrave), pp. 105–122.

Philips, M. (2006) *Londonistan: How Britain is Creating a Terror State Within* (London: Gibson Square).

Pipes, D. (2001) The Palestinians are a miserable people ... and they deserve to be, *Washington Report on Middle East Affairs* (July).

Pipes, D. & Hedegaard, L. (2002) Something rotten in Denmark?, *New York Post*, 27 August.

Rose, F. (2004) The threat from Islamism, *Jyllands-Posten*, 29 October. Translation available at http://bellaciao.org/en/article.php3?id_article=10253.

Rose, F. (2006) Why I published the cartoons, *Washington Post*, 19 February p. B01.

Simons, M. (2005a) Muslim women in Europe claim rights and keep faith: embracing Islam and independence, *New York Times*, 29 December, p. 3.

Simons, M. (2005b) Living with Islam: the new Dutch model?, *The Economist*, 2 April, pp. 24–26.

Smith, C. S. (2006) Adding newsprint to the fire, *New York Times*, 5 February, p. WK5.

Sriskandarajah, D. (2006) Britain must look at that other group of migrants, *Financial Times*, 7 August, p. 11.

Steger, M. B. (2005) American globalism 'Madison Avenue-style': a critique of U.S. public diplomacy after 9/11, in: P. Hayden & C. el-Ojeili (Eds) *Confronting Globalization: Humanity, Justice and the Renewal of Politics* (London: Palgrave), pp. 227–241.

Storper, M. (2001) Lived effects of the contemporary economy: globalization, inequality and consumer society, in: J. Comaroff & J. L. Comaroff (Eds) *Millennial Capitalism and the Culture of Neoliberalism* (Durham, NC: Duke University Press), pp. 88–124.

Tiryakian, E. A. (2003) Assessing multiculturalism theoretically: *E pluribus unum, sic et non, International Journal on Multicultural Societies*, 5(1), pp. 20–39.

Vidal, D. (2004) France: hate and the hijab, *Le Monde diplomatique*, 4 February.

Waever, O. (1996) European security identities, *Journal of Common Market Studies*, 34, pp. 03–132.

Wallerstein, I. (2005) The inequalities that blazed in France will soon scorch the world, *The Guardian*, 3 December.

Weisman, S. R. (2006) Rice is seeking millions to prod changes in Iran, *New York Times*, 16 February, pp. A1–12.

Wieviorka, M. (2004a) The stakes in the French secularism debate, *Dissent* (Summer), pp. 71–73.

Wieviorka, M. (2004b) The making of differences, *International Sociology*, 19(3), pp. 281–297.

Jan Nederveen Pieterse, Professor of Sociology at University of Illinois Urbana-Champaign, works on globalization, development studies and intercultural studies. Recent books are *Ethnicities and Global Multiculture: Pants for an Octopus* (Rowman & Littlefield, 2007), *Globalization or Empire?* (2004), *Globalization and Culture: Global Mélange* (2004) and *Development Theory: Deconstructions/Reconstructions* (2001).

Cohering Culture on *Calle Ocho*: The Pause and Flow of *Latinidad*

PATRICIA L. PRICE

Querying Culture through *Latinidad*

> [C]ultural coherence in the face of heterogeneity and porous boundaries, complexity, and complicity across far-reaching networks are some of the most challenging and intriguing issues in cultural theory today. (Duncan and Duncan, 2004, p. 391)

In this article I explore the coming together of certain place-specific social relations; in Duncan and Duncan's (2004) words, cultural coherence. To do so, I will examine *latinidad*, a term which implies (among other things) pan-Latinismo (García, 2003; Aparicio and Chávez-Silverman, 1997). The ethnic solidarity at the root of *latinidad* is a concrete example of cultural coherence. This defines culture as a fluid terrain, one that emphasizes process, performance, and encounter, standing in contrast to a concern with defining the precise contents of what does or does not count as 'culture'. Thus, in my examination of *latinidad*, I will emphasize the productive tension between flow and pause in the strategic composition of pan-ethnic identity. This is an interplay which is mirrored at a broader level in my discussion of globalization, as well as more narrowly in the role of city streets from which the examples to illustrate the pause and flow of *latinidad* are drawn.

The images used to illustrate the discussion throughout this essay were taken by me and my sometimes-Latina daughter, during the 2006 *Calle Ocho* street festival in Miami's Little Havana neighborhood. Held once a year as part of Lent festivities, *Calle Ocho* is an afternoon-long street fair that sees 23 city blocks along Southwest Eighth Street closed to vehicular traffic and devoted instead to a crush of pedestrians bent on eating, drinking, and listening to the live music blaring from 30 stages. Billed as 'a signature event that celebrates the city's cultural heritage' (Bradley, 2006, p. 1A), *Calle Ocho* has evolved from its inception in 1978 as a venue for introducing non-Hispanic Miamians to their Cuban neighbors, to the city's showcase celebration of its diverse Latino cultures. 'There has been a shift in the faces, food, souvenirs and sound—reflecting Miami's evolving Hispanic community' (Bradley, 2006, p. 2A).

In the media coverage of *Calle Ocho*, as well as in the festival itself, an uncomplicated *latinidad* is vigorously promoted. Reveler Julietta Chávez, quoted in the *Miami Herald*, stated that 'We're all one heart here. There are no distinctions of race, of country or culture' (Bradley, 2006, p. 1A). Chávez's statement invokes the larger, strategic valorization of all things Latino in opposition to Anglo society's devalorization of them, or at best their political neutralization under the term 'Hispanic'. But, in practice, *latinidad* is complicated. As with other sodalities, whether based in perceived ethnic, racial, gender, regional, or other similarities, diversity within is submerged in the name of the greater political good to be gained in unity. The question, with *latinidad* as with other such alliances, is whether this is politically justifiable or whether it merely produces other layers of suppression.

Though I make no claims to resolving these difficult questions here (though see Price, 2004, esp. pp. 61–82), I do note that the issues surrounding *latinidad* are at the heart of a project that I and my colleagues are conducting in gentrifying inner-ring ethnic enclave neighborhoods in Miami, Phoenix, and Chicago (Arreola *et al.*, in progress). In this research, we utilize surveys (n = 400 in each site), in-depth interviews (n = 40 in each site) and focus groups (n = 4 in each site) to explore the negotiation of literal and figurative turf. In the study neighborhoods, established groups of Latino/a residents are faced with an influx of very poor new arrivals, at the same time as they are faced with a significant transition in the physical space of their neighborhoods due to luxury condominium construction and an influx of relatively wealthy gentrifiers. Data analysis is in the preliminary stages as of mid-2007, thus any conclusions on my part would be premature and lacking in the comparative empirical data needed to buttress them. However, Miami's Little Havana neighborhood is far more diverse in terms of country of origin of its residents as compared to both Pilsen (in Chicago) and Garfield (in Phoenix), whose Latino/a residents are overwhelmingly Mexicano/a.[1] Thus the question of pan-Latinismo may perhaps be best addressed in Little Havana, given that national origin forms one of the strongest bases of intra-Latino/a solidarity (amongst co-nationals) and cleavage (amongst different national groups).

Because Latino/a enclave neighborhoods such as the ones in our study concentrate Latino/a populations spatially, a potential base for pan-ethnic solidarity, resource mobilization, and political empowerment is hypothesized by some (Villa, 1999). This has been evidenced in practice in strategic political alliances in the United States (García, 2003; Cabán, 1998; Torres, 1998) as well as in assumptions, such as Roberto Suro's (1998, p. 159–178), that

Miami is just one big 'barrio without borders' (see also Fox, 1997). Yet as García (2003) has noted, there is no reason to assume a natural basis for pan-ethnicity amongst Latinos/as in the United States, who span over 20 national origins, times of arrival varying from hundreds of years ago to very recently, socio-economic locations ranging from the wealthiest to the poorest, and the gamut of ethno-racialized identifications. Too-easy assumptions of ethnic solidarity inhibit recognition of deep divisions amongst Latinos/as (Torres-Saillant, 2002). Some scholars have suggested that the assertion of ethnic identities in the United States is in fact leading to a profound redefinition, and possible fragmentation, of the public sphere (Cabán, 1998; Torres, 1998; Rosaldo and Flores, 1997; Horton, 1992).

What research in the arena of civic engagement narrowly (i.e., participation in political activities and formal civic organizations) and broadly (i.e., participation in community life through the labor and housing markets, churches, schools, and social networks) has uncovered about the existence of intra-ethnic tensions and solidarities is rich and suggestive. For example, Ochoa (2004), Menjívar (2000), Mahler (1995), and Chinchilla, Hamilton, and Loucky (1993) document instances of friction and divisiveness arising amongst Latino communities along lines of gender, national origin and even co-nationals by time of arrival. Stepick and Grenier's (1993) analysis of the apparent solidarity amongst cubanos/as in Miami, for example, reveals that assumptions of solidarity in fact mask significant racism against both African-Americans and Afro-cubanos/as, discrimination by economic class and gender, and workplace segmentation by race, gender, and national origin (see also Alberts, 2005; Grenier and Stepick, 1992). Thus in-depth research has revealed intra-Latino/a relations to be complex and place-specific, and to include elements of solidarity as well as contention.

Questions surrounding *latinidad* are not unique to Miami. In arguably the nation's most important contemporary demographic event, high levels of Latino/a immigration have met with higher-than-average rates of population increase for those Latinos/as already in the United States, leading Hispanics to surpass Black Americans as the most numerically significant 'minority' population as of 2003. Because Latinos/as are notably urban in their residential patterns, this has meant that many US cities are particularly affected by this demographic sea change. This so-called Latinization of the US has the potential to profoundly reshape the parameters of democracy, citizenship, and national identity. Indeed, the implications of the transformations wrought by Latinization are hemispheric in scope, potentially forging trans- or post-national identities that will eclipse older solidarities.

It is typically the automobile-induced suburban sprawl, strip mall vernacular architecture, and the service-oriented labor base that are cited as what makes cities such as Las Vegas, Phoenix, Miami, and Los Angeles tick as templates for contemporary urban studies in the United States (e.g., Dear and Flusty, 2001). That these cities inhabit the cutting edge of urban studies in the United States is not, however, accidentally related to the fact that these cities are, or have long been, Latinized. Recent urban research points to the specific contributions of Latinos/as, both longtime residents and recent arrivals, as contrasted to earlier 'ethnic' groups. Findings have begun to counter assumptions of theories of urban change that pre-date widescale Latinization of so many US metropoles, as is the case with the models dating from the early to mid-twentieth century: for example, the black–white binary's paradigmatic status, the (desir)ability of assimilation into the Anglo mainstream as the fate of all 'ethnics', knowledge of who participates in neighborhood revitalization and how, or the traditional modeling of residential geography along the 'ethnic wedge' template (Arreola *et al.*, in progress; Davis, 2000; Villa, 2000). Latinos/as are revealed to be the engine behind the revitalization of decaying industrial zones, older working-class neighborhoods, and aging inner city ethnic neighborhoods in

New York City (Miyares, 2004), San Francisco (Godfrey, 2004), Los Angeles, (Curtis, 2004), and San Diego (Herzog, 2004). In Little Havana, YUCAs (young upwardly-mobile Cuban-Americans) are the main agents behind the gentrification of the neighborhood, partly out of nostalgia and partly for the same reasons all fairly wealthy, young professionals gentrify: relatively undervalued housing stock located near revitalizing downtown financial centers (Arrreola *et al.*, in progress). Gentrification is seen by many neighborhood residents as on balance a good thing. Some believe—rightly or wrongly—that the construction of condominiums in vacant lots, tearing down derelict strip malls, and the upgrading of existing housing stock will bring a larger tax base, more residential stability, higher property values, and an increased level of pride in place to their neighborhoods. This sets common wisdom on gentrification on its ear, and counters assumptions that deny Latinos/as agency of the sort that gentrifiers enact.

It is relegation to the status of non-agents that is most deeply interrogated by work that makes its way past the dazzling façade of postmodern urban theory and into the *barrios*. In otherwise careful scholarship, there exists a tendency to view 'ethnic' and racialized minorities, immigrants, and the urban poor as constituting victims of processes beyond their control. For example, Zukin (1996, p. 49) describes the global city in terms of a 'vernacular landscape of the powerless', composed of 'women, racial minorities, immigrants, certain types of workers, and the homeless' (p. 43). She contends that this vernacular landscape is under pressure of replacement by a 'new landscape of power' (p. 49). While there is certainly no denying that such pressures exist, it is surely a mistake to assume away the participation in, negotiation of, or resistance to these pressures. Or to disregard the notion that 'women, racial minorities, immigrants, certain types of workers, and the homeless' might actually craft powerful landscapes of their own, to which global forces need to respond. On 10 March 2006, for example, the streets of downtown Chicago became the site of a stunning gathering of up to half a million Latinos/as and their supporters, marching in protest against HR 4437, the Sensenbrenner immigration bill, legislation that would have extended the border fence between Mexico and the United States and criminalized undocumented immigrants as well as those who assist them. Though when it occurred the protest constituted practically a non-event for the mainstream media, the message that 'we are here in great numbers, we contribute in vital ways to this region's economy, and we are not about to be bordered-out of the future' was disseminated widely over alternative venues (word of mouth, email, and Spanish language media) and resonated with a huge number of Chicago's, and the nation's, residents. This initial protest crested in a wave of huge metropolitan-based protests throughout the late spring and summer of 2006. Though the notion that Latinos/as and the spaces they inhabit in global cities are relatively disadvantaged may well be true at a certain level of abstraction, there is no natural extension from this observation to the idea that poor, immigrant, or marginalized peoples constitute homogenous populations that passively allow larger structural changes to occur in uniformly disadvantageous ways.

An alternate tactic has involved the pinpointing of Latinos/as as particular sorts of agents, as opposed to discounting them as such; specifically in the guise of 'Hispanic culture'. Samuel Huntington's (2004) much decried 'The Hispanic Challenge' epitomizes this approach. Huntington singles out 'Hispanic immigrants' as a force threatening to divide the nation culturally and politically thanks to their sheer numbers and inability or unwillingness to assimilate. Huntington's many critics have understandably spent a great deal of time discussing the myriad errors of fact, erroneous assumptions, illogical extensions, and outright prejudice that comprise the tight weave holding this treatise together, and I will not replicate those discussions here.[2] Rather, I wish to underscore the fact that rather than attempting to silence the issue altogether—as with the mainstream US media's treatment of the Chicago protest, or urban theory's persistent blind spot with respect to Latinization—Huntington faces his demon square on and gives it a name: culture. For it is 'Hispanic culture' that is seen to fly in the face of the mainstream (Anglo-Protestant in values, White in race, English-speaking, and harkening back to English political institutions and notions such as the rule of law), threatening to plant a boulder dividing the mainstream in two, 'two peoples with two cultures (Anglo and Hispanic) and two languages (English and Spanish)' (Huntington, 2004, p. 32).

Both of these arguments—Latinos/as as non-agents and Latinos/as as monolithic agents—turn on culture. For it is 'Latino culture' that is seen, in the first instance, to inhibit civic engagement, and, in the second, to promote the destructive agency of the sort invoked by Huntington. Culture is thus in no way ancillary to this discussion of *latinidad*. I make this seemingly straightforward observation despite strong claims that we now inhabit a post-cultural era, or that invoking 'culture' necessarily treads too-dangerous ground (Benhabib, 2002; Mitchell, 1995). Rather, I will suggest, along with others, that culture provides an especially salient avenue for critical inquiry, not so much because culture exists in some abstract fashion, but because it is reified so persistently as to take on a currency and power that are undeniably real. 'Abstract ideas, meanings, and intangible processes of meaning-making are just as real as material things. They interact with and through objects, becoming material culture' (Duncan and Duncan, 2004, p. 392).

If culture is, then, not so much a transcendent thing as it is a contingent and place-specific constellation of social, economic, and political relations made to fall under the rubric of culture, the process of coherence comes to the forefront. In defining culture as a coming together of certain place-specific social relations, the notion of situational coherence, decomposition, and recomposition is central. In other words, culture involves a dynamic interplay between flow and pause. In this sense, flows and pauses, and the dynamic tension between these two polarities, can be seen to be at the heart of *latinidad* as cultural coherence. Importantly, there is much room for the strategic composition, decomposition, and reconstitution of identities within this view of cultural coherence. Latinos/as, far from being passive recipients of changes beyond their control, or constituting monolithic behemoths forcing change by dint of their stubborn otherness, are (at least potentially) every bit as resourceful in their deployment of *latinidad* as those who would deploy it against them. 'Latin@s use different voices to speak as members of different groups at different times, even at the same time' (Zentella, 2002, p. 321).[3]

In the context of this essay, then, how is it that *latinidad* is successfully cohered—in protests like the recent immigration marches, but also in festivals, neighborhood redevelopment, tourism, electoral politics, etc. (the list is a long one)—despite the ready axes of cleavage that always-already exist within this social formation? What of reality that the Latinos/as involved in the Chicago protest, for example, hail from over a dozen Spanish-speaking nations (or from the United States)? What of the fact that marchers occupy a plethora of racialized, gendered, sexualized, or class positions, or that marchers may well occupy other social locations altogether? The Nation of Islam as well as evangelical Christian groups were prominent participants in the Chicago marches, as were Irish-Americans and Chinese immigrants, members of labor unions, and myriad others, yet the Chicago protest and subsequent marches were organized and widely understood as 'Latino' events. How and why is it, in other words, that the notion of pan-Latinismo circulates despite the diverse valences cohered within the category? How and to what end is culture conjured in specific contexts?

In this paper, I examine more closely the broader coherence of culture at various scales, ranging from street-level encounters to larger notions of culture and its deployment under the banner of *latinidad*. In the next three sections I turn to a grounded exploration of daily life in a Miami neighborhood, with an eye toward an understanding of the public spaces of streets, sidewalks, parks, and cafes, as moments in the local where *latinidad* coheres. I will illustrate by way of example what has already been discussed in more general terms above: the tension between pause and flow that defines *latinidad*, the performativity of *latinidad*, the fraught interplay between exclusion and inclusion contained within *latinidad*, and *latinidad*'s situational coherence. As a precursor to these illustrations, the larger-scale intersections of *latinidad* with global cities is discussed as a context within which the narrower Miami-focused discussion resides, for solidarities forged along the lines of *latinidad* promise to productively challenge existing maps of meaning at multiple scales.

Calle Ocho: Local Encounters in a Global City

To my knowledge, there is next to nothing published specifically from a global cities perspective that foregrounds the role of global cities in encouraging human encounters at the scale of lived, quotidian experience. Rather, the emphasis is overwhelmingly on flux (see also Pratt, 2005). Perhaps this is due to the fact that, as Castells (1996) has noted, global cities are better connected to other global cities whilst becoming progressively disconnected from their local populations— or perhaps it is this *perception* that has driven analysis of global cities in particular ways. And it is precisely this sense of disconnection that resides in much scholarship on globalization, and by extension global cities, that I wish to address in this paper.[4] For all its emphasis on flows—of people, ideas, goods, services—and movements that have become ever faster, ever less centered, ever more efficient or brutal—the human element has seemed to drop out of work on globalization. To be sure, recent work on globalization and global cities has begun the process of critical inquiry regarding the huge human asymmetries obscured behind the façade of the global. Recent publications on neoliberalism's nefarious occlusion of enormous increases in disparities of human well-being, for example, have called globalization-as-rhetoric what it is: a discourse used by powerful actors (states, the IMF, large multinational corporations) to wring an economic advantage (that accrues invariably to the wealthiest in society) out of the already, and the newly, disenfranchised (Pratt, 2005; Yúdice, 2003). In addition, there exists a corpus of creative production that undertakes the ground-level focus on daily lives lived in global cities as its point of departure, and it is toward this work that this paper gestures. One might think particularly of films, such as *Amores Perros* (set in Mexico City), *Cidade de Deus* and *Central do Brasil* (both set in Rio de Janeiro), *María Llena de Gracia* (set partly in New York City), *Lost in Translation* (set in Tokyo), and *Crash* (set in Los Angeles) that do a good job of capturing the enduring need for human encounter in the midst of the movement, change, disconnection, and loss that have become symbolic of global cities.

Not all of life under globalization is in flux. And, despite the well-placed critical focus on the nefarious human consequences of neoliberalism, not all of life under globalization is abject misery. We still go about our daily lives: even in the cruelest of global urban dystopias, even under conditions of virtual labor slavery, even as members of the most excluded sectors of society. To be sure, folks certainly do grapple with malnutrition, stress, ill health, exploitation as laborers, violence in the streets and at home, involuntary dislocation, and a host of other maladies exponentially incremented under the auspices of 'globalization'. But they also dwell, raise families, break bread with one another, joke, beautify themselves and their surroundings, and appreciate a sunrise or a baby's smile. The lives of the vast majority of the planet's inhabitants are not only flow and abstraction, but also pause and connection.

I will suggest that the very local scale provided by street studies provide a heuristic that grants insight into spaces of heightened inflection found in global cities. Eighth Street distills and channels the international flux of human and commercial traffic in Miami and across South Florida's peninsula. It scripts the place-ballets (Jacobs, 1992) or urban encounters (Liggett, 2003) performed by people brought together from increasingly disparate places and walks of life. Next, I will briefly discuss a series of pauses along this street, for it is the encounters between people and place that, ultimately, define globalization as lived experience, one predicated in part on the choreography of pause and flow.

Sidewalk Talk

> Lowly, unpurposeful and random as they may appear, sidewalk contacts are the small change from which a city's wealth of public life may grow. (Jacobs 1992, p. 72)

Calle Ocho is a long thoroughfare that changes name and character several times as it crosses the state of Florida connecting the cities of Tampa on the northwest coast to Miami on the southeast coast.[5] As it leaves Miami to the west and heads through the Everglades, across the Florida peninsula and up the West Coast to Tampa, it is called Highway 41. This roughly 350-mile stretch of highway is also referred to as the Tamiami Trail, which is a combination of the names of the two cities it connects: Tampa and Miami. Only the relatively small portion of the street that runs through Miami's Little Havana neighborhood is referred to as Calle Ocho. But Calle Ocho is the name that locals and outsiders alike are most familiar with. And it is certainly a street in a global(izing) city where public life, far from declining, is in full swing. Plazas, parks, street corners, and the buffers par excellence of the public/private urban interface—sidewalks—are definitely used here.

Jane Jacobs's classic rejoinder to modern urban planning in the United States, published in 1961 as *The Death and Life of Great American Cities*, saw the sidewalk as integral to what makes the city a great (safer, less lonely, more interesting) place to live. This is in part due to the element of choice that exists in cities between solitude, one-on-one exchange, and operating as part of a crowd. The choice, in other words, between pause and flow, between becoming part of a collective or highlighting one's uniqueness. Jacobs contrasted the lively, if sometimes confrontational, daily rhythms of sidewalk flows and pauses to the deadened suburbs where human contact is of the 'all or nothing' model. In the suburbs, according to Jacobs, there is no public pedestrian life at all: streets are used to transport vehicles from home to work to shopping and back again, and socializing takes place indoors. As such, sidewalks—where they exist at all in the suburbs as functional elements between the public places of streets and the interiors of homes and commercial establishments—do not fulfill the same function of facilitating the semi-public human encounter, of providing a 'realm of casual public trust'. Rather, people must gather in one another's' homes; a leap of faith that, Jacobs asserts, few suburbanites are willing to make.[6]

Other scholars have noted the key function of streets and their sidewalks in the facilitation of psycho-socially acceptable encounter between neighbors and strangers. This is not to say that all have viewed sidewalks with the same enthusiasm as Jacobs (or suburbs with the same disdain, for that matter). Notably, the paradigmatic modern urban planner Le Corbusier erased corridors of pedestrian flow in his Radiant City, replacing them with multi-leveled thoroughfares for vehicular traffic alone. When an adapted version of Le Corbusier's plan was finally implemented in the 1950s with the building of Brasilia in the Amazonian jungle, the results were, predictably,

Figure 1. Sidewalk talk during the 2006 *Calle Ocho* festivities. Photo taken by the author

deadly, speaking figuratively of the public sphere. As James Scott (1999) notes, public spaces—street corners, sidewalk cafes, plazas—exist in profusion and at a human scale in Brazil's longstanding capital city of Rio de Janeiro. Forging a modern Brazil, however, involved forcing the 'Brazilianness' out of Brazilians, according to Brasilia's planners, and there was no better way to do this than to get people off of the streets and sidewalks, out of the cafes and plazas. No, modern Brazilians would not waste time on idle chitchat with their fellow urbanites (and, not incidentally since Brazil would by 1964 be controlled by its right-wing military, this includes potential subversion, public protests, strikes, and the like—planner Lúcio Costa's public discourse notwithstanding); they should move efficiently from home to work and back again in their automobiles. Small wonder that Brasilia to this day has a floating population of bureaucrats who fly back to Rio on the weekends to join families that refuse to move permanently to this deadened city.

In his comparison of preindustrial Brazilian urbanization patterns with the modern urban design of Brasilia, James Holston (1999, p. 250) notes that the street 'constitutes the architectural context of the outdoor public life of Brazilian cities'. Its absence in Brasilia in mixed pedestrian–vehicular form, without intersections forming street corners, has led to a city without crowds and the social life that is associated with crowds. Brasilia has achieved nothing less than a reconfiguration of the relationship between public and private, a reconfiguration with profound civic consequences. For example, Holsten discusses the resistance of Brasilienses to the architectural denial of the *rua* (the street) through tactics of reversal and conversion of the service backs of commerce planned to face the street, into store fronts. Yet the administrative powers-that-be have fought back with tighter planning controls and have ceased to make any gestures at all to pedestrians in the form of green spaces, pedestrian shopping, parking, or even providing for safe passage around and across roadways. For their part, sidewalks have been separated from the streets as arcades in front of discrete buildings in some areas, and simply do not exist in others.

[T]his design precludes the possibility of street life by severing the street from the place of exchange. It eliminates sidewalk contact between the two and considers each separately, demoting the street to the single function of transport and sequestering all commerce into self-contained, detached mini-malls. In the absence of a continuous sidewalk edged with facades, not only is 'strolling down the avenue' impossible, but, moreover, the urban flaneur is now confronted with extinction. (Holsten, 1999, p. 272)

Democracy might be said to reside on the sidewalks. For sidewalks encourage the encounters between public and private, self and other, that provide a necessary counterweight to the state and its repressive tendencies. Sidewalks also provide a space for initiating, strengthening, and renewing friendships, for performing identities of all sorts (gendered, racialized, classed, sexualized, national, age-related, and so on), for watching and being watched, to a variety of ends ranging from the safety Jacobs considered so vital to the pure pleasure of watching that is at the (admittedly problematic) heart of the *flaneur*, and for undertaking the much-maligned-of-late commercial exchanges that allow us to eat, drink, and be merry. In our example, they make the 'small change' of daily encounters that allows the coherence necessary to conjure *latinidad* in contexts such as Little Havana's *Calle Ocho* festival. It is these performances of motion, exchange, and connection that are considered next.

El Bailongo

It is a complex order. Its essence is intricacy of sidewalk use, bringing with it a constant succession of eyes. This order is all composed of movement and change, and although it is life, not art, we may fancifully call it the art form of the city and liken it to the dance. (Jacobs, 1992, p. 50)

Human movement is at the heart of *Calle Ocho* festivities. To be sure, the relentless forward movement of the crowd provides the inescapable arterial choreography for the event. But movement comes in more scripted forms as well. Beside the many planned musical performances conducted at scheduled times on stages throughout the afternoon, drummers and singers in the crowd occasionally break into song, while the people nearest them shift gears from their inexorable forward crush, to dance. Different national styles of Latin music are highlighted, from Cuban *rumba*, *mambo*, and *son*, to Colombian *cumbia*, Dominican *merengue*, and Puerto Rican *bomba* and *plena*, and those Cubanas/os, Colombianas/os, Dominicanas/os, and Boricuas/os in the crowd cheer emphatically for their own national styles, but also dance the ubiquitous tropical salsas and enjoy the rhythms of other nations, as do the many Black and Anglo Americans also in the crowd.

Jane Jacobs (1992) coined the enduring phrase 'street ballet' to signify the repetitive everyday movements and interactions of people she came into contact with on a daily basis on Hudson Street, where she lived in Greenwich Village. She saw the street ballet in its predictability, temporal rhythm, and inclusiveness as central to maintaining safety, fostering human contact, and socializing children. Her observations echo Henri Lefebvre's (2004) notion of rhythmanalysis as a method for understanding the patterned interactions of space and time in everyday urban life. Certainly, as both Jacobs and Lefebvre note, the built elements of cities—streets, sidewalks, public spaces—shape the movement of people within them. Miami's gridded street layout, for example, prioritizes automobile travel and channels human movement along either a north–south or east–west axis. Addresses are generally easy to find, and distances easy to calculate. But these movements also shape cities. One might go so far as to suggest that it is the sedimented, ritual acts of movement and encounter between people, and between people and the other elements (animate and inanimate) that in concert conjure the city itself as a cultural being.

Several important elements are crystallized in the metaphor of dance as applied to understanding the patterned spatio-temporality of urban engagement constituted by, and constitutive of,

Figure 2. Dancers during the 2006 *Calle Ocho* festivities. Photo taken by Nina Price

cities. First of all, dance involves bodies. Thus, understanding cities through the prism of dance necessitates that bodies be centralized, a point that feminists (Wilson, 1992) and others (Thrift, 1997; de Certeau, 1984) have emphatically made. Second, dance is all about the tension between rules and improvisation. The *Calle Ocho* revelers danced specific dances, encouraged by music scheduled and performed at predetermined places and times, with the correct steps. But the spontaneity of sidewalk drumming and lone male dancers attempting to show one another up was equally entertaining for dancers and spectators alike, though it did not appear anywhere on the schedule. Third, and related to the previous two points, dance is a prime example of performance, which has of late provided a productive conceptual lens onto a multitude of socio-spatial phenomena. Fourth, and perhaps most importantly for my purposes here, dance—both as metaphor and literally—is centrally about negotiating self and other. All of these points bear important resonances with identity as an embodied, negotiated, performed choreography that triangulates between self and other. Dance, in other words, is about flow and pause. The productive tension between the identities on parade during the *Calle Ocho* festivities, and the solidification, disintegration, and recompositon of these identities through movement and encounter, are central to understanding the situational operation of *latinidad*.

Mediations

> [F]or many of us those commodified signs we may gaze upon, or simply catch out of the corner of the eye, we use as one of the numerous resources in making sense of where—and who—we are, and the place, street, we move through. (Crouch, 1998, p. 172)

In much of the literature on public spaces in an era of globalization, the dominant refrain is that late or global capitalism is inexorably appropriating, commodifying, and surveilling public urban spaces (Mitchell, 2003; Smith, 1997; Davis, 1992). Global cities like New York and Los Angeles are as a result becoming mosaics of exclusionary zones. The poor, minorities, and immigrants are becoming progressively shut out of these public spaces and thus shut out of citizenship. To be sure, this argument has its merits, and Miami is no exception to this trend. In many ways Miami is the epitome of exclusionary urban spaces, with its gated neighborhoods, lack of public transportation, unaffordable housing, high levels of poverty, and the ubiquitous shopping malls that blanket the landscape and provide the preferred form of local family entertainment. And the *Calle Ocho* festival itself, despite its self-promotion as a cultural venue where the material artifacts of 'Hispanic culture'—food, music, dance, souvenirs—can be enjoyed by all, is also at its core a commercial event. The primary points of interaction are points of sale, in the many booths that line the sidewalks selling food, drink, jewelry, CDs, cell phone plans, and t-shirts. Police are mounted in elevated surveillance towers in the center of the street in the center of every block keeping watch over the crowd, scanning constantly for thieves, fights, and drunkards. Many merchants close their doors, fearing the crowds, theft, and people wanting to use their restrooms.

Underlying the shift from open and democratic urban public spaces to closed and exclusionary ones lies the romantic fiction that in other cities—cities outside of the US, pre-industrial cities, or in cities as they existed before globalization reshaped them—public space and human encounters in those spaces were all that they are not today: unmediated by the almighty monetary transaction, democratic, liberating, inclusive. But have cities ever really been sites of truly unmediated spontaneity? Even the idealized Greek polis limited citizenship, not to mention participation in the public civic life of the city-state, to freeborn resident males only, thereby excluding females, children, slaves, and foreigners. Though I am not a scholar of urban history, I suspect that in all cities everywhere and throughout history productive tensions exist over what Lefebvre (2004) termed 'the right to the city' and those who would sell that right or exclude some from it.

Anthropologist Setha Low, in her study of Costa Rican plazas (1999), conversed with a long-time user of San José's Parque Central. This elderly gentleman, who at the time of their interview spent most of his day sitting in the park with his friends, had once worked as a guard in the park. He noted that the park's gates used to be locked at night, and not everyone was allowed in during daylight hours, whereas today that sort of overt surveillance had been abandoned in favor

Figure 3. Buying a coco frío during the 2006 *Calle Ocho* festivities. Photo taken by the author

of more surreptitious gate keeping, including plainclothes police and the requirement that vendors purchase a license to sell their wares in public spaces such as the Parque Central. Thus, Low (1999, p. 124) observes, it is not that public spaces have somehow become more restrictive or commodified than before; rather, they have become differently restricted and commodified: 'control over who is in the plaza is apparently maintained less openly and more subversively than it used to be'.

Without losing sight of the commodified, exclusive, and surveilled aspect of *Calle Ocho* festivities, and Miami's urban landscape more generally, it is important to maintain a balance. Particularly in the case of immigrants from the Americas (who make up 88% of Little Havana's population, as per Arreola *et al.*, in progress), more intensive use patterns of public space are prevalent.

> Across the vast pan-American range of cultural nuance, the social reproduction of *latinidad*, however defined, presupposes a rich proliferation of public space . . . Latin American immigrants and their children, perhaps more than any other element in the population, exult in playgrounds, parks, squares, libraries and other endangered species of US public space, and thus form one of the most important constituencies for the preservation of our urban commons. (Davis, 2000, pp. 54–55)

Not all of Little Havana's public spaces have been appropriated by any means. Little Havana is a neighborhood noted for its vibrant street life, public protests, and café culture. And even where exchange is mediated through monetary transaction, there is unmediated joy to be had in the conversation shared with the merchant, seeing fellow *paisanos* rejoice at the sight of a favorite treat seldom found in the US, and in consuming that *coco frío*.

Exile Memories and the Shaping of Miami

> One can say that the city itself is the collective memory of its people, and like memory it is associated with objects and places. (Rossi, 2000, p. 172)

Contemporary urban theory is replete with musings about nomads, exiles, and the role that memories play in the shaping of cities as interplay between the imagined and the real. And this emphasis is well placed, given the operation of so much of 'the urban' as disjuncture and reconfiguration in the lives of a city's inhabitants. But here, as with so much provocative work on cities and culture, the literature tends toward a frustrating abstractness. *What* city? *Which* exiles? For better or for worse, Miami's Latino/a landscape has acquired the peculiar affective patina provided by over 40 years of Cuban exile presence, in the form of memories that act to shape it literally and figuratively, the imposition of a master narrative rooted in these memories and a particular political agenda, and the powerful demographic, affective, and political presence of this waning, but still important, sector of its overall Latino/a population. As such, while Miami can ground theory that purports to explore 'the city' as site of 'memory' and 'exile' in a real city with real memories of real exiles, it cannot fully speak for other Latino/a populations in the US, or even for those within Miami who do not share the Cuban exiles' particular history and concerns.

Miami is self-consciously constructed utilizing the memories of Cuban exiles as its literal and figurative scaffolding. Such memories reside in diverse places: Sunday afternoon accounts of life in Cuba before and after the revolution, stories of family members still living there, whether one should or should not travel to Cuba or even say a positive word (or any word at all) about Cuba; yard shrines to La Virgen dela Caridad del Cobre; the name and sayings of poet José Martí memorialized in streets, parks, and plaques throughout the city; shops along Eighth Street designed to attract tourists with names like *Mi Vieja Habana* (My Old Havana); the list goes on. In many ways, Miami is a city looking south, not just as the gateway to the Americas, but also casting a short gaze across 90 miles of ocean and nearly 50 long years. 'Return' is an enduring theme that links these memories: of course we will return, can we ever really return, would we return if given the chance? The ever-present interrogative and problematic 'we', musings that have reached fever pitch as Fidel Castro's health deteriorates.

For Cuban exiles, Miami functions as a collective sort of home away from home. Memories that circulate in the built environment, in conversation, and in rhetoric about Miami as a place, provide a way of nurturing the theme of return in the collective exile imaginary. Gaston Bachelard (1994 [1958], p. 56) wrote poignantly about the configuration of home, loss, and memory, at about the time of the Cuban revolution:

> If we go from these images, which are all light and shimmer, to images that insist and force us to remember farther back into our past, we shall have to take lessons from poets. For how forcefully they prove to us that the houses that were lost forever continue to live on in us; that they insist in order to live again, as though they expected us to give them a supplement of living. How much better we should live in the old house today!

This is not to say that Cuban exiles are the only ones who have played a role in shaping the rhetoric and design of this city, nor that all Cuban exiles have the same memories or agenda.

Figure 4. Cuban Memorial Way (SW 13th Ave). Photo taken by the author

Indeed, there is a disciplinary coherence of 'Cuban memories' around which there exists a signi-ficant, frequently punitive, politics of inside and outside. I have found that people who have not lived for some time in Miami, and who do not speak Spanish, have difficulty appreciating the depth of this coherence and the extent of the discipline that enforces it.

The variable hegemony of the Cuban exile voice in Miami's deployments of *latinidad* can be illustrated by three recent examples (though these of course do not provide sufficiently thorough analysis of this complex topic). The first involves the World Baseball Classic, held in March 2006 in Puerto Rico. When the Cuba versus Japan game was played, the pressing question among many Miamians was, 'Who will you cheer for'? Because rooting for one or the other team carried significance far beyond baseball (though baseball for many Cubans is in and of itself quite significant). Cheering for the Cuban team, seen by many Miamians as the natural home team, was tantamount to betrayal for exiled Cubans. Rooting for the Cuban team meant—as with other gestures, including sending money or medicines to relatives on the island, traveling to Cuba, or attending concerts by musicians from the island—a defiance of the embargo. It meant supporting Fidel Castro. Thus exiles such as Emilio Buitrago, interviewed in the exile-run Playa Café on Miami Beach, 'traced an imaginary gash across his chest. "In my heart, there are wounds that I will never forget, and that is why I am for Japan"' (quoted in Menendez, 2006, p. 1B). Other Hispanics viewing the game rooted for the Cuban team in an apparently unproblematic expression of solidarity for the Latinos. Pan-Latino solidarity in this case failed to solidify around the Cuban exile vision of solidarity and betrayal.

The second example regards the fate of the so-called Freedom Tower, a building that dates from 1925 and sits on a piece of what has lately become prime real estate in downtown, adjacent to Little Havana's east end. Dubbed by some as 'Miami's most iconic landmark' (Menendez, 2005, p. 1B), the building was constructed in 1925 to house the *Miami Daily News*, and was utilized as an assistance center for Cuban refugees in the 1960s. Since then, however, the building had remained unused and unoccupied. Purchased by the Terra Group in 2003, it was slated for partial demolition and eclipse by a 62-story condominium, one of many to 'grace' Miami's downtown during the recent condominium construction boom. Cubanos/as rallied against the plans, lobbying instead for the building to be left intact, while some wanted to see it designated as a national historic landmark, thus insuring that it would be protected from such compromising schemes in the future. Marches to preserve the tower included non-Cubanos/as, who saw the Freedom Tower as a broader beacon to the receptiveness of Miami toward Latinos/as. Thus, unlike the Japan versus Cuba baseball game, pan-Latino solidarity did cohere around the issue of historic preservation of a Cubano/a immigrant landmark versus high rise development (a game wherein, by the way, many of the players are Cubano/as). In the end, Terra Group's Pedro Martín decided to donate the building to Miami Dade College, and while the condominium construction would proceed, it would not physically incorporate the Freedom Tower. Rather, it would provide a glass façade behind the Tower to, Martín argued, better showcase this building. Martín was reported to be 'overwhelmed by emotion', and 'genuinely moved by the tower's place in the city's memory and his own personal connection to it as a Cuban American' in his decision to undertake the costly redesign of the project (Menendez, 2005, p. 1B).

The third and final example concerns the best-known of the three outside of Miami: the strange case of Elián González. For those few readers who may have lived far from the US media hype surrounding this event, this case involved a nearly six-year-old boy who was found floating in an inner tube several miles off the coast of Fort Lauderdale on Thanksgiving day, 1999. The men who rescued Elián brought him to shore where he was treated at a local hospital and released to his relatives in Miami. Along with the 11 passengers who perished on the handmade boat attempting to cross the Strait was Elián's mother, but his father (who was divorced from Elián's mother) was alive and well in Cuba and made it clear that he wanted his son returned to him. The Miami Gonzálezes, however, disagreed that the best place for Elián was in Cuba with his father. They began a protracted attempt to keep the boy with them in Miami.

The story is complex, and distills many fascinating aspects of contemporary culture in a globalizing world. Here I am particularly interested in the solidarities that did, or did not, cohere around the case. Many commentators have remarked that, much as with the Mariel boat-lift 20 years earlier, the Elián González affair constituted a watershed in how Cubanos/as were viewed. The decision to return Elián to Cuba, and the violent Miami exile reaction to it, had the effect of 'recast[ing] the image of *cubanas/os* from law-abiding, model minorities to fanatical freaks seeking to keep a father and son apart' (Hernández-Truyol, 2001, p. 708). Cubanos/as were painted as ungrateful immigrants who had no right to criticize the authorities responsible for deciding Elián's fate. US flags flew from Anglo-owned cars, while Cuban flags or upside-down US flags flew from Cubano/a-owned cars, and the one-upmanship reached ridiculous pro-portions as some Miamians sported full-sized flags flapping from car windows in an attempt to make their point. Anti-immigrant rallies saw confederate flags flying and calls to 'send them all back!' (Stepick *et al.*, 2003, p. 7; Santiago and Dorschner, 2000, p. 4B). In their expressions of nativism, Anglo and Black Miamians were united in a way they have not been before or since. Non-Cubano/a Latinos/as and many Cubanos/as not directly connected to the exile community remarked feeling more sympathetic toward the 'rule of law' logic that reunited Elián with his father in Cuba than to the González family's argument, but did not feel at liberty to express this dissent (Hernández-Truyol, 2001). And some younger Cubanos/as experienced a 'reactive ethnicity', including a curiosity to know more about their parents' history, a desire to make their home in Miami, and an invigoration of activism on behalf of the exile cause (Santiago and Dorschner, 2000).

These incidents, which in some universe would remain rather trivial, telescope the profound and at times anguishing sense of betrayal that many exiles feel when family crises arise, that many Cubanos/as who do not consider themselves exiles must negotiate, and that non-Cubanos/as in Miami struggle to understand. As journalist Ana Menendez (2006, p. 1B) remarks, Miami's exile community inhabits what is seen by many as a topsy-turvy universe, where

> 'We' means 'they,' unless you're exiled, in which case 'us' means 'here,' 'Cuba' means 'them' and 'home' means something else entirely. Anywhere else, the Playa Café would exist in an inverted universe. Here, it sits quite comfortably at the center of the Miami cosmos, a place defined not by reason, but by loss.

The difficult coalescence of *latinidad* around the Elián González affair illustrates the place-specific nature of pan-ethnic solidarity. The historical inflections of Miami's *latinidad* drew boundaries around inside and outside, boundaries that shifted as one moved from the local to the national scale, boundaries that some suffered in silence while at the same time catalyzing new identifications.

Conclusion

In the examples above, I have only touched the surface of the conceptually intriguing, politically difficult, and empirically complex issues surrounding *latinidad* as cultural coherence.

Rather than striving for generalizability, I have suggested avenues for further comparative, systematic research on *latinidad*, culture, and globalization, such that the emerging contours of belonging in a globalizing world can be better limned, both empirically and theoretically. In conclusion, I wish to emphasize three points that might prove useful as this collective project moves forward.

First, *latinidad* is a scale-shifting identification. *Latinidad* ranges from the very local scale of the individual and his or her immediate zone of inhabitance—a block, a neighborhood, a street— to nations and world regions that are hemispheric in scale. 'Shifting among several identities— for example, one linked to a specific nation in Latin America, another linked to a pan-Latin@ formation in the United States, another linked to the ideals of the United States, and still others identified with local cities, neighborhoods, *bloques* (blocks), and individual gender, racial, and class classifications—is commonplace for U.S. Latin@s' (Zentella, 2002, p. 321). It is this very scale-jumping that makes *latinidad* so useful in world where borders literal and figurative do not work the way we expect, and so frustrating to those who conceive of culture in static terms.

Second, *latinidad* is place-specific. As geographers have long emphasized, place specificity is important to keep in mind regardless of the object of study. With regard to conceptualizing pan-Latino solidarity, examples such as the Miami-based ones I discuss here serve as a corrective to the overwhelmingly Mexicano/a focus of much Latino/a studies in the US. Specificity should not be sacrificed in the name of unity (see also Torres-Saillant, 2002). On a more concrete level, Miami's particular inflections both shape, and are shaped by, the city itself. Over the ten years that I have resided in Miami, the aging demographic profile of exile Cubans, compounded by in-migration from other Caribbean and Latin American nations, has diluted the exile hold on Miami's landscape. The notion of culture as difficult and contextual coherence will come to bear strongly in deciding what will be allowed to define Miami as a place.

Third, I have emphasized that *latinidad* has important ramifications for national, trans-national, hemispheric, and even global, modalities of belonging; but that to grasp its shifting, situational, and strategic deployment one must not overlook the local scale of quotidian encounters. I have suggested that the study of global culture can benefit greatly from sticking close to home. The Latinization of important (and not so important) cities in the United States constitutes perhaps the most significant contemporary globalizing force at work. Thankfully, most of the world's cities are *not* Brasilia, and thus retain at least components of their more mundane public spaces in which such encounters have always, problematically, been negotiated. The situationally specific, flexible coalescence of identity around a variously imagined *latinidad* provides fertile conceptual and empirical terrain for understanding how culture coalesces at the scale of quotidian human encounters. By taking these human encounters up close and seriously, our understanding of globalization and culture is further nuanced, at times challenged, and always enriched.

Acknowledgements
The dialogic conference 'Globalizations, Cities, and the Production of Culture' provided a supportive critical environment in which to develop this article. I wish to thank Mark Amen, Kevin Archer, and Martin Bosman for orchestrating this event and providing detailed feedback, as well as editorial guidance, throughout the various iterations of this manuscript. Conference attendees also provided invaluable input, particularly Edmond Keller, who was this paper's discussant, and I wish to thank them all. Damián Fernández also commented on an early version of this article.

This material is based in part on work supported by the National Science Foundation Human and Social Dynamics program under Award No. 433947. Any opinions, findings, and conclusions or recommendations expressed in this publication are those of the author and do not necessarily reflect the views of the National Science Foundation.

Notes

1 Despite its name, the census tracts comprising the commonly accepted boundaries of the vernacular neighborhood of Little Havana are, as of the 2000 Census, only 47% Cuban or Cuban-American. Over one-quarter (26%) identify themselves as from Central America (primarily Nicaragua and Honduras), a growing number (4%) are from South America (especially Colombia), and a significant portion (18%) does not identify primarily by national origin but rather as 'other Hispanic or Latino'. Overall, 92% of Little Havana residents identified as Hispanic or Latino.

2 See statement issued by MALDEF and LULAC, 23 April 2004, 'MALDEF and LULAC Rebuke Samuel Huntington's Theories on Latino Immigrants and Call on America to Reaffirm its Commitment to Equal Opportunity and Democracy', available online at http://www.maldef.org/publications/pdf/MALDEF_LULAC_Statement.pdf (accessed 19 March 2007), see particularly the citations gathered in footnote 2 of this document.

3 'Latin@s' spelling in original quote. There is a group of Latino/a scholars that use this spelling to signify both the femine 'a' and masculine 'o'.

4 The question of whether Miami is a truly global city is debatable (see Nijman, 1996; Sassen and Portes, 1993). While Miami might prove to be a bit thin with regard to the strength and size of its economic linkages to other global cities, or its commanding role in the development of a global city-region in South Florida (or the circum-Caribbean), there is certainly evidence enough of a high and sustained level of international movement, investment, and boosterism on the part of the city that Miami warrants a deeper look into the cultural dimensions of globalization in a city (Yúdice, 2003).

5 A version of this description appeared as 'Calle Ocho' in Oboler and González (2005, p. 253).

6 In our Little Havana surveys we corroborated this observation (Arreola *et al.*, in-progress). Few interviewees socialized inside a neighbor's home nor did they invite neighbors into their homes. Rather, socialization with neighbors occurs as people enter and leave their homes or during outside activities such as gardening.

References

Alberts, H. (2005) Changes in ethnic solidarity in Cuban Miami, *The Geographical Review*, 95(2), pp. 231–248.
Aparicio, F. R. & Chávez-Silverman, S. (1997) Introduction, in: F. R. Aparicio & S. Chávez-Silverman (Eds) *Tropicalizations: Transcultural Representations of Latinidad* (Hanover, NH: University Press of New England), pp. 1–17.
Arreola, D., Fernández, D., Lukinbeal, C., Price, P., Ready, T. & Torres, M. (in progress) Comparative civic and place engagement in three Latino enclave neighborhoods in transition. Study funded by the National Science Foundation Human and Social Dynamics Program.
Bachelard, G. (1994 [1958]) *The Poetics of Space*, Trans. M. Jolas, Foreword J. R. Stilgoe (Boston: Beacon Press).
Benhabib, S. (2002) *The Claims of Culture: Inequality and Diversion in the Global Era* (Princeton, NJ: Princeton University Press).
Bradley, T. (2006) Calle Ocho beckons hemisphere's revelers, *The Miami Herald*, 13 March, pp. 1A, 2A.
Cabán, P. (1998) The new synthesis of Latin American and Latino studies, in: F. Bonilla, E. Meléndez, R. Morales & M. Torres (Eds) *Borderless Borders: U.S. Latinos, Latin Americans, and the Paradox of Interdependence* (Philadelphia, PA: Temple University Press), pp. 195–215.
Castells, M. (1996) *The Rise of the Network Society. Volume 1: The Information Age; Economy, Society and Culture* (Oxford, UK and Cambridge, MA: Blackwell).
de Certeau, M. (2002 [1984]) *The Practice of Everyday Life*, Trans. S. Rendall (Berkeley and Los Angeles: University of California Press).
Chinchilla, N., Hamilton, N. & Loucky J. (1993) Central Americans in Los Angeles: an immigrant community in transition, in: J. Moore & R. Pinderhughes (Eds) *In the Barrios: Latinos and the Underclass Debate* (New York: Russell Sage Foundation), pp. 51–78.
Crouch, D. (1998) The street in the making of popular geographical knowledge, in: N. Fyfe (Ed.) *Images of the Street: Planning, Identity and Control in Public Space* (London & New York: Routledge), pp. 160–175.

Curtis, J. (2004) Barrio space and place in Southeast Los Angeles, California, in: D. Arreola (Ed.) *Hispanic Spaces, Latino Places: Community and Cultural Diversity in Contemporary America* (Austin, TX: University of Texas Press), pp. 125–141.

Davis, M. (1992) *City of Quartz: Excavating the Future in Los Angeles* (New York: Vintage).

Davis, M. (2000) *Magical Urbanism: Latinos Reinvent the US City* (London: Verso).

Dear, M. J. & Flusty, S. (2001) The resistible rise of the L.A. school, in: M. J. Dear (Ed.) *From Chicago to L.A.: Re-visioning Urban Theory* (Thousand Oaks, CA: Sage), pp. 3–16.

Duncan, J. & Duncan, N. (2004) Culture unbound, *Environment and Planning A*, 36, pp. 391–403.

Fox, G. (1997) *Hispanic Nation: Culture, Politics, and the Construction of Identity* (Tucson, AZ: University of Arizona Press).

García, J. A. (2003) *Latino Politics in America: Community, Culture, and Interests* (Lanham, MD: Rowman and Littlefield).

Godfrey, B. (2004) Barrio under siege: Latino sense of place in San Francisco, California, in: D. Arreola (Ed.) *Hispanic Spaces, Latino Places: Community and Cultural Diversity in Contemporary America* (Austin, TX University of Texas Press), pp. 79–102.

Grenier, G. & Stepick A. (1992) On machines and bureaucracy: controlling ethnic interaction in Miami's apparel and construction industries, in: L. Lamphere (Ed.) *Structuring Diversity: Ethnographic Perspectives on the New Immigration* (Chicago: University of Chicago Press), pp. 65–93.

Hernández-Truyol, B. E. (2001) On becoming the other: Cubans, Castro, and Elián—a LatCrit analysis, *Denver University Law Review*, 78(4), pp. 687–718.

Herzog, L. A. (2004) Globalization of the barrio: transformation of the Latino cultural landscapes of San Diego, California, in: D. Arreola (Ed.) *Hispanic Spaces, Latino Places: Community and Cultural Diversity in Contemporary America* (Austin, TX: University of Texas Press), pp. 103–124.

Holston, J. (1999) The modernist city and the death of the street, in: S. Low (Ed.) *Theorizing the City: The New Urban Anthropology Reader* (New Brunswick, NJ: Rutgers University Press), pp. 245–276.

Horton, J. (1992) The politics of diversity in Monterey Park, California, in: L. Lamphere (Ed.) *Structuring Diversity: Ethnographic Perspectives on the New Immigration* (Chicago: University of Chicago Press), pp. 215–245.

Huntington, S. (2004) The Hispanic challenge, *Foreign Policy* (March/April), pp. 30–45.

Jacobs, J. (1992 [1961]) *The Death and Life of Great American Cities* (New York: Random House).

Lefebvre, H. (2004) *Rhythmanalysis*, Trans. S. Elden & G. Moore (London & New York: Continuum).

Liggett, H. (2003) *Urban Encounters* (Minneapolis, MN: University of Minnesota Press).

Low, S. (1999) Spatializing culture: the social production and social construction of public space in Costa Rica, in: S. Low (Ed.) *Theorizing the City: The New Urban Anthropology Reader* (New Brunswick, NJ: Rutgers University Press), pp. 111–137.

Mahler, S. (1995) *American Dreaming: Immigrant Life on the Margins* (Princeton, NJ: Princeton University Press).

Menendez, A. (2005) A building breathes, and a city sighs, *The Miami Herald*, 3 December, p. 1B.

Menendez, A. (2006) Wistful Cubans had to reconcile hearts, principles, *The Miami Herald*, 22 March, p. 1B.

Menjívar, C. (2000) *Fragmented Ties: Salvadoran Immigrant Networks in America* (Berkeley: University of California Press).

Mitchell, D. (1995) There's no such thing as culture: towards a reconceptualization of the idea of culture in geography, *Transactions of the Institute of British Geographers*, n.s. 20(1), pp. 102–116.

Mitchell, D. (2003) *The Right to the City: Social Justice and the Fight for Public Space* (New York: Guilford Press).

Miyares, I. (2004) Changing latinization of New York City, in: D. Arreola (Ed.) *Hispanic Spaces, Latino Places: Community and Cultural Diversity in Contemporary America* (Austin, TX: University of Texas Press), pp. 145–166.

Nijman, J. (1996) Breaking the rules: Miami in the urban hierarchy, *Urban Geography*, 17(1), pp. 5–22.

Oboler, S. & González, D. (Eds) (2005) *The Oxford Encyclopedia of Latinos and Latinas in the United States*, vol. 1 (New York: Oxford University Press).

Ochoa, G. L. (2004) *Becoming Neighbors in a Mexican-American Community: Power, Conflict and Solidarity* (Austin, TX: University of Texas Press).

Pratt, M. L. (2005) Why the Virgin of Zapopan went to Los Angeles: reflections on mobility and globality, in: J. Andermann & W. Rowe (Eds) *Images of Power: Iconography, Culture and the State in Latin America* (New York: Berghahn Books), pp. 271–289.

Price, P. (2004) *Dry Place: Landscapes of Belonging and Exclusion* (Minneapolis, MN: University of Minnesota Press).

Rosaldo, R. & Flores, W. V. (1997) Identity, conflict, and evolving Latino communities: cultural citizenship in San Jose, California, in: W. V. Flores & R. Benmayor (Eds) *Latino Cultural Citizenship: Claiming Identity, Space, and Rights* (Boston: Beacon Press), pp. 57–96.

Rossi, A. (2000) Typological questions, and The collective memory, in: M. Miles, T. Hall & I. Borden (Eds) *The City Cultures Reader* (London: Routledge), pp. 171–173.

Santiago, F. & Dorschner, J. (2000) Outside image bewilders exiles, *The Miami Herald*, 23 April, p. 4B.

Sassen, S. & Portes, A. (1993) Miami: a new global city, *Contemporary Sociology*, 22(4), pp. 471–477.

Scott, J. (1999) *Seeing like a State: How Certain Schemes to Improve the Human Condition have Failed* (New Haven, CT: Yale University Press).

Smith, N. (1997) Social justice and the new American urbanism: the revanchist city, in: A. Merrifield & E. Swyngedouw (Eds) *The Urbanization of Injustice* (New York: New York University Press), pp. 117–136.

Stepick, A. & Grenier G. (1993) Cubans in Miami, in: J. Moore & R. Pinderhughes (Eds) *In the Barrios: Latinos and the Underclass Debate* (New York: Russell Sage Foundation), pp. 79–100.

Stepick, A., Grenier, G., Castro, M. & Dunn, M. (2003) *This Land is our Land: Immigrants and Power in Miami* (Berkeley: University of California Press).

Suro, R. (1998) *Strangers among Us: How Latino Immigration is Transforming America* (New York: Alfred A. Knopf).

Thrift, N. (1997) The still point: resistance, expressive embodiment, and dance, in: S. Pile & M. Keith (Eds) *Geographies of Resistance* (London: Routledge), pp. 124–151.

Torres, M. (1998) Transnational political and cultural identities: crossing theoretical borders, in: F. Bonilla, E. Meléndez, R. Morales & M. Torres (Eds) *Borderless Borders: U.S. Latinos, Latin Americans, and the Paradox of Interdependence* (Philadelphia, PA: Temple University Press), pp. 169–182.

Torres-Saillant, S. (2002) Problematic paradigms: racial diversity and corporate identity in the Latino community, in: M. M. Suárez-Orozco & M. M. Páez (Eds) *Latinos Remaking America* (Berkeley: University of California Press), pp. 435–455.

Villa, R. H. (1999) Aquí estamos y no nos vamos: place struggles in Latino Los Angeles, in: G. Leclerc, R. H. Villa & M. J. Dear (Eds) *La vida Latina en L.A.: Urban Latino Cultures* (Thousand Oaks, CA: Sage), pp. 7–17.

Villa, R. H. (2000) *Barrio-logos: Space and Place in Urban Chicano Literature and Culture* (Austin, TX: University of Texas Press).

Wilson, E. (1992) *The Sphinx in the City: Urban Life, the Control of Disorder, and Women* (Berkeley: University of California Press).

Yúdice, G. (2003) *The Expediency of Culture: Uses of Culture in the Global Era* (Durham, NC: Duke University Press).

Zentella, A. C. (2002) Latin@ languages and identities, in: M. M. Suárez-Orozco & M. M. Páez (Eds) *Latinos Remaking America* (Berkeley: University of California Press), pp. 321–338.

Zukin, S. (1996) Space and symbols in an age of decline, in: A. King (Ed.) *Re-presenting the City: Ethnicity, Capital and Culture in the 21st Century Metropolis* (New York: New York University Press), pp. 43–59.

Patricia Price is a human geographer, exploring broad issues of human/land interaction. She specializes in cultural and urban geography. She has published a number of journal articles on the US–Mexico borderlands, the body, popular religiosity, and urban social movements. Her field research has taken her to Mexico for extended periods, including Veracruz, Mexico City, and Guadalajara, as well as the border cities of Ciudad Juarez and Tijuana. Her book, *Dry Place: Landscapes of Belonging and Exclusion*, was published by the University of Minnesota Press in 2004.

Whose Culture? Globalism, Localism, and the Expansion of Tradition: The Case of the Hñähñu of Hidalgo, Mexico and Clearwater, Florida

ELLA SCHMIDT

The Cultural Dialectics of Mutuality

Some 20 years ago, while doing fieldwork in Chiapas on decision-making patterns regarding the cultivation of native varieties of corn among farmers in the area, we came to the house of a reasonably prosperous *campesino*. He greeted us with cold glasses of the Mexican drink *atole* with chocolate added and, with a welcoming smile, he excitedly invited us into his home. We then started to explain to him that we were working on a research project aimed at discerning the decision-making patterns concerning micro-environments and the different native varieties of maize that farmers used in response to these environmental challenges. He looked particularly pleased and said: 'Finally, you anthropologists came to visit me. All these years I have been watching these educational programs on TV and have watched other people all over the world being interviewed by people like you, and I always wondered when was it going to be my turn.' He then proceeded to show us the different micro-climates that his farm encompassed and to explain the elements he considered (i.e., wind, sun exposure, rain, etc.) when deciding what corn variety to plant in which plot.

Having worked in the Peruvian Andes and observed the many households that could afford a battery-run TV in the middle of nowhere, or the many men—and women—who would go about their daily chores with a little portable radio for company, this particular incident only took my interpretation to another level. Indeed, compared to the Peruvian Andes, the Mexican country-side has relatively better access to electricity and phones, thus easing and promoting knowledge of different ways of thinking and lifestyles (whether they were attainable or not). The distinction between farmers in the Andes and their equivalent in the Tuxtla Gutierrez area is based largely on the degree of access to the outside world. Both, however, are impacted by their increasingly accelerating transactions with broader market circuits.

Seeing this 'exchange' as a unidirectional transaction ignores the transformations that ensue when farmers and other rural people not only appropriate some of the messages or products being promoted by the radios or TVs they can afford, but also transform and share this infor-mation with others while they visit or work in other areas. This exchange of cultural elements through technology and the movements of people is marked by constant fluidity and trans-formation. Certainly, those of us who long to travel to far-away places first dreamt of those places with the help of images conveyed by magazines, radio or television, or by a neighbor or relative who emigrated. In fact, we do not need to go anywhere to be changed and, like others, we often reshape that transformation by selectively appropriating elements that make sense to us (or that we find appealing) and then expressing them through our clothing, housing, or ways of thinking.

Many of the Hñähñu—an indigenous Mexican group of the Mezquital Valley in Hidalgo, Mexico—have been profoundly transformed without having ever left their communities of origin by their neighbors and relatives who have made Clearwater, Florida, one of their chosen destinations in the US. With the levels of male out-migration reaching up to 70% in some of the indigenous communities of the Mezquital Valley, this transformation has only inten-sified. It has also profoundly changed those indigenous migrants who travel back and forth and, when possible, send presents, remittances, talk over the phone, write as well as send documents and pictures through the internet. As discussed above, this transformation is not unidirectional. Migrants are being changed in their communities of destination and help in the transformation of their communities of origin. They are, however, also continuously being transformed by those relatives who for a myriad of different reasons have remained in their place of origin.

With the help of remittances from relatives who made the trip to *el norte*, for instance, some bilingual teachers are advancing and disseminating their indigenous traditional culture through local programs in their communities of origin (i.e., cultural festivals, radio programs, etc.). In other instances, women who usually face the brunt of the challenges of male out-migration are promoting indigenous cottage cooperatives that are helping redress local gender inequalities and ecological degradation imposed by centuries of oppression and marginalization. This support for traditional practices at the local level is enhancing a sense of their indigenous identity abroad which also helps transform their communities of destination.

Focusing on the economic, social, and cultural transactions of the Hñähñu in Mexico and the United States and the new socio-cultural and economic spaces that these transactions are creating, this paper emphasizes the need to go beyond dichotomous analyses which assume that the impersonal global forces of capital, labor, and information and the culturally specific local identities and ways of life are irreducible and mutually exclusive.

The article is divided into four sections. The first section offers a short description of the history of the Hñähñu. The second discusses the politics of selective cultural reception and appropriation that challenge the purported hegemony of the global. The third section describes two instances—*Radio Bilingüe* and *Mujeres Reunidas*—that illustrate the dialectic processes of a politics of reception and appropriation that selectively (re)formulates and (re)negotiates the local and the global as co-constituents of (re)defined socio-spatial locations which defy rigid geopolitical boundaries of both. Finally, the conclusion offers a glance at the dialectics of the 'traditional' that ensue.

The Hñähñu: A History of Conquest, Resistance and Solidarity

Builders of the ancient city of Tula while under Toltec domination, the Hñähñu have been present in the Mezquital Valley (State of Hidalgo, Mexico) since around 250 BC. Actively resisting conquest by the Aztecs and Spaniards, among others, the Hñähñu decided to retreat to the most arid and desolate areas of the valley. This strategy imposed serious limitations on their economic participation in the region. Over time they became exploited as cheap and submissive labor by *caciques* who settled in the area with the aim of concentrating available irrigated land into large landholdings. The Hñähñu, like many other ethnic minorities, lived in relative isolation from the nation state, ignored by the great majority of Mexicans (Schmidt and Crummett, 2004).

In 1948, in an effort to bring indigenous communities into the twentieth century and integrate them into the Mexican nation state (Aguirre-Beltrán, 1955), the Mexican government created the *Instituto Nacional Indigenista* (INI) (National Indigenous Institute). At the time, an indigenista movement could not decide whether the 'indigenous problem' was one of culture or biology. In 1951, the *Patrimonio Indígena del Valle del Mezquital* (PIVM) (Indigenous Patrimony of the Mezquital Valley) was created by presidential decree at the strong recommendation of social scientists and presidential consultants like Manuel Gamio, who combined their efforts to draw attention to the problems of desolation and the abject poverty to which the Hñähñu population had been endemically subjected (Schmidt and Crummett, 2004). These efforts were not free of the contradictions created by clientelist relationships between the Mexican government and different regional and local factions that could not agree whether indigenous organizations should be autonomous or subject to the central government's or local elites' interests (Fox, 1994). At any rate, the PIVM was created as an agency to promote the development and economic integration of the indigenous population in the area. Shortly thereafter, the PIVM fell into the hands of local *caciques* who owned extensive property in the highly productive irrigated sections of the valley, especially Ixmiquilpan. This situation started to change when Maurilio Muñoz, a Hñähñu anthropologist, was appointed director of the PIVM which was later renamed the *Consejo Supremo Hñähñu* (Supreme Council of the Hñähñu) in the 1970s. The appointment of Muñoz turned out to be critical to the indigenous communities of the region. In an effort to restore the dignity and a sense of agency to the Hñähñu, Muñoz changed the nature of the interactions between them and the PIVM. The paternalist and *clientelista* transactions imposed by PIVM representatives on the indigenous population were replaced by more egalitarian interactions in an effort to recognize rural communities as active partners in the development process (Schmidt and Crummett, 2004).

Even though the ties with the Institutional Revolutionary Party (PRI) have a long history in the Mezquital region (Kugel, 1996), the Hñähñu council members stress their interest in advancing the political, social, and economic agendas of their indigenous group (Schmidt and Crummett, 2004).[1] They often invoke their common indigenous origins and culture along with their opposition to the *mestizo* power structure in the Mezquital Valley (Kugel, 1996). However, the walls of the offices of the *Consejo Supremo* in Ixmiquilpan are usually covered with political statements supporting different PRI candidates. Interestingly, in November of 2004, the PRI candidate for governor of the state of Hidalgo, which is where the home communities of most Hñähñu are located, appeared at a political rally in Clearwater accompanied by the Hñähñu senator from PRI. This current alliance with the PRI power structure obviously raises interesting political issues of representation that will be affected by the emergence of new and younger leaders (Pietro Hernandez and Utrilla Sarmiento, 2003), both in Ixmiquilpan and in Clearwater. At this time, the roles of the Supreme Council in Ixmiquilpan and of its counterpart in the United States—the *Consejo Mexicano de la Bahía de Tampa* (Mexican Council of the Tampa Bay Area)—have been to provide leadership and advocacy as well as to serve as brokers between the Hñähñu community both in Ixmiquilpan and Clearwater with the Mexican and American authorities. These efforts yield obvious political and economic benefits for the leaders, as well as for those being served. These efforts also are key to the creation of diasporic politics involving host and home communities that furthers the transnational nature of the Hñähñu communities. Issues such as access to drivers' licenses in the US, or border/highway safety in Mexico for returning migrants, are among the items that are regularly discussed in meetings of both the *Consejo Supremo Hñähñu* in Ixmiquilpan and the *Consejo Mexicano de la Bahia de Tampa* in Clearwater thereby furthering the creation and organization of a Hñähñu socio-cultural space that disrupts—or at least questions—neat geo-political divisions.

Interviews conducted in 2002 disclosed that the Supreme Council's leadership role among Hñähñu migrants had led to the creation of the Office in Support of the Hidalgo Community in their Home State and Abroad (*Coordinación General de Apoyo al Hidalguense en el Estado y el Extranjero*) in the State of Hidalgo. This organization supports many of the political and cultural events in Clearwater. With an obvious political interest in maintaining their presence among the migrant communities in the US, the Hidalguense government has been crucial in sponsoring dancers and traditional crafts, as well as in providing Mexican teachers for cultural festivals and summer educational programs in Clearwater (Schmidt and Crummett, 2004). Now that the Mexican Federal Government is going to allow people living outside Mexico to vote, one suspects that the presence of Mexican politicians in Clearwater may become more frequent.

At the same time, the Hñähñu culture, centered around family and collective responsibility, has been at the forefront of channeling migrant remittances into Mexican community development (Bada, 2003; Goldring, 1998). According to data collected in Clearwater, between two and four million dollars a month are sent back to families in the Valle del Mezquital. In fact, the Hñähñu code of ethics, based on defining the individual as a citizen of his/her community, is strongly associated with the active participation of each member in community projects and issues. Citizenship is contingent on participation in, and fulfillment of these responsibilities and is defined not by individual but by social activities based on group solidarity. Community members in the area of the Valle del Mezquital unanimously expressed the importance of complying with the requirements that being a *ciudadano* (citizen) entails (Schmidt and Crummett, 2004). Interestingly, this information contrasts sharply with information gathered by Galinier (1997) in the highlands of the Sierra Madre Oriental northeast of Tulancingo, indicating the disappearance (or lack of a rebirth) of traditional communal structures and practices in that area.

Through the building of sewage and potable water systems or the paving of streets, remittances do not only allow Hñähñu communities to improve their families' well-being and their communities' infrastructure. They are also promoting and, in some cases, rebuilding Hñähñu indigenous culture. Although some elements of 'symbolic resistance' (Hall and Fenelon, 2003) might be present in the efforts of Hñähñu culture (re)building, we should also bear in mind the opportunities that those remittances offer for the assertion and promotion of their indigenous cultures. This is in no way, therefore, a 'conservative resistance' based on an attempt to cling to old ways (Perry, 1996). As much as their location in 'the geographical peripheries of the states' (ibid., p. 237) allowed them, indigenous groups throughout history have carefully and selectively worked at adapting, adopting, and manipulating state and market impositions to their benefit. Being flexible has not been a luxury but a necessity of cultural survival.

Whether they resist or adapt to outside forces, they offer indigenous people what they badly need: jobs, technologies, and markets that allow them to participate, though many times at the local level, in the global scene. While they do that, they are also asserting their right to support and promote a variety of traditional cultural practices that promote a sense of responsibility towards their communities and indigenous identity. Indigenous peoples have since 'time immemorial' been developing strategies that help them pursue their own interests (Perry, 1996). One fundamental difference is that they are currently acting on several scales simultaneously (Langer and Muñoz, 2003) at a speed and intensity that only remittances and the technologies available can afford them.

From Hegemonic Leadership to Scattered Hegemonies: How Cultural Appropriations Get Misrepresented

Dismissed by members of the Mexican elite as an invention of the federal government's National Indigenous Institute, the Hñähñu illustrate a powerful instance of reappropriation of cultural symbols (Dening, 1986) and social and cultural space. Hñähñu identity and history, rich with struggles for cultural, social, and economic advancement, serve as the context for ways in which the Hñähñu from Ixmiquilpan have negotiated and continue to negotiate their social and economic environment in both the United States and Mexico (Schmidt and Crummett 2004).

This history 'from the bottom up' not only illustrates the resilience of indigenous populations who have suffered through centuries of extreme marginalization and poverty, forced assimilation, and, in many instances, ethnocide (Langer and Muñoz, 2003; Perry, 1996). It also seriously questions the possibility of a hegemonic power to impose and shape differences into monolithic entities ignoring local agencies and their intermediations with history, gender, class, ethnicity, and the counter-power relations that ensue. The production of a Hñähñu 'ethnoscape', of a sense of locality (as a 'structure of feeling, a property of social life, and an ideology of a situated community' as Appadurai (1996, p. 183) would have it) has been under assault for centuries. The Hñähñu, however, illustrate an instance in which the negotiations and redefinitions of cultural (re)production called for the selective appropriation of imposed (cultural) knowledge and its reformulation to fit their need for cultural and social survival. The transactions and negotiations with the colonial or neocolonial powers that ensued illustrate the articulation of the differences among the Hñähñu, as well as those between their community and the invading powers. The Hñähñu are not unique in these transactions. Once under the yoke of conquest and neo-colonialism, many indigenous communities in Latin America and elsewhere have reinforced their traditional communal structures, cultures, and identities in an effort to counteract attacks on their ways of life, ideology, and culture by external powers. At the same time, they have also tried to carve out spaces and build political power within and without the state (Langer and Muñoz, 2003).[2] These careful politics of reception, appropriation and (re)production are then at the basis of a renewed effort to build and consolidate a new sense of cultural and political empowerment both within and beyond the Mexican and American states.

Paraphrasing Appadurai (1996) this process of articulation of differences is a relational one; it is an everyday social project in which individuals and groups seek to annex that which they per-ceive as positive additions to their own images of themselves and their communities. Though Appadurai is referring to the 'global' and the 'modern', his insights are quite useful in this context, as the Hñähñu—like many other indigenous populations worldwide—have been dealing with the 'global' and the 'modern' for some centuries already. At present, however, Hñähñu migration and their use of electronic media for remittances and to keep in contact not only 'coconstitute a new sense of the global as modern and the modern as global' (Appadurai, 1996, p. 10) but have definitively sped up the mutual processes of cultural nego-tiation and appropriation. These processes of negotiation and appropriation, however, remain dependent on the Hñähñu historical and cultural understandings of themselves as indigenous people and their sense of solidarity and responsibility towards their fellow Hñähñu in the US and in their native communities. This 'global flow of images, news, and opinion now provides part of the engaged cultural and political literacy that diasporic persons [and those who stay put in their communities of origin] bring to their spatial neighborhoods' (Appadurai, 1996, p. 197) which, for the Hñähñu, include their communities in the Mezquital Valley in Mexico and in the city of Clearwater, Florida, among other places in the US.

As Janet Wolff (1997, p. 167) indicates, 'cultures are constructed in relation to one another, produced, represented and perceived through the ideologies and narratives of situated dis-courses'. These situated discourses, moreover, are the product of local (and global) negotiations and appropriations brought about by individual members of particular communities which are products of specific historical circumstances. No grand sociological theory can override the insights—and tensions, Wolff (1997, p. 163) would add—that concrete ethnographies can afford us while trying to understand how everyday practices of identity are immersed in cultures and histories that responded to, and were impacted by, colonial and neocolonial powers.

Grewal and Kaplan (1994, p. 5) caution that center–periphery models 'inaccurately reflect the circulation of ideas and social practices in contemporary life on a global scale' as they tend to favor the existence of universal categories and to ignore local specificities. Socio-spatial location ('localities' for Appadurai) is key to understanding specific manifestations of new, many times, transnational, formations as is the case of the Hñähñu communities. Theirs is a unique socio-spatial formation which is the result of specific articulations of the local and the global. Other-wise put, it is a 'particularity historicized' through a comparison of 'multiple, overlapping, and discrete oppressions rather than [through the] construct of a theory of hegemonic oppression under a unified category of [ethnicity or race]' (Grewal and Kaplan, 1994, pp. 17–18).

Hñähñu everyday practices—their cultural formations and identity—need to be understood within a politics of cultural reception and appropriation that allows for the selective reformula-tion of old and new cultural elements. This selective reformulation is strongly mediated by both the Hñähñu who have migrated but also by those who have stayed behind and continue to live in their communities of origin. Their locality—their structures of feelings and identities—are also the product of particular historical articulations with colonial and neocolonial dynamics that have created what Grewal and Kaplan (1994) call 'scattered hegemonies', which are, as we have seen, the product of particular impositions and negotiations at the local level. Though one could readily be tempted to emphasize the hegemonic character of 'outside' influences represented by the remittances and images along with discourses of those who now live in the US, theirs are also 'scattered hegemonies', being a product of their own location as ethnic minorities in the US.

The two cases that follow illustrate the dialectic process of this politics of reception and appropriation that selectively (re)formulates and (re)negotiates the local and the global as co-constituents of this same dialectic process.

Local Pressures on the Global: The Case of *Radio Bilingüe* and *Mujeres Reunidas*

Radio Bilingüe[3]

The state of Hidalgo—the state with the fifth largest indigenous population (17.9%) in Mexico—is considered a non-traditional migratory region. However, the Mezquital Valley, place of origin of the Hñähñu discussed in this paper, shows a rate of out-migration of 2.79% per year which is more than the national average of 1.68%, making it the ninth highest area of international out-migration. In the Mexican census of 1995–2000, 7% of households had at least one of their members working in the US versus a national rate of 4.14% (Quezada, n.d.).

By the 2000 census, 96% of the population living in the municipality of Ixmiquilpan—one of the main areas of origin of the Hñähñu in Clearwater—continued to be classified as indigenous by INEGI (*Instituto Nacional de Estadística e Informática*—National Institute of Statistics). Indigenous presence in the surrounding municipalities of the Mezquital Valley ranged between 88.5% and 99.7%. This overwhelming indigenous presence is the product of a historical trend acknowledged by federal authorities as far back as the 1930s. At that time, the Lázaro Cárdenas government established 29 indigenous boarding schools in the region, with one in the community of Remedios in the municipality of Ixmiquilpan.

Forty years later, when Maurilio Muñoz was brought into the *Patrimonio Indígena del Valle del Mezquital* (PIVM—Indigenous Patrimony of the Mezquital Valley), he not only continued to support the bilingual teacher program promoted by the *Instituto Nacional Indigenista* at the national level, he also developed and supported leadership training programs for communal leaders as the legitimate representatives of their communities of origin, with the right to negotiate, as equals, with government representatives and other political agents (Schmidt and Crummett, 2004). These community leaders were, in many instances, rural teachers trained in bilingual indigenous schools founded by Cárdenas whose mission was to promote Mexican culture and Spanish language, in other words, to *castellanizar* (hispanicize) the indigenous populations (Baumann, 1975; Kugel, 1996). This was an effort to help the central government bring them into 'modernity', as they were perceived as living marginal lives and were seen as one of the biggest obstacles to developing the Mexican nation since the rise of liberalism in the nineteenth century. The social prestige thus acquired by teachers, and their regular transactions with the institutional world, helped them to be seen as an indigenous elite that could negotiate with the institutional world (Kugel, 1996).

Maria Crummet and I first encountered the association of rural teachers with leadership positions during fieldwork in Ixmiquilpan while interacting with members of the *Consejo Supremo Hñähñu*. This structure was one of the 56 supreme indigenous councils created by President Luis Echevarría during the 1970s in an effort to give representation to ethnic minorities while at the same time making sure that the central government could control them. Almost all the official positions in the *Consejo Supremo* (i.e., president, secretary, treasurer) were, and had been, filled by rural teachers who had either retired or were on professional leave at the time of our visit (Schmidt and Crummett, 2004).

Some of these rural bilingual teachers are also involved in *Radio Bilingue*, a weekly radio program that showcases everything Hñähñu, from herbal medicine, to ancient ways of life, tales and legends, to music and contemporary educational news. The program is both Spanish and Hñähñu and is broadcast through Radio Cardonal, a local radio station with a broad audience in the Valley. The 'miscellaneous informative program' as one of our informants described it, is made possible through minimal support from the Mexican government. The program staff work out of a couple of offices in the state-owned civic center in Ixmiquilpan which they receive rent-free. The programs are put together by a team of bilingual teachers who work for this project on a voluntary basis. Talking with Ms. Sanchez, one of the leaders of the radio program, we learned that her husband, a teacher, had left for the US in 1986 and works as a construction worker in Clearwater. Since he shares housing and food costs with two of Ms. Sanchez's sisters who are in Clearwater, her husband is able to send money back home on a very regular basis. In fact, his support made it possible for two of their children to go to the university and become teachers themselves. Their other two sons spent three years each in the US. One now owns a print shop and the other bought a house in El Fitzi, a neighborhood of Ixmiquilpan.

Ms. Sanchez's clear mission to support and disseminate the Hñähñu culture and language could not be possible without her husband's remittances from Clearwater. All the members of *Radio Bilingüe* buy office supplies and tapes out of their own pockets on a regular basis. It is obvious that her salary as a teacher barely covers living expenses. In a surprising twist, then, remittances are not only helping her family survive materially, they are also enabling her to promote and disseminate traditional culture in the valley, thus assisting in the cultural survival of the community. Although she wears imported clothes and enjoys relatively expensive gadgets that her ties to the US allow her to obtain, Ms. Sanchez is not an agent of 'Americanization'. In fact, her migrant husband's hard work in the US makes it possible for her to participate in an ambitious effort to revitalize indigenous culture, as well as sending the message that migration, modernization, and indigenous traditions are not mutually exclusive. In this case, at least, the actors at play, their sense of identity and of locality, along with structures of feeling, are articulated with other actors, identities, and localities where negotiations, reformulations, and selective appropriations take place in a way that makes cultural and historical sense to all concerned. The above example makes it impossible to claim, as some have, that *migradólares* are simply agents of 'modernity' and cannot help with the revitalization of traditional cultures.[4]

Mujeres Reunidas

El Alberto, a 20-minute ride in a microbus from Ixmiquilpan, consists of approximately 650 families and shows the great impact emigration has had on the way the community looks. To be sure, from a trickle in the late 1980s to waves in the early 1990s, 70% of males—the great majority of them between ages 16 and 30—are in the United States, mainly working in construction in Las Vegas. Their very modest landholdings, often less than one hectare (2.2 acres), are not enough to feed their families (Schmidt, 2006).

In only two decades, El Alberto has undergone an impressive transformation in its material culture. Even though some streets are still unpaved, many are lined with two-story houses that combine US and Mexican architecture and were gradually built as remittances from community members arrive from the United States. These 'built-by-installment' houses (Frye, 1996) stand imposingly at different stages of construction and are a testament to migrants' dreams of returning. They also attest to the transformations of their consumption patterns, styles, and tastes.

At the time of our visit, the main community project was the Town Hall, designed by a migrant who had been working in Las Vegas for a big construction company since 1989. With its 'Roman' arches and columns, it was reminiscent of faraway casinos along the Las Vegas strip. But, it also stood for something more profound: the clear and unwavering support and commitment to the community of all members regardless of whether they were working in the United States, or on their small plots in El Alberto. Indeed, this building, whose construction started three years before our visit, was being built through *faenas* (communal work) by those who remained in the community. Remittances from the *norteño* migrants and those who could not comply with the labor investment of the *faenas*, were used to buy locally necessary construction materials (Schmidt, 2006).

But community transformations have not only occurred in material culture. The great majority of those who have stayed behind are women and their children. To a significant degree, these women have taken over the day-to-day communal responsibilities of their parents, husbands, or partners.

This area of the Mezquital Valley, with very little water and great expanses of arid land, used to have big plantations of maguey (century plant) which were used in the production of *pulque*, a fermented beverage with an alcohol content similar to beer. By the eighteenth century, this beverage was one of the leading sources of taxes for the colonial state. Attitudes embraced by the Mexican elites and middle classes in their modernizing efforts considered *pulque* as one of the sources for drunkenness and backwardness among indigenous populations. In the 1970s, this stigma led to the replacement of traditional weavings of *ayates*—made of the maguey fiber—with plastic and synthetic fibers leading to the abandonment of maguey plantations and the disappearance of small but important sources of income for women.

Under conditions of economic uncertainty and facing productive and reproductive stresses in order to support themselves and their families, the women in El Alberto have turned for income once again to more readily available traditional resources, although in a limited way, and have again begun spinning and weaving the maguey fiber. For the last 12 years, with the support of NGOs that promote cottage industries for women, they have been weaving a variety of bath products—mainly sponges—that are very successfully sold internationally through the Body Shop, illustrating the plasticity of 'local knowledge' (Schmidt, 2006).

Conflict, however, is also present. At the time of our visit, 117 women were active members of a cooperative—*Mujeres Reunidas*—and 200 more were eagerly waiting to join. Issues of demand and the need to open new markets were limiting the numbers allowed into the cooperative. Members of the Executive Board expressed their frustration with the situation. Having benefited tremendously from this enterprise, they understood the eagerness of other community women to participate. Though requiring extremely intense labor—women members of the cooperative would cut, roast, carve, wash, dry, comb, and spin the materials themselves— they were able to weave or crochet between 10 and 12 sponges per week and earn around 50 pesos a day when working. This income compared positively with the 32 peso daily wage typical in the area (domestic work excluded).

The administrative structure of the cooperative mirrors the communal structures of leadership based on a rotational system that requires every member of the community to serve in administrative, leadership, and representational positions. The cooperative thus very closely follows traditional organizational structures that have existed since pre-colonial times and that ensure citizenship rights and obligations. Women have held these positions of authority and influence, though not through direct participation in public assemblies (Nash, 1988), by accepting the responsibilities of *mayordomías* in the female sphere of patron saint celebrations (Hamilton, 1998) and decision-making processes. Such participation has ensured that women play an important role in production and, indirectly, political decisions.

The benefits did not end there. Besides a renewed interest in 'reforesting' the area with maguey plants to revive the centuries-old tradition of maguey production and consumption, women were learning how to keep account books, write checks, and plan for the acquisition of materials and establish work routines necessary to fill orders for their products. The women elected to the different positions in the cooperative administration were learning to deal with formal and financial institutions along with governmental agencies. They were also transforming—in fact, bringing back equity to—their gendered transactions and negotiations within their household and their community. Thus, a centuries-old tradition of complementarity and reciprocity among genders was being positively revived by development efforts that have, for the last 50 years at least, privileged gender divisions of labor and decision-making based on an assumed public male hierarchy (Schmidt, 2006).

After centuries of external impositions, including forced segregation, taxation, indentured labor, and coerced participation in the market, traditional indigenous communities in Latin America continue to exist, demonstrating their extraordinary resilience. Whether working to counteract ecological challenges (Murra, 1975) or legal and imperial impositions on their well-being and humanity (Silverblatt, 1987; Stavig, 1999), indigenous communities have survived by calling on centuries-old communal definitions of citizenship, gender complementarity, community participation, solidarity, and civic responsibility. Targeted for their supposed economic inefficiency and lack of rationality, they were forced many times to give up traditional ways in favor of 'progressive' ideas. As a consequence, many indigenous communities suffered a regression. Women were ignored and set aside and everybody was denied their indigenous identity (Cooper and Packard, 1997) as it did not fit within a developmentalist discourse supported by urban and westernized elites who insisted that the Indians were an obstacle to progress and modernization.

Though restricted in their movement by their familial and communal responsibilities, the women of *Mujeres Reunidas* opted to create ways to benefit from their 'traditional' domestic tasks. Knitting and tending their gardens and small plots (now their maguey plantations) allows them to continue to take care of their children and the elderly. As these women, however, continue to fuel low-cost production of articles sold in international markets, feed and care for their children and extended families, and ultimately invest in communal projects, the perils of a triple exploitation (Gills, 1999) are clear. The benefits that the Mexican state is reaping from these hard-working women are also obvious.

By the same token, these activities have stopped being 'domestic' and have been transformed into a new combination of international and domestic responses to specific changes brought by global forces. Women's encounter with global forces has pressed them into negotiations and accommodations. However, they are the ones picking and choosing what makes sense to them and what they perceive as beneficial, not because some outside force—in this case the NGOs—has imposed it, but because it makes cultural and economic sense to them (Long, 1996). Indeed, they are applying their indigenous knowledge of maguey production and their centuries-old tradition of maguey fiber processing into *ayates* and other woven products to the production of highly valued items in northern nations. These 'sophisticated' markets are discovering the benefits of indigenous knowledge that focuses on readily available and renewable natural resources that ensure the sustainability of workers and their environment. It is true that these women are now conducting transactions with banks and multinational corporations, and they have fundamentally changed their own perceptions of themselves. But those 'global' forces are also being changed by these women's resilience and strong belief in their families, communities, and understandings of citizenship. These women's ability to selectively transform and adapt to internal and external pressures is key to remaining loyal to their indigenous values and identities. In fact, one could say that the 'global' is helping them remain 'local', albeit transformed. This cultural dialectics questions the assumed unidirectionality of cultural transformation processes.

Conclusions: Whose Culture? Selective Appropriation and the (Re)creation of the Traditional

Ironically, the global forces that created the 'third world' as a category and which are, in part, behind migration, are now, more than ever, engaged with the local. In fact, they are the economic foundation behind an effort by indigenous communities like El Alberto and Ixmiquilpan to help rescue and promote traditional social and cultural structures and processes that aim at securing the material and cultural well-being of their citizens. All researchers, myself included, should be encouraged to look more closely at the articulations and interactions of the local, many times viewed as traditional and indigenous, and the global, usually viewed as cosmopolitan and modern (Ferguson, 1997). We need to be reminded that the traditional is not something isolated, static, or fixed that can be stuck in a museum and that the global is not homogeneously dynamic and hegemonic. There is plenty of space in which to negotiate, contest, and transform—to better respond to—that which is imposed or sometimes seen as inevitable.

The impact that global forces are having on the Hñähñu both in the Valle del Mezquital and in the United States cannot be ignored. The mass emigration, primarily of men at the height of their productive lives, has an impact on those who stay behind. Though the economic impact of the absence of men is considerable, women are responding to these challenges by creating female cooperatives that are revitalizing and finding new markets for the traditional cottage industry of maguey processing which had been all but destroyed in the 1970s. On the other hand, women are recovering key roles in household production and decision-making that pre-date the Spanish conquest. Therefore, this ability to adapt to new (global) challenges and to develop new strategies to pursue their own culturally and socially defined interests is not new. One could say that what has fundamentally changed is the scales at which these transactions are being negotiated. These exchanges illustrate not only the resiliency of indigenous groups, but their selective appropriation of new elements that, at this time, reinforce a solidarity and communal ethos of social responsibility to their families and communities. These everyday practices reinforce their indigenous identities and values, albeit transformed.

Should we assume that what the women of El Alberto are doing is becoming more 'traditional' in the face of the challenges imposed by the absence of their fathers, husbands, or partners and the economic impact that their migration entails (De la Cadena, 1995)?

Should we infer that their revival of traditional maguey fiber processing is, in fact, an act of resistance to outside homogenizing global forces?

As we have seen, efforts to revitalize and promote the traditional Hñähñu culture, like *Radio Bilingüe* cannot depend exclusively on state or federal financial support. It is with the support of hard-earned *migradólares* that the Hñähñu culture—rich in legends, myths, songs, and solidarity—is once again promoted in the Mezquital Valley. But this a complex process that eludes facile explanations. Are the bilingual teachers committed to disseminating the Hñähñu culture in a region where people are stuck in an ideological past and refuse to 'modernize'? Or, in contrast, are they redefining what it means to be modern and indigenous without having to give up either of those projects?

The responses of the women of El Alberto and the bilingual teachers of *Radio Bilingüe* need to be analyzed within a framework that takes into consideration the active processes of selective appropriation and transformation of both local and global forces and realities by actors who need to make sense of their world in their own cultural terms (Mintz, 1998). These actors selectively appropriate and transform the 'global' factors that, combined with their 'local' understandings and skills, make cultural sense to them. It is these transactions that provide the intricate connection between impersonal global forces and very specific cultural realities. It is in these contexts that reformulations of structures of meaning, feelings, and identities get localized in specific histories. It is in this selective process that the traditional gets regularly negotiated and (re)created. This is the stuff of localities, or ethnoscapes that Appadurai talks about. This is where 'historicized particularities'—those scattered hegemonies (Grewal and Kaplan, 1994)—are articulated and define the meaning of localities, of the traditional with a global flavor.

Hñähñu everyday practices—their cultural formations and identity—need then to be understood within a politics of cultural reception and appropriation that allows for the selective (re)formulation of old and new cultural elements. This selective (re)formulation is strongly mediated by both the Hñähñu who have migrated, but also by those who continue to live in their communities of origin. This short essay on the dialectics of culture has highlighted the many levels at which differences get articulated and mediated by social actors, thus creating multiple configurations of practice that respond to specific historical realities, economic articulations, and struggles for power, making projections of possible assimilation, revitalization, indigenization, or rejection hard to predict.

Notes

1   This political activism continues to this date. During our visit in the summer of 2003, a Hñähñu bilingual teacher from Ixmiquilpan had been elected to the state senate. Another young Hñähñu had been elected to the state legislature in early 2000 and headed the state assembly's international migration committee. Both visit the Hñähñu communities in the Tampa Bay area on a regular basis.

2   For a thorough account of how indigenous populations incorporated colonial requirements of their labor into their traditional community offices and cargos, see Stavig, 1999. For other cases, see Hall and Fenelon, 2003; Langer & Muñoz, 2003; Perry, 1996.

3   Funding for this research was provided by the Globalization Research Center of the University of South Florida (now the Patel Center for Global Solutions) as part of a broader project on the connections between economic integration and civic participation of transnational communities and the effects these connections have on the host communities and communities of origin of the Hñähñu, an indigenous group from the Valle del Mezquital in Hidalgo, Mexico.

4   In fact, there is a long tradition of this since the *enganche* system in the nineteenth century.

References

Aguirre-Beltran, G. (1995) Theory of regional integration: the coordinating centers, *América Indígena*, 15, pp. 29–42.

Appadurai, A. (1996) *Modernity at Large. Cultural Dimensions of Globalization*, Public Worlds series, Volume 1 (Minneapolis: University of Minnesota Press).

Bada, X. (2003) Mexican hometown associations, *Citizen Action in the Americas*, No. 5. Interhemispheric Resource Center. Available at: http://www.americaspolicy.org.

Baumann, W. (1975) Economic development and culture change in an Otomí village: a critical analysis. MA Thesis, Goddard College.

Cooper, F. & Packard, R. (1997) Introduction, in: F. Cooper & R. Packard (Eds) *International Development and the Social Sciences: Essays on the History and Politics of Knowledge* (Berkeley: University of California Press).

De La Cadena, M. (1995) Women are more Indian: ethnicity and gender in a community near Cuzco, in: B. Larson, O. Harris & E. Tandeter (Eds) *Ethnicity, Markets, and Migration in the Andes: At the Crossroads of History and Anthropology* (Durham, NC: Duke University Press).

Dening, G. (1986) Possessing Tahiti, *Archeology in Oceania*, 21(1), pp. 103–42.

Ferguson, J. (1997) Anthropology and its evil twin: development in the constitution of a discipline, in: F. Cooper & R. Packard (Eds) *International Development and the Social Sciences: Essays on the History and Politics of Knowledge* (Berkeley: University of California Press).

Fox, J. (1994) The difficult transition from clientelism to citizenship: lessons from Mexico, *World Politics*, 46(2), pp. 151–42.

Friedman, J. (1990) Being in the world: globalization and localization, in: M. Featherstone (Ed.) *Global Culture: Nationalism, Globalization and Modernity*, A *Theory, Culture and Society* special issue (London: SAGE Publications).

Frye, D. (1995) *Indians into Mexicans: History and Identity in a Mexican Town* (Boulder, CO: University Press of Colorado).

Galinier, J. (1997) *The World Below. Body and Cosmos in Otomi Indian Ritual* (Boulder, CO: University of Colorado Press).

Gills, D.-S. (1999) *Rural Women and Triple Exploitation in Korean Development* (New York: St. Martin's Press).

Goldring, L. (1998) From market membership to transnational citizenship. The changing politicization of transnational spaces, *L'Ordinaire LatinoAméricain*, 173(43) (July–December), pp. 167–42. Reprinted in Red Internacional de Migración y Desarrollo. Available at http://migracionydesarrollo.org and as Working Paper No.23 of the Chicano Latino Research Center. University of California, Santa Cruz.

Grewal, I. & Kaplan, C. (1994) Introduction, in: I. Grewal & C. Kaplan (Eds) *Scattered Hegemonies. Postmodernity and Transnational Feminist Practices* (Minneapolis, MN: University of Minnesota Press).

Hall, T. (2006) Indigenous movements and globalization. What is different? What is the Same? Paper presented at the International Studies Association Meeting, 22–25 March, San Diego, forthcoming in *Globalizations*.

Hall, T. & Fenelon, J. (2003) Indigenous resistance to globalization: what does the future hold?, in: W. Dunaway (Ed.) *Emerging Issues in the 21st Century World-System: Vol. I: Crises and Resistance in the 21st Century World- System* (Westport, CT: Praeger).

Hamilton, S. (1998) *The Two-headed Household: Gender and Rural Development in the Ecuadorean Andes*, Pitt Latin American Series (Pittsburgh, PA: University of Pittsburgh Press).

Kugel, V. (1996) Les instituteurs: Formation d'une nouvelle elite indienne? (Valle del Mezquital, México). Ph.D. Thesis, Université de Toulouse-le-Mirail.

Langer, E. & Muñoz, E. (2003) *Contemporary Indigenous Movements in Latin America*, Jaguar Books on Latin America, No.25 (Wilmington, DE: Scholarly Resources).

Long, N. (1996) Globalization and localization: new challenges to rural research, in: H. L. Moore (Ed.) *The Future of Anthropological Knowledge* (London: Routledge).

Mintz, S. (1998) Localization of anthropological practice. From area studies to transnationalism, *Critique of Anthropology*, 18(20), pp. 117–42.

Murra, J. (1975) *Formaciones ecológicas y políticas del mundo andino* (Lima: Instituto de Estudios Peruanos).

Nash, J. (1988) Cultural parameters of sexism and racism in the international division of labor, in: J. Smith (Ed.) *Racism, Sexism, and the World System* (New York: Greenwood Press).

Perry, R. (1996) *... From Time Immemorial. Indigenous Peoples and State Systems* (Austin, TX: University of Texas Press).

Pietro Hernandez, D. & Utrilla Sarmiento, B. (2003) Ar Ngú, Ar Hninim Ya Meni. La Casa, el Pueblo, la Descendencia. (Los Otomíes de Querétaro), in: S. Millan & J. Valle (Eds) *La Comunidad Sin Límites. Estructura Social y*

Organización Comunitaria en las Regiones Indígenas de México, Etnografía de los Pueblos Indígenas de México II (México, DF: Instituto Nacional de Antropología e Historia (INAH)).

Quesada, M. F. (n.d.) La migración de la población indígena en el Estado de Hidalgo. Manuscript.

Schmidt, E. (2006) Sustainable community for sustainable development. A case study of the Mujeres Reunidas Cooperative in Hidalgo, Mexico, *Journal of Developing Societies*, 22(4), pp. 379–42.

Schmidt, E. & Crummett, M. (2004) Heritage re-created: Hidalguenses in the United States and Mexico, in: J. Fox & G. Rivera-Salgado (Eds) *Indigenous Mexican Migrants in the United States* (La Jolla, CA: Center for Comparative Immigration Studies and Center for U.S.–Mexican Studies).

Silverblatt, I. (1987) *Moon, Sun, and Witches: Gender Ideologies and Class in Inca and Colonial Peru* (Princeton, NJ: Princeton University Press).

Stavig, W. (1999) *The World of Túpac Amaru. Conflict, Community and Identity in Colonial Peru* (Lincoln, NE and London: University of Nebraska Press).

Wolff, J. (1997) The global and the specific: reconciling conflicting theories of culture, in: A. D. King (Ed.) *Culture, Globalization and the World-System. Contemporary Conditions for the Representation of Identity* (Minneapolis, MN: University of Minnesota Press).

Ella Schmidt is Assistant Professor in the Interdisciplinary Social Sciences Program at USF St. Petersburg. He received her MA in Cultural Anthropology from the Université Paris VII-Jussieu and her Ph.D. from the University of California at Davis. She has done research on Mexican farmworkers in West Central Florida and changes in their construction of identity. Currently her research focuses on transnational Mexican migrants in Clearwater and Valle del Mezquital, Hidalgo, Mexico and the creation of new social formations in both home and host communities. She serves on the international editorial board of *Globalizations*.

Hegemony/Counter-Hegemony: Imagining a New, Post-Nation-State Cartography of Culture in an Age of Globalization

KEVIN ARCHER, M. MARTIN BOSMAN, M. MARK AMEN & ELLA SCHMIDT

Introduction

The preceding articles make clear that the cultural implications of globalization are nothing if not diverse. It is also clear that determining precisely what these implications may be is driven by what one imagines both culture and globalization to 'be', as discussed in the Introduction to this volume. The articles by Marcuse and Wilson, for example, are pretty straightforward in their portrayal of globalization as a force pressuring local and regional cultural agents to conform, in specific ways via specific means, to certain exigencies, quite beyond much modification. Whether understood more as a real process from without or, as Wilson rightly points out, a more discursive trope to which locally- and regionally-based agents tend to conform in their agency, globalization is understood as a pressing planetary macro-process that must be either accommodated or resisted by these latter. For obvious reasons, we will call this sort of take a more 'global' imaginary of the cultural implications of globalization which necessarily produces more macro-structural accounts, both theoretical and empirical, of the issue.

The articles by Marston *et al.* and Nederveen Pieterse are produced on the basis of an alternative imagining of the global–culture nexus which suggests that the global is less a macro-cultural force from without and more a force co-constituted by precisely the agency of situated people in situated places. Marston *et al.* are quite explicit about this theoretical move while Nederveen Pieterse's thick, thoroughly theoretically informed, empirical narrative profoundly illustrates the interpenetration of the 'global' and the 'local' at different spatial scales of analysis and praxis. We will call this a 'global–local' take on the cultural implications of globalization which is the basis of a much broader literature on transnationalism, cultural hybridity, post-modern post-coloniality, etc. (Bhabha, 2005; see Introduction).

Finally, the articles by Price and Schmidt take the analysis of culture and globalization more to the popular streets by closely examining the ways in which specific collectivities actually make use of global–local cultural resources. Within this imaginary, greater knowledge of what is happening in the street(s) necessarily renders a better understanding of greater diversity in the culture(s) of globalization than is rendered by more macro-structural analyses. Such an approach renders a cultural world less sensitive to the cultural exigencies attributed to globalization and more sensitive to 'its' contingencies as the 'global' is imagined and revealed as nothing but the conjuncture of such human relational contingencies. We will call the imaginary revealed in these papers more 'local–global' to suggest both a greater similarity to the global–local one than to that of the macro-global and, yet, a very real difference nonetheless.

Of interest here is that these varying imaginings of the cultural implications of globalization appear to be the result of disciplinary, as well as what can be called scalar, bias in terms of both theoretical and empirical strategy. While certainly debatable, we suggest that such biases go far in determining both what one makes of 'culture' and 'globalization' and, then, how one goes about revealing the impacts the 'former' may have on the 'latter' and vice versa. If this is indeed the case, it goes a long way towards explaining why it is so very difficult to construct a truly trans-scalar, transdisciplinary imaginary, particularly in the context of an ever more rapidly proliferating discipline-based literature on globalization and culture, ongoing in all possible directions with all possible disciplinary-specific tropes, rhetoric, methodologies, and, then, empirics.

A more productive way of achieving such transdisciplinarity would be to consciously rethink the problem in a broader meta-theoretical manner. Toward this end, we suggest making creative use of the notion of 'social imaginaries' as recently articulated by Gaonkar (2002) and his colleagues on the basis of the earlier work of Castoriadis (1987). As the former puts it, a social imaginary is 'an enabling but not fully explicable symbolic matrix within which a people imagine and act as world-making collective agents' (Gaonkar, 2002, p. 1). Such an imaginary includes both explicit and implicit or tacit knowledges on the basis of which humans make sense of the world and act on the basis of this 'common sense'. At this point in our analysis, we are discussing most directly the differences in the social imaginaries involved in different scalar and disciplinary scholarly matrices which lead to a particular view of the cultural implications of globalization and then the practical research activity initiated as a result of this view. To carry the critical analysis of specific scalar and disciplined scholarly imaginaries much further, however, is beyond the scope of this essay.

We wish to underscore that, regardless of the scale by which 'it' is viewed or the discipline from whence knowledge of 'it' is produced, the modern Western imaginary of 'culture' is inherently related to that of 'nationhood', 'nationalism', and what we call the whole 'nation-state-to-international' matrix of cultural relations established by the globalization of the terms of the Peace of Westphalia of 1648, as a result of Western imperialism. In turn, the prevailing Western imaginary of 'globalization' is strongly influenced by this version of institutionalized, internationalized 'cultural' relations. In this, we agree with Gaonkar (2002, p. 5) that 'the *national people* is a paradigmatic case of modern social imaginary' spread not only globally by imperialism but also between more scholarly contemplation to more popular understandings, if unevenly so. 'Nations' are how most Westernized individuals now imagine culture, and that between 'nation states' is how they imagine cultural relations globally. It is necessary, then, to critically examine this prevailing cultural–global imaginary in order to both get beyond scalar and disciplinary bias and to possibly construct alternative imaginaries. In short, *it is necessary to break the now essentialized link between 'nationality' and 'culture' which has been so tightly forged in the imaginaries of Westernized people over the last few centuries*, in order to better imagine and understand cultural relations in today's increasingly globalized world.

But this notion of social imaginaries points to how, specifically, to break this imagined link between nationality and culture by directing our focus not only on how Westernized scholarly elites may consider this link differently but also on how non-Westernized elites, as well as non-elites, imagine their own cultural relations. A focus on the construction and maintenance of social imaginaries renders it necessary to determine more precisely what those 'quite Other' and 'elsewhere' as well as those 'on the street' actually make (or not) of the 'cultural implications of globalization'. Identifying and then recognizing, by giving stronger voice to, these other imaginaries of the cultural implications of globalization renders these implications differently, both discursively and in reality. This opens the way for a more thorough consideration of potentially alternative forms of cultural relations within alternative forms of globalization.

Nations and Nation States as the Cultural Project of Western Modernity

Coming to terms with the cultural implications of globalization necessitates coming to terms with the historical legacy of a post-colonial, if not a post-imperial, world. Specifically, human relations across the planet have been organized and regulated in something called the international system, based on the colonial imposition of what we will call political–territorial envelopes understood in the Western imagination, more or less consciously, as 'nation states'. This latter is a territorial imaginary of enclosures of self-determining, or sovereign, states bounding one against the other, juxtaposing the difference of internal domesticities and possible external 'relations' with others. Yet it is also an imaginary that is complexly confused in substance. As often noticed (Cocks, 2002; Delanty and O'Mahony, 2002), really existing 'national' states do not envelope a single cultural collectivity, a nation, but are all multicultural-national to very real extents. Similarly, identified or self-identified cultural groups considered actual 'nations' in the world do not always have states and the self-determining sovereignty this would entail.

That this reality of the 'international' system has been much noticed, however, has not meant that the imaginary which conjured it has receded from dominance. Those who self-describe, or are described by third person analysts, as 'ethno-nationalists', for example, would be more apt to describe the weakening of the cultural functions and regulation of existent states brought on by deepening globalizing flows to be hastening a system of more truly inter*national* relations. From this perspective, what we have now, if weakening, is not an inter*national* order but, instead, an inter*state* one, with nations mixed up within or across extant state boundaries. It is from this global imaginary that springs ethno-nationalist notions, such as the ethno-Quebecois would have an easier time protecting their cultural traditions if they separated from Canada and joined the United States, or that the ethno-Flemish people would similarly be better off in a united Europe, outside the restrictive confines of the 'oppressive' Belgian state.

This discursive confusion within the imaginary of nation-states-in-international relations is extremely important for the problematic we are developing here because it bestrides the problem of characterizing both globalization and culture. Those who believe that current trends signify new, 'global', forms of human interaction generally emphasize the novelty by comparing it to this inter-nation-state system, which is presumed to be breaking down under the weight of increasing flows of capital, images, and peoples across state boundaries. Similarly, attempts to imagine the cultural implications of presumed globalizing trends tend to characterize these as either leading to an increasingly hybridizing 'post-nationalist' era or, quite the opposite, to a increasingly dangerous world of rapidly proliferating projects of reifying and of actively, even violently, opposing cultural difference. In both instances, a 'pure', homogeneous ethnic 'nationality' is assumed as an actual possibility and, perhaps, a reality.

Going beyond this nation-state-to-international imaginary requires a rethinking of the discursive construction of 'nation' and the experience of the attempted project of its material instantiation. This rethinking is difficult because of the slippery nature of the terms used. The idea of 'nation' is the dominant way in which the modern West has characterized 'culture' in this imaginary. So when the cultural implications of globalization are considered, the fate of the 'nation' is the assumed object of first concern to be investigated; hence, the oft-used terminology of post-*nationalism*, ethno-*nationalism*, trans-*nationalism*, etc. The main question here is: are the cross-border flows of globalization leading to a breakdown in the coherence of national identities or, quite the converse, their resurrection? One's imagining of the cultural implications of globalization, as well as the process of globalization itself, thus hinges on what the 'nation' is considered to be in the currently transforming inter*national* system.

The marriage of nation to state in the imagined 'nation state' renders this rethinking much more difficult. The scholarly and policy-oriented authors of a recent book critically considering the experience of 'nation building' in war-torn Afghanistan and Iraq, for example, speak hardly at all about the cultural traditions—let alone the actual inhabitants—of this area of the world. They singularly focus on what went wrong in the rebuilding of the two *states*. The implicit, background assumption is that once the states are successfully rebuilt the 'nations' of Iraq and Afghanistan again be furnished with the protection of sovereign power (Fukuyama, 2006). There is no apparent doubt on the part of these authors that an Iraqi or an Afghani 'nation' actually exists (perhaps always has?) within the boundaries of the states so identified, problematic as such an assumption surely is, on even a cursory view of the current 'cultural' situation there.

Similarly, on this implicit assumption of nation state, if one were to look at the same case from the point of view of the impact of global flows on these 'nations' it would no doubt suggest that either such flows are breaking down in terms of their cultural coherences or leading to essentially reactive projects of reification and opposition. The point is that the nation-state imaginary itself biases those who engage it toward essentializing and territorializing cultural relations, which thereby appear to be increasingly 'impacted' by more fluid and supposedly 'deterritorialized' global flows. These 'impacts' can be imagined either positively or negatively, depending on the focus and interests of those so imagining.

Yet simply noticing this problem with the nation-state-to-international cultural imaginary in varying disciplinary ways does not immediately suggest a better one. Much more work has to go into unpacking the meanings behind these imaginings. While the term 'nation' may have an ancient history, the connotation of this term in the modern West is thoroughly confused at its roots. Indeed, the modern Western imaginary of nationhood has both a dual imaginary lineage and a thoroughly mixed reality. It shares the ancient imaginary of nations as shared bloodlines through time, or what has come to be known in modern terminology as 'ethnic groups'. As Smith (1986) elaborates, modern nations, even those born of more enlightened ideals, all have more primordial roots in a longer distant past of common descent, or ethnicity. Indeed, this image of a longer cultural past can even accommodate the seemingly quite contrary notion that nations are really only 'imagined communities' of the recent

European past (Anderson, 1983) as even the 'invented traditions' (Hobsbawm and Ranger, 1983) these communities commonly conjure up are mostly just newly elaborated ethnic traditions of this longer cultural past.

This view of the primordial roots of modern nationhood has a much longer tradition in Western imaginaries, arising as it does in the reaction of the Romantics to the Rationalists of the Enlightenment. The idealization by the former of the ways of life of traditional, agrarian, communal relations as these faced the onslaught of modern, utilitarian social relations involved in the spread of revolutionary, urbanized, industrial society is a well-enough known historical narrative that it does not need rehearsing here. Of specific interest is that the Romantics imagined such traditional 'ways of life' not just as differences between, say, rural and urban life, but also as that among cultural 'nations'. So stood Herder (1969), for example, in opposition to the humanist universalisms of the Enlightened rationalists, with the notion of relative human difference based on equally legitimate 'national' values (see also Eagleton, 1991; Thompson, 1997).

This primordial ethnic imaginary of nationhood is thus co-birthed with the Enlightenment imaginary, the basis of the apparently 'invented' alternative suggested above. The Enlightenment version of this latter, more recently conjured imaginary is sourced in the Rationalist ideal of human relations conducted on the basis of reason, and not on that of faith, blood, traditional inheritance, or emotion. This rational imaginary of nationhood is not that of descent but of modern construction, a civic-*project to be completed* (Kedourie, 1994). While there exists a wider, multidisciplinary discussion of this dual heritage, it is clear that the two imaginaries of nationhood emerging out of the Enlightenment are more than merely different, they are actively opposing. They are, in fact, evil discursive twins co-birthed in the Enlightenment and co-present in the modern Western imaginary and praxis. The one twin, what we will call Nationhood 1, is imagined as an ethnic group regarded politically, or, in some versions, an ethnic group mobilized for political goals such as state power and sovereignty. The other twin, Nationhood 2, is conversely imagined as the overcoming of ethnicity via the construction of reasonable relations among groups and individuals within larger collective communities. That this imaginary confusion is real in its consequences is more than clear with the recent disintegration of Yugoslavia. Not only was imagined Nationhood 1 mobilized with the most tragic results, this mobilization was rewarded with formal sovereignty, heightening the hopes of Nationhood 1 elite culture-brokers the world over.

The confusion, however, is even more profound than this. Not only are there two apparently opposing Western imaginaries of nationhood, they actually interpenetrate each other in specific ways with specific, often equally tragic, bloody results. A Nationhood 1, imagined as a politicized ethnic group, must go through some process of politicization in order to act politically as a group. In reality, this process has been undertaken by elite culture brokers who have appealed as much to reason as to bloodline, depending on the context. More importantly, the stark rationalism entailed in the Nationhood 2 imaginary belies a reality of Nationhood 2 building that has rested squarely on the foundation of quite irrational, Romantic imaginaries and praxis. There is nothing rational, for example, about swearing allegiance to flags or singing 'national' anthems or cheering national sports teams or wearing specific uniforms to kill other equally rational human beings (in different uniforms) in the name of the nation. And yet these types of rituals and emotions, not reason, are what have molded human behavior in even the oldest Nationhood 2 projects. These aspects of the Romantic imaginary are what actually inspire and reinforce collective belonging to the 'nation', as Appadurai (2000a, p. 130) makes clear:

Love of nation, it is evident, is no mere figure of speech. Parades bring people to their feet. National anthems produce lumps in the throat and flags induce tears in the eye. Insults to national honor can greatly assist internal mobilization and violations of national sovereignty can create irate mobs. Sacrifice, passion, anger, hate are all part of the symphony of affects in which love—here love of nation—is the orchestrating force. So regularly has love of nation been invoked by nationalists through every medium of communication that we have ceased to pay attention to its peculiarities.

On the basis of such confusion within the imaginary of Western nationhood it is clear that imagining 'nation states' already begins confused. The consideration of which people are allowed self-rule and sovereignty is thus open as, again, best exemplified by the experience of the former Yugoslavia where sovereignty was most recently granted on the basis of 'pure' ethnicity. This confused imaginary was born with a territorial basis that was then spread materially throughout the world via Western imperialism. This territorial legacy of the Peace of Westphalia of 1648 renders it that much more difficult to think through, or outside of, this confused imaginary as distinct 'nations' become affixed to distinct 'states' in an elision which essentializes non-essences (nations) thereby according 'them' agency. In fact, there never has been such a thing as a *nation* state in cultural substance, only states regulating territorial limits inhabited by groups and individuals with different sets of collective and individual cultural identities with varying amounts of social and political power. What Westphalia bequeathed to the imperial(ized) world was a new territorial cartography of fixed boundaries, not frontiers, maintained by internal and external power-brokers in the name of territorial 'sovereignty'. From the beginning, these boundaries enclosed different cultural groups with different interests, sometimes conflicting. It was of immediate elite concern to maintain territorial integrity in the midst of such potentially conflicting internal relations. One way to do this is by force, of course, as wars became civil, but a more enduring way is by forced consensus, as politics became civil in the form of the cultural project of the 'nation'. In this context, the cultural groupings which controlled the power of the newly sovereign state determined the cultural evolution of the projected 'nation', while other groups either assimilated culturally or were marginalized, exiled, or exterminated.

Within this well-known, but often forgotten or ignored, cultural history 'after Westphalia' are some hidden paths towards understanding the cultural implications of globalization today. First is consideration of the importance of state power in the production of modern nations. Control of state power becomes an object of desire for elite culture-brokers, thereby inherently politicizing cultural processes and constructions. Second, this territorially bounded cartography of cultural relations makes clearer the ways in which 'nations', 'ethnic groups', and, then, 'cultures' are in actuality actively projected social constructions instead of human essences. Focusing on this new cultural cartography also reveals the varying ways in which such constructions have been built by more or less active culture-brokers vying for state power. Third, looking closely at this new cultural cartography makes it clear that the project of cultural assimilation/marginalization necessitated after Westphalia has been not only violent but also a very unevenly successful process, both in old states of the global post-colonialist North and particularly of today's post-colonial states in the South. Finally, this post-Westphalian understanding of the essential role of the state in the cultural creation of modern nations makes it clear that any weakening of the power of sovereign states via global flows will *necessarily* lead to the emergence of different forms of cultural identities and belongings, both individual and collective and both violently and non-violently birthed.

Imagining a New Cultural Cartography for a Global Age

The Western nation-state imaginary thus fixes the space–time of cultural processes in a mental and material cartography of artificial territorial boundaries, the escape from which, both theoretically and actually, remains quite difficult. Yet, by elaborating on the four previous assertions we can help construct an alternative cultural cartography more suited to this age of globalization. The first move toward this new imaginary is to recognize that the modernist territorial state, which hitherto has provided the framework for some groups to construct cultural power over others, is now under siege as a result of globalization. The question that needs to be addressed here, then, is what new spatial framework of cultural regulation—global, regional, sub-regional, etc.—is going to be constructed in lieu of the nation state? This is surely one of the main issues in the interdisciplinary discussion over the production of socio-spatial scales (Brenner *et al.*, 2003; Swyngedouw, 1997) and that concerning new forms of global governance (Held and McGrew, 2002; Jessop, 2002). As Held *et al.* (1999, p. 32) put it, globalization is leading to an increasing 'deterritorialization of politics, rule, and governance', meaning for King (1997, p. 6) that '[c]ulture', itself, 'is increasingly deterritorialized'. While we take issue below with this notion of deterritorialization, these authors certainly are on to something culturally important taking place beyond the confines of the nation state.

The second move is more profound. One of the main results of the nation-state imaginary was to 'fix' collective cultural identity to the territory of autonomous, sovereign, states. As alluded to above, this fix biases this imaginary to the reification and essentialization of the nation/culture by 'placing' it in separate territorial envelopes of inside sameness and outside difference. Even in recent discussions of globalization, this nation-state discourse proceeds with these hidden, unreflected assumptions and terms of spatial fixity and unitary agency. Imagining the nation-state instead as a severely unfinished cultural 'project', however, renders both the idea of culture and cultural space less fixed or essential. Cultures and cultural space are revealed as ever open to transformation with ongoing transformations in human relations.

Recognizing the nation state as an unfinished project leads to reconsideration of other cultural 'facts' of salience for understanding a post-nation-state cultural world. After reviewing dictionary definitions in 12 separate languages, Bauman (1999, p. 31) found that the definitions for 'ethnic group' and 'nation' were virtually the same: 'based on descent', 'often recognizable by looks', 'sharing cultural traits (language, outlook, etc.)', 'said to be acquired by birth', and 'forming a community of destiny and some form of political organization'. Surely such a similarity of definition could be constructed for that virtual human categorization of 'race'. And, of course, what of that of 'culture' itself?

Scholarly attempts at more refined definitions of these social 'things' not only do not usually add much profundity or significant nuance but also tend to simply proliferate as a result of whatever qualification might be added, as alluded to in the Introduction with regard to the proposed definitions of 'culture' and 'globalization'. Other than the significant similarity in definitions, which are decidedly real in their theoretical and social effect, the point here is twofold. First, attempting to define ethnic group, race, or culture on the basis of these traits each somehow includes 'fixes' them within this list of extant traits. This imagined fixation, like that of the nation state, biases those who take it into reifying by essentializing the object itself. Second, this reifying image necessarily renders this object, be it ethnic group, nation, or culture, 'thing-like', to be discovered or recovered, in its authentic form in reality, if the image is calibrated properly.

Yet, like that of the imagined 'nation state', if this fixation is loosened, a quite different imaginary can arise. This new imaginary portrays these 'things' as less thing-like and more the specific spatio-temporal structuration of ongoing processes. It is important to recognize the extent to which the essentialist fixation of culture lingers in the scholarly, and, even more so, in the popular imaginary, perhaps particularly in this age of globalization. Grillo (2003, p. 160), considers the 'old model' (we would say 'ever present' model) of such a reifying definition of culture as suggesting that '[c]ultures (static, finite and bounded, ethnolinguistic blocs labeled 'French', 'Nuer' and so on) determine individual and collective identities, and the subject's place in social and political schemas. Cultural membership is thus virtually synonymous with ethnicity'. This essentialist image of culture—what he calls the 'culturalist' image—has the additional view of 'it' as 'historic', 'rooted', 'authentic', and 'traditional'. Indeed, pertinent to our purposes, Grillo (2003, p. 160) goes on to say that this 'old model' thus implies that:

> people(s) may be deprived of their culture, and thence there is a need for 'cultural conservation', a mode of thinking (often present in multiculturalism), in which cultural authenticity must be protected like a rare species. This perspective may also entail a form of biological determinism, with cultural traits and differences seen as 'bio-cultural' . . . and inheritable.

Clearly, there is a tight linkage among the (equally) potentially essentializing imaginaries of culture, ethnicity, race, and nation. And this is solely within the discussion of the scholarly literature. More important is that the overwhelmingly dominant popular understanding of such 'things' appears both essentialist and reifying. Whereas Friedman (2002, p. 32) may be right (although we would argue the point) that this conception of an old scholarly model of essentialism is merely a 'straw man' put to fire by new model interested scholarship, it is clear that essentialism still exists in the streets. As Bauman (1999, p. 86) puts it, 'the essentialist view of culture cannot be written off as mere rubbish; precisely because so many people espouse it'. In fact, it is precisely the cultural essentialism being constructed and mobilized in the street—the concrete manifestation of the evil twin of Western modernist nationhood—that has led to so much bloody conflict as the nation-state cultural project has increasingly weakened.

Indeed, this latter is no less than the tragic outcome of what Grillo (2003) and Arthurs (2003) identify as the disconnect between the scholarly and popular cultural imaginaries. Many scholars may be moving on to an anti-essentialist imaginary of cultures, but most people live in an essentialized or rapidly essentializing world, with real life and death struggles over their cultural 'essences'. As Grillo (2003, p. 167) elaborates:

> Often enough, rightly or wrongly, people really are concerned about 'their' culture, and often enough their ideas are grounded in essentialism. *Pace* anthropologists and others who espouse alternative accounts, it might be argued that many people insist on an essentialist reading of culture seeing in it something which represents them in some deep sense and that defines their 'real' selves.

Moreover, these struggles are escalating precisely because of what he calls the 'cultural anxiety' that many people feel in this time of relatively rapid geo-social transformation. While the power of nation states seems to be breaking down under the weight of global flows, this modern-traditional cultural 'fixity', however unevenly felt, is disappearing for many people, thus causing anxiety as a result of growing ontological uncertainty and a sense of insecurity.

Such cultural anxiety, of course, is felt and acted upon in different ways, by different people, in different contexts. Class, gender, and place would have to be included in the empirical investigation of such to render it appropriately noticeable. But it is relatively clear that new cultural 'fixes' are emerging on the basis of three foundations: ethnicity, religion, and some form of Western civic republicanism. The first two represent renewed essentialisms as a result of the uneven and now declining cultural project of the nation state. The third foundation is a recast, rescaled, and re-narrated version of the Enlightened ideal of reasonable nationhood. In any case, all three cultural fixes are being constructed by elite culture-brokers in every part of the world. The first two appear to be most important in those states where the national project was least successful, while the third foundation appears to be most important where this project was most successful.

These general assertions, however, must be rendered more precise if they are to serve as guideposts toward new imaginaries of global cultural relations. The territorial nation state is far from disappearing from the stage of global and local governance, but its functions are nevertheless being radically transformed in the wake of globalization. As Delanty and O'Mahony (2002, pp. 170–171) and many others have argued with regard to the nation state, there has been a 'transference upwards to the transnational level and downwards to the subnational or regional levels of many of its functions', including those involving the promotion and regulation of the national project. As a result, these authors contend, traditional national-cultural public legitimation of the state:

> is less significant today simply because of the growing number of global spaces, stateless spaces and normative vacuums. Thus, the increased visibility of nationalism in the world today is merely a manifestation of this anarchic situation of extreme social fragmentation, which can of course also be described as one of offering new opportunities for cosmopolitan community. Lacking a political form—akin to the nation-state—'nations' as articulated by anti-systemic forces all over the world are rebelling against states.

In this context, these authors continue, the 'nation code has been opened up to new codifications of belonging' on the basis of new 'cultural opportunities for self-determination'. Others, of course, have underscored this transformation of state regulation in similar ways (Held and McGrew, 2002; Jessop, 2002). This particular rendition is nonetheless significant because it clearly focuses attention on four specific aspects of the present, potentially post-nation-state situation in such a concise manner.

First, it points, if rather pejoratively, to new 'spaces' (and we would add 'places') of 'anarchic' socio-cultural 'fragmentation' let loose from the nation-state regulatory matrix. While we would argue that there are no 'normative vacuums' in these spaces (and places), it is clear that this spatial rescaling of cultural norms and belongings is, indeed, taking place.

Second, the emphasis on 'nations' and 'nationalism' as a means to describe new cultural spaces and movements clearly maintains the Enlightenment understanding of the political–cultural nexus. Culture becomes, on this view, a political project to be achieved, not something inherited as tradition. This helps clarify what is at stake in the transformation of the nation-state in these globalizing times. Today's 'anti-systemic' forces are 'rebelling against states' as a means to achieve self-determination within a continually existing international system of sovereign states. In this context, culture, whether ethnic, religious, or 'national' is politicized by necessity, both discursively and on the ground, in the attempt to obtain sovereign self-determination.

Third, the authors point to the dual nature of this 'anarchic situation of extreme social fragmentation': that is, that it can lead, and has led, *either* to what we underlined above as cultural anxiety and renewed, cultural essentialism *or* to an expansion of the Enlightenment project of reasonable cultural–political community on the basis of a renewed cosmopolitanism. Indeed, the vast and rapidly growing literature on globalization is largely split between those who underscore growing ethnic essentialism and those who underscore growing cosmopolitanism. On the basis of our earlier discussion, however, we would argue that this is not an '*either/or*' but a '*both/and*' global cultural situation, due to the 'evil twin', reasonable–romantic, nature of politicized cultural relations after the Enlightenment and ensuing Western imperialism.

Finally, the authors speak directly to what they call new 'codifications of belonging' and this focuses attention quickly and clearly on what needs to be closely examined as the nation state is being transformed. It used to be, as Hedetoft (2003, pp. 139–140) points out, that 'belonging' was a notion that only racists (or 'culturalists' as this term is used above) employed in their quest for maintaining authentic, natural, ethnic boundaries among peoples or nations. Now, he argues, it has infiltrated the lexicon of even many 'liberal cosmopolitans'. In short, belonging 'has become not just a much more diverse and legitimate notion than it used to be; it has undergone a far-reaching *essentialization* process'. 'Belonging', in this (re)new(ed) imaginary:

> goes to our very roots, the core of our existential dilemma, it would seem. We may struggle over where, how and why we belong, to one or multiple sites, but *that* we need to belong is beyond question: belonging as axiom, or in Bourdieu's terminology, as *doxa*. Identity *is* belonging, though certain (elite) groups can afford the luxury of cultivating the idea of their global non-belongingness. (Hedetoft, 2003, p. 140)

Viewing the transformation of the nation state through this four-sided prism—new cultural spaces, the political–cultural nexus, social fragmentation–renewed solidarity, and changing cultural belongingness—the cultural implications of globalization not only become more apparent, they can also be seen more clearly as fluid, on-going processes nowhere (literally) stabilized completely, let alone institutionalized (like nationalism) in state or state-like constructions. Substituting this more fluid imaginary for that of the fixed nation state thus makes it easier to determine what is at stake in the different cultural projects already set forth in the literature and on the ground. The emancipation of 'culture' from the discursive and material project of the nation state thus opens the way for both a more profound critique of the latter and a more sophisticated understanding of the former as an ever evolving and therefore contestable discursive/practical phenomenon or condition.

Cultural Identity and Belonging in a Neoliberalizing Global Context

There is a vast, ever-growing literature pointing in the direction of this new imaginary of global cultural flows, fluidity, openness, hybridity, and so on. But we have taken the specific direction that we have toward this goal in order to emphasize two main issues we think are important in relation to the adoption, or not, of such an imaginary. The first issue, already discussed, is the difficulty many have in thinking past the nation-state project when it comes to cultural relations. The second issue figures more prominently at this point in the discussion: that is, the continuing relevance of the nation-state cultural project even in this age of global social fluidity. More precisely, the key to the nation-state project is to construct collective identity, a sense of 'belonging', among individuals increasingly being individuated as competing beings by primitive accumulation, the division of social and factory labor, market competition, reformed Christianity through secularism, democratic citizenry, utilitarian-rational bureaucracy, and so on. It is this 'state of nature' that has to be overcome if social alienation/anomie is not to violently overcome 'society' itself. That the nation-state imaginary was born 'confused', is because of what appears to be an essential complication in this very project. The ever expanding and deepening commodity relations of capitalism render enduring collective social relations well-nigh impossible on a state-wide basis. Individual and group competition essentially rules in this context, not solidarity with, or belonging to, a greater socio-cultural collective or 'nation'.

Not only that, but this is a version of modernity in which, quite necessarily given its characteristics, 'all that is solid melts into air', including previous understandings of self, group, home, and place in the cosmos. And in the latter's place emerge new understandings which only with difficulty, if at all, fill human hearts with security or connection with their fellow human beings. As Eagleton (2000, p. 67) puts it:

> It is hard for a way of life whose priorities are secular, rationalist, materialist and utilitarian to produce a culture adequate to these values ... This, to be sure, was always a headache for industrial capitalism, which was never really able to spin a persuasive cultural ideology out of its own philistine practices. Instead, it was forced for this purpose to exploit the symbolic resources of the Romantic humanist tradition, and in doing so betrayed the discrepancy between its utopian ideal and its sordid reality.

The nation-state project, in other words, attempted to suture a collective cultural 'belongingness' on an ever-expanding material basis of necessary social fragmentation due to individual competition. This was attempted not only by appealing to these 'symbolic resources of the Romantic humanist tradition' articulated in the citation by Appadurai (2000a, p. 130) above concerning engendering 'love' of nation. But nation-state projects also more or less embedded these ever expanding commodity relations within political-regulatory frameworks which helped to attenuate their most severe social fragmentary nature. As Bobbit (2002, p. 177) puts it, the idea is that the 'nation-state is supposed to be doing something unique in the history of the modern state: maintaining, nurturing, and improving the conditions of its citizens'. This social welfare function of the state thereby enhanced social solidarity within its space–time envelope which, in turn, provided material legitimation for just these Romantic 'symbolic resources'. Moreover, this state-generated social welfare, as it emerged in different ways in different states, was increasingly imagined as variations of 'capitalism' which had everything to do with the cultural variations of the 'peoples' of these states. Indeed, this is the very foundation of the 'variety of capitalisms' argument most prominent, for example, in regulationist (Boyer, 1986; Boyer and Saillard, 1995) and institutionalist (Polanyi, 1944; Beckert, 2002) accounts.

These observations suggest that with the transformation 'upward' and 'downward' of regulatory functions of the hitherto nation-state project, not only do symbolic resources of collective cultural solidarity have to be adjusted but also the material welfare functions which underpin them. But this is nowhere near happening in the same sense as that of the homogenizing project hitherto embodied in the nation state. Rather, this latter appears to be devolving to the greater particularities of cultural or 'identity' politics in the rich North and both universalizing and particularizing religious and ethnic cultural politics in the poor South.

Or, perhaps, this is really not the case, as the citation above by Delanty and O'Mahony (2002, pp. 170–171) suggests. Perhaps this increasing transformation of the nation-state cultural project has opened up the greater possibility for a true, universalizing, multicultural cosmopolitan project on a global scale (Beck, 1997). Perhaps recognizing the Other via a transformed, post-nation-state imaginary of cultural identities will allow for the emergence of greater, more global social solidarity based on mutual respect and tolerance of the cultural Other in an emerging global civil society. This would, in this respect, be a continuation of the Enlightenment project, now globalized.

'Perhaps' is the key term in our narrative here in two very significant ways. First, it suggests that all of these possible cultural projects are just that, *projects* to be discursively constructed and actualized. Here, again, the emergence of various, often conflicting, post-nation-state social imaginaries is important in the on-going struggle for hegemony and hegemonic actuality. This suggests that the disconnect between the scholarly move toward anti-essentialist understandings of cultural phenomena and the continuing essentialism in the streets is in serious need of more thorough analysis. This is particularly the case given the very real material circumstances of the transformation of the nation state in the poor South. Overall, as Bobbit (2002, p. 228) describes, nation states have largely lost control over more than symbolic resources for collective solidarity:

> no nation-state can assure its citizens safety from weapons of mass destruction; no nation-state can, by obeying its own laws (including its international treaties) be assured that its leaders will not be arraigned as criminals or its behavior be used as a legal justification for international coercion; no nation-state can effectively control its economic life or its own currency; no nation-state can protect its culture and way of life from the depiction and presentation of images and ideas, however foreign or offensive; no nation-state can protect its society from transnational perils, such as ozone depletion, global warming, and infectious epidemics. And yet guaranteeing national security, civil peace through law, economic development and stability, international tranquility and equality, were the main tasks of the nation-state.

While one can quibble over the details of these assertions, this account quickly summarizes the globalizing forces transforming the cultural role of the nation state. The question is what sort of state-like regulatory institution is going to emerge which will provide these and similar types of protections of 'social' security? As to this, the discursive battle at the global level—that is, the view 'upwards' from the nation state—is, we suggest, taking place along threefold lines. There is a battle, largely among Westernized observers, between those who argue, either implicitly or explicitly, that global cultural solidarity will be based on relative cultural homogeneity, and those who argue, conversely, that a new cultural solidarity will be based on the accommodation of multicultural 'difference', including hybrid cultural bricolage. Among the former are those who have initiated and actively promoted what Harvey (2006, p. 146) calls the 'neoliberal revolution' those who argue on the basis of a superficially rehashed modernization theory, now concentrating very specifically on how politics can change 'cultures' so that all can 'develop' appropriately (Harrison and Huntington, 2000; Harrison, 2006; Harrison and Berger, 2006; Harrison and Kagan, 2006). Among the latter is a much more diverse group arguing either historically—that is, all cultures have ever been hybrid and open to change, even through the nation-state era—or more contemporarily—that is, new and more rapid flows of mediatized images and products as well as people are creating increasingly hybrid cultural identities—that there is a transnational culture in the making and that this transnational culture, now freed from nation-state constraint, has not only reactionary but also emancipatory possibilities (Beck, 1997; Scholte, 2000; Bhabha, 2005).

Both accounts, however, incorporate the nation-state ideal, the first in terms of cultural assimilation, the second in terms of cultural accommodation. Both, in other words, assume a similar goal of collective cultural solidarity, now global in extent, if along different paths: a sort of universal cosmopolitanism based on the one hand on cultural similarity and, on the other hand, on difference within a greater, reasonable unity of mutual endeavor. The third discourse at the newly emerged global level, however, is decidedly different in both substance and form. This is a non-Western, universal discourse of public religiosity, freeing itself, with the help of globalizing flows of people and information, from the Western nation-state project of secularism. This discourse has evolved most rapidly in those very unevenly successful colonial 'nation state' projects, but it is one that has truly global resonance as an alternative basis for global solidarity, even from within more successfully 'completed' nations of the rich North. Because the substance of this discourse—be it Islam, Hinduism, Sikhism, etc.—does not consider any separation among politics, economics, culture, and religion, its form is less conducive to a disconnect between scholarly and popular accounts. It is also a discourse, for this very reason, that speaks the language of traditional non-Western cultural belongingness much better than that of post-Enlightenment Western discourse. This newly globalized and spreading non-Western universal discourse, then, represents a truly alternative modernity in the making.

The discursive battle at the sub-state level—that is, the view 'downwards' from the nation-state—is less about substance and more about intent. Overall, the emerging discourse of post-nation-state collective identity and belonging is about a return, in varying ways, to more 'authentic' ethnic origins in the context of the existing international geopolitical context. That is, this is a 'return' to what are considered ethnic roots but with the goal of obtaining sovereign state status in a modern global, inter-nation-state community. So-called ancient hatreds so often invoked in commentaries on recent ethnic conflicts, are really nothing but more recent constructions within this modernist framework. Particularly in the rich North, this revitalized ethnic reconstruction is aimed at establishing fairer, post-nation-state representation and participation of these 'nations' within a larger 'multi-cultural' federation. This version has affinities with the universalizing post-Enlightenment views of greater collective solidarity among cultural differences. Particularly in the poor South, ethnic reconstruction is more exclusivist, veering toward racism and the profound belief in strict cultural borders enclosing blood-based homogeneity within and heterogeneity without. Both ethnic revivals share, however, a common bias in the understanding of an authentic, traditional, organic or blood-like collective cultural belongingness so that, even with the more 'Western' intent of the former, racism and ethnic cleansing are potentially active cultural resources on which such a discourse essentially draws, both in the richer North (e.g. Yugoslavia) and in the poorer South (e.g. Rwanda).

Competing Cultural Imaginaries and the Quest for Hegemony

These diverse discourses of imagined post-nation-state global cultural relations have real consequences in the world, and that is why it is absolutely necessary to continue to engage in discussions like the present one. It is also important to understand what the arena of discursive discussion consists of. As to this, we underscore again the disconnect between scholarly and popular imaginaries of globalization and cultural relations. The scholarly battle for more decent, anti-essentialist, even hybrid human understandings and relationships is meaningless if the streets remain essentialist. But it is also important to understand power relations in the construction and real instantiations of social imaginaries. As Hedetoft (2003, p. 91) reminds us:

> In the real world of politics and influence, certain nationalisms, certain cultures, certain ideas, certain interpretations are more transnationally powerful, assertive and successful than others. Where the less influential ones are not necessarily less self-congratulatory, they are certainly more inward-looking and always carry the label of national specificity. The more powerful ones (actually or in the making), on the other hand, tend toward a universality of meanings, impact and acceptance, as their national-cultural currency becomes transnationally adopted ... In this way, globalization is a very non-symmetrical process and constitutes anything but a level playing-field.

As Bartolovich (2002, pp. 12–13) says, in a world of so unevenly rich and poor, powerful and powerless, there are 'vast discrepancies in "being heard"' at the table at which the global cultural conversation is taking place. What she calls the 'dizzying disequilibria (of power, resources, social agency) exhibited in the contemporary world system are ... literally *irreducible* without closing the gaps in *material* inequalities among peoples'.

Of the two Western-oriented global imaginaries, by far the most powerful, in this respect, is neoliberalism which, according to Harvey (2006, pp. 145–146) and many others, has become common sense among post-Cold War political elites in both the rich North and the poor South. This discourse of 'private property rights, individual liberty, free markets and free trade' renders the political project for the state merely one of facilitating the spread of such practices, not, in our terms, of attenuating by politically embedding the nefarious social effects these practices inevitably engender. Hence, the expanding instantiation of neoliberal praxis is at the very core of the decline of nation-state cultural practice as a result of the intentional political disembedding of capitalist relations. The power of this discourse derives from the end of the Cold War—'won' by the capitalist West, to be sure—but also from the fact that, as Harvey contends, 'the advocates for the neoliberal way now occupy positions of considerable influence in education . . . in the media, in corporate boardrooms and financial institutions, in key state institutions . . . and also in those international institutions such as the IMF and the WTO that regulate global finance and trade'.

This economistic neoliberal discourse is being reinforced by that discourse engendered by the scholars and policy makers involved in the rehashing of modernization theory within the recently initiated scholarly/policy project generally entitled 'culture matters'. Harrison (2006), one of the (re)originators of this cultural discourse, asserts frankly that culture can be disaggregated into broad categories like 'worldview', 'values, virtues', 'economic behavior', and 'social behavior', and that, furthermore, all cultures can be examined according to whether they are 'progress-prone' or 'progress-resistant'. The explicit assumption is that those cultures which adopt Western cultural characteristics will be labeled the former while those which continue in their non-Western traditional ways will be labeled the latter. It is no wonder then that Huntington helped to found this 'culture matters' project its adaptation of his notion of a global 'clash of cultures'.

This neo-modernizing take on culture, however, runs into the same problem as the Enlightenment project of collective solidarity and the cultural legitimation of capitalist social relations. As Harvey (2006) makes clear, the neoliberal agenda, while highly successful in initiating the transformation of many a state, has not delivered on its promise of growing prosperity for all as global income and wealth has polarized and increasing numbers of people, in both poor and rich countries, have been economically marginalized as a result of such policies. In this respect, adopting 'progress-prone' cultural characteristics has resulted not in 'progress' but in cultural regress and increasing social fragmentation due to the increasing political disembedding of globalizing capitalist relations.

In the end, the intensifying global spread of neoliberal cultural characteristics of competitive individualism, privatism, secularism, materialism, and utilitarianism renders collective solidarity, let alone belongingness, the major social problem on both a global and local level. This is why, in addition to the loosening of the nation-state project's monopoly on it, there has been such a widespread 'cultural turn' in Western social sciences and humanities. Thus the major question that arises is: what will replace the nation-state cultural project of collective belonging and at what geopolitical scale?

At the global level, we think the best way to answer this question is to more thoroughly investigate the two evolving universalizing projects discussed so far: that is, first, the evolution of the continuing Western project, now embodied best, not in the actually cultureless, utilitarian 'culture matters' form, but in the form of the continuing regionalization of Europe and, to a lesser extent, North America and East Asia and, second, the alternative universalizing religious movements, best exemplified by globalizing Islam. To what extent has there been a growth in cultural affectation among European 'citizens' for the European Union, on what basis, to the exclusion of which groups, etc? In other words, the cultural characteristics of the European political–economic union must be better interrogated as the newest form of the nation-state project which, given the asymmetric power relations of the global political economy, has been adopted in other emerging 'regions' of the world.

A more thorough investigation of alternative modernities included in the discourse and practice of the universalizing religionist and particularizing ethnic movements is equally important. It is on this basis that we can find the lingering effects of the Western nation-state cultural project and possible alternatives for global and local cultural collectivity. These are modern, not traditional movements, and they include not just reactionary protestations but also hopeful future imaginaries, the latter largely ignored in the mostly Westernized literature on culture and globalization. It is necessary to reconsider how the confused nature of the nation-state project impacted different groups within designated state borders in both the colonial and the colonialized world. The current reactive side to these alternatively modern movements is a direct result of the imposition of the nation-state project and what Cocks (2002, p. 159), following Fanon (1963) and Berlin (1992), calls the 'historical experience of humiliation, resentment, and anxiety' of minoritized and colonialized groups sensing historically and, now, contemporarily 'a fear of impending loss'. This is another way to approach the issue of 'cultural anxiety' discussed above. Cocks discusses the main sources of this cultural humiliation that, we think, need more thorough investigation:

> The economic sources of group humiliation: domination by an imperial power for purposes of exploitation; the arrival of modernity in the form of a violent incursion from the outside; the uneven development of capitalism, with its greatest injuries for people and classes at the losing end of progress; the assault on rural life by the forces and agents of industrialization. The political sources: state conquest, state collapse, and state building, each inciting fears that one group will be stepped on and over by another, or that some groups will be stranded, stateless and rightless, out in the political cold. The social sources: the contempt of a more powerful ethnic, racial, or national group for a less powerful one; minor disparities between peoples living in close proximity, who seem more like than unlike one another to all eyes but their own; a sudden move by one population to tout itself as separate and unique, with boomerang effects on its neighbors. (Cocks, 2002, p. 159)

She goes on to describe other, historical and perceived, humiliations, the most important (for the present purposes) being the active construction of humiliation by elite culture brokers, not necessarily yet as gut-felt by most members of the group.

It was just this sort of cultural humiliation on the part of newly minoritized groups within new state borders that needed to be assuaged by 'nation' formation. This humiliation was not thoroughly assuaged even within the longer term national projects of the rich North, to say nothing of the very young, very unevenly instituted projects of the poor South. These latter projects included the imperial imposition and enforcement of 'national' majority/minority or power/powerless formation within borders drawn by Western outsiders so that, once this imperial imposition was withdrawn, suppressed humiliations erupted in active conflict, even well before the current phase of intensive globalization. The key here, however, as Cocks (2002, pp. 160–161) points out, is that 'humiliation' is an *emotion*, heartfelt and fully absorbed, that cannot be assuaged on the basis of reason alone. Here, then, we have come full circle to the very necessity of confusion in the birth of the modern Western imagining of cultural nationhood: Romantic, embodied, humanism actually must needs be merged with Enlightenment rationalism in order to ensure collective solidarity of both cultural humiliators and humiliated alike within designated state boundaries. By such a diversion of emotional attention, over time, the latter must be enculturally assuaged in order to feel any sort of cultural belongingness with the oppressing former.

Humiliation, in this respect, is an emotion felt mostly as a loss of social respect, social prestige, social power practically manifested in the loss of control over one's, or one's cultural group's, destiny. The contemporary onslaught of neoliberal globalizing forces and the concomitant transformation of nation-state functions upward and downward necessarily signals a rapidly growing context of humiliation (or cultural liberation and a reactive scramble to regroup) based on what Cocks suggests above is an 'impending sense of loss' of control over the processes most affecting individual and collective lives. As Mittelman (2004, p. 15) argues, for 'many people, a major propellant of resistance is experiencing neoliberal globalization as a loss in the degree of control—for some actors, however little to begin with—exercised locally', that is, in their day-to-day lives. Major changes in individual and collective lives are being affected by decisions made elsewhere without any input from those most affected by such decisions. Is it any wonder that many, even scholars, as Marston *et al.* point out, see 'globalization' as a giant force that comes from without, or that individual and group alienation and humiliation as well as reactive liberationist revenge might be on the rise in today's world?

Finally, it needs to be underscored again that the alternative modernities enunciated by universalizing religionist imaginaries and particularist ethnic imaginaries are not just reactions to Western modernity. They may also be positive projections of the proper basis for good individual and collective lives that can be quite different from that projected by the Western capitalist culture-nation imaginary. Particularly in a time of growing uncertainty, these alternative, equally modern, imaginaries possess advantages, as Smith (2001, p. 37) quite rightly underscores, 'denied to other modes of national identification', that is, 'a definite standard of authenticity, a clear criterion of communal belonging and a powerful basis for a sense of collective destiny' both, we would add, in this life and the next. As Melucci (1989) similarly points out, such alternative imaginaries raise important questions about the rights of cultural collectivities to be different, to develop autonomously on the basis of different social norms and goals, even if in the minority, locally or globally:

> The 'innovative' components of ethno-nationalist movements, albeit a minority issue bound up with their struggle against discrimination and for political rights, also has a predominantly cultural character. The ethnic appeal launches its challenge to complex societies on such fundamental questions as the goals of change and the production of identity and meaning ... Difference is thereby given a voice which speaks of problems which transverse the whole of society. (Melucci, 1989, p. 92)

While both Smith and Melucci make specific reference to renewed ethnic claims, we would argue that the same 'innovative' characteristics pertain to more universal religionist imaginaries on a more global scale.

Unfortunately, these imaginary projections come through the glass darkly in the globally hegemonic Westernized imaginary, which generally perceives Others through the lens of itself. 'Cultures' only 'matter' to the extent that they are like the West. Of vital importance in today's globalizing world is thus to clear this glass and switch lenses, so that alternatively modern imaginaries can be seen more clearly and considered more deeply as potential alternatives to globally hegemonic Western neoliberalized cultural discourse and praxis. This can only happen, however, if we allow these other imaginary spaces to emerge and instantiate and the voices of those who adopt them to be better heard, both from the heights of non-Western scholarship and from the popular streets below.

Towards the Construction of a New, Global Cultural Cartography

Translating the foregoing attempt to establish a new, global post-nation-state-international cultural imaginary into a specific research program must needs be tentative, much like this imaginary itself. As mentioned in the Introduction to this volume, the specific papers published here come at the problem of globalization and culture both from identifiable disciplinary angles and with their own imaginaries, some, like Marston *et al.*, Nederveen Pieterse, and Schmidt, explicitly so, others less explicitly. As already suggested, these different imaginaries can be considered, quite broadly, as being either more global, like that of Marcuse and Wilson, or more global–local, like that of Marston *et al.* and Nederveen Pieterse, or more local–global, like that of Price and Schmidt. Each paper presents important empirical details about the ways in which cultural relations are changing in the wake of globalization, in both the rich North and the poor South.

Within this broad categorization of the results of this attempted transdisciplinary project, this final essay obviously takes its lead from the more theoretical investigations of Marston *et al.* and Nederveen Pieterse, as a means to provide a more comprehensive context for the efforts all of our authors have put forth. We have adopted the term 'imaginary' in lieu of what some of our contributors call 'ontology', because it suggests something less abstractly technical and closed. We have, however, taken a more singularly theoretical path toward our objective than the latter author. Nevertheless, all of the interventions published here add to this emerging imaginary, as this itself remains as unfinished as the cultural characteristics of the rapidly transforming post-nation-state-international world. The key is that such an imaginary-in-the-making should be considered not just an unfinished project—there is no forced consensus here—but also as an intervention in the ongoing struggle for hegemony among (similar) imaginaries, both scholarly and on the street, with very uneven power to be instantiated, globally and locally.

Having said this, there are several specific epistemological entailments that we consider to have emerged on the basis of our evolving imaginary and this is where all the papers in this special issue play a central role, both theoretically and empirically. The post-nation-state-international imaginary recognizes explicitly that the forces of globalization are leading to a transformation of states, thereby underscoring theoretically what Marcuse and Wilson elaborate more empirically with regard to art policy in New York City and urban development in the mid-western United States, respectively. Such global forces are being felt strongly, according to these accounts, in the richest, most powerful 'nation state' in the world. The suggestion here is that more investigation of the impact of global flows on US state power (illegal immigration, NAFTA regionalization, etc.) would provide a clearer picture of the precise nature of these global forces potentially transforming all states, especially the much less powerful.

Similarly, we suggest the way to imagine the evolving transformation of the nation-state cultural functions and regulation, as either an 'upward' move to global or regional institutions, or a 'downward' move to sub-state, even urban institutions. Marcuse's and Wilson's papers have something to say about this latter, but we believe that Marston *et al.*'s and Nederveen Pieterse's papers speak more directly to the unfinished 'fixity' of these new culturally regulatory spaces. Marston *et al.* are very explicit about this, as they explore the shortcomings of the most prominent 'ontologies' of globalization writ large as a means to arrive at what they consider to be the need to investigate specific 'sites' of intersecting globality–locality, like Nollywood, to know what 'globalization' actually entails. Similarly, Nederveen Pieterse's theorized empirical examples of cultural hybridity and its uses, both on a macro-scale of politico-religious conflict and on a micro-scale of individual identity, overwhelmingly suggests a cultural world in flux, with fixity a matter of political will, but not an inevitability at any specific spatial scale. Indeed, these accounts of cultural flux and flow and the investigation thereof have contributed greatly to our own understanding of what we call the 'structured coherences' of global cultural characteristics.

Finally, our developing imaginary suggests that there is a serious disconnect between emerging scholarly takes on nation, culture, ethnicity, race, and individual identity and the more popular takes evolving in the streets. Our first cut at this disconnect considered the more and more widely accepted anti-essentialism of the former and yet the prevailing essentialism of the latter. Our imaginary suggests a similar disconnect between Westernized scholarship on globalization and culture and possible alternative imaginaries. The work of both Price and Schmidt helps to transcend these disconnects by listening more carefully to the streets and paying more careful empirical attention to the ways in which 'global' neoliberal forces are made use of by different people in different places in, perhaps, non-neoliberal ways. The key here, in both cases, is to try to get at how the 'street' actually is impacted by global forces, what is made of these on the street, and how knowledge of this gets us closer to determining possible alternatively modern counter-hegemonic cultural globalizations and localizations.

Our conclusion has been an attempt to combine the insights of all the contributors into a more comprehensive theoretical framework. As to this, it is clear that the Western neoliberal cultural project is hegemonically powerful in both its enunciation and instantiation, given the globalization of capitalism and its ideological baggage via the global standardization of economic and business education as well as public policy (Chorev, 2005; Harvey, 2006; Soederberg, *et al.*, 2005). However, as our contributors suggest this hegemonic discursive power is far from being completely successful either in forcing discursive closure, even among Westernized scholar-elites, or in its acceptance and instantiation on the culturally varied streets of the world. Similarly, on the streets of Amsterdam and Miami, in Africa's Nollywood, and among the Hñähñu of Clearwater/ Hidalgo, such 'global forces' are culturally refracted by the 'recipients' turning them into resources potentially quite different from those 'sent'. Indeed, the overall message of our papers is that *this refraction itself is really what cultural globalization is*, not the coverage of the world with cultural standardization and homogenization, no matter how powerful the discursive and material forces behind these processes may seem to be.

In the end, more specific implications of our post-nation-state-international cultural imaginary could serve as a preliminary foundation for further transdisciplinary research. First, much more needs to be known about the 'success' of the original cultural-national projects in real existing states and, then, how precisely these quite varyingly 'completed' projects have been transformed as a result of global pressure. Second, the cultural implications of the transformation of nation-state functions and regulations are still quite unevenly known empirically, particularly the extent to which new institutional fixes at the supra- and sub-state level may have emerged to take the place of the nation state. At the supra-state level, more investigation of the *cultural* implications of the European Union, and alternative religionist universalisms, would pay great dividends, as would that of the cultural implications—both positive and negative or reactive and progressive—of ethnic particularisms (see Weiler, 2000, for a start at the former).

What needs to be kept uppermost in our imaginary is that the cultural implications of globalization are in as much flux as globalization itself. The discourse of neoliberal globalization has not yet been successfully instantiated, a fact which should be ever kept in mind as a rallying call for alternative discourses in the hegemonic struggle. It suggests that the cultural implications of globalization can only be fully understood by taking these more macro-processual imaginings 'to the streets' to determine how (or, indeed, whether) they actually play themselves out in popular discourse and practice. What we suggest is that while the world may be a 'world of flows', as Appadurai (2000b, 1996; see also Castells, 1996) argues, these flows are not and, in fact, cannot be 'deterritorialized' as is often asserted. This notion suggests the lingering imaginary of the fixed nation-state/territory cultural nexus is now somehow 'transcended'. Rather, cultural relations are being reterritorialized, if quite away from this particular nation-state space–time cultural envelope. Whether this reterritorialization is best imagined as a 'site', as Marston *et al.* argue, or, as we argue, a structured coherence of unevenly powerful flows, is open to debate. The point is that what Appadurai calls the 'disjunctural flows' of 'ethnoscapes', 'financescapes', 'technoscapes', etc. that constitute contemporary globalization always are instantiated in inevitably varying ways in particular 'places', as these places themselves are constituted by particular confluences of these flows.

Nollywood, in this respect, is less an African, 'Nigerian' or ethnic phenomenon, and more a global–local one, as more global cultural forces reterritorialize *with* more local cultural forces at this particular 'site'. However, the significance of calling this reterritorialization of local and global flows a 'structured coherence' of cultural forces is, we suggest, twofold. First, this imaginary implies a structurating reterritorialization of global–local cultural flows, but without the implication of complete closure to these reterritorializing flows. Following Appadurai (2000b), the emphasis here is on imagining a 'process geography' of ongoing cultural relations instead of one based, as is usually the case, on more fixed cultural 'traits'. Second, and following from this, imagining a structurating coherence of cultural relations directly necessitates determining by what means, processes, group and individual behaviors such a spatial 'coherence' has come about. This puts the focus on the need for more precise investigation of how global and local flows intersect, and on how they become structured one way and not another: why is it, for example, that certain global flows, like mediatized filmmaking, are more ascendant in Nollywood and not other places? Who were the main global–local agents of this ascendance? And who, if anyone, was against it? Or why has a certain religious imaginary like Islam become ascendant in some parts of Amsterdam and not other parts of the city, or other places in Europe, in the same way? (Or has it? And in what ways?) The point here is that investigating the ongoing structuration entailed in the reterritorialization of cultural relations necessitates a close critical look both at how scholars have imagined this process and at how this reterritorialization is being imagined and instantiated in the streets. Much more needs to be heard directly from those global–local agents now in the process of structuring Nollywood, or parts of Amsterdam, or the local–global agents of Hidalgo/ Clearwater and Miami, as relatively coherent reterritorializations of cultural relations. Is the global–local imaginary being employed by these agents the same way as that imputed to them by third-person scholarly observers?

Finally, this attempt to bring voice to the globalization of cultural relations in the streets also entails a greater sensitivity to alternatively modern cultural imaginaries, both more globally and more locally oriented. Paying greater attention to these not only helps with critically thinking through and perhaps beyond the Western nation-state/capitalism imaginary but also about the real cultural implications of a shrinking human world. As Cocks (2002, p. 164) puts it so well, successfully 'transcending' the Western 'development metaphors' entailed in imaginaries like the 'culture matters' group would mean that:

> the route to and meaning of well-being would no longer be equated with an objective process of development along Western or American lines. In the absence of that equation, the whole world would be able to embark on a truly open-ended consideration of the classical political philosophical questions: 'What is the good life?' and 'What is the good society?' But if these questions must no

longer be answered by a single country or region for the rest, neither can they any longer be answered by each country or region solely for itself. Given the intensified intermingling of peoples and cultures, in combination with the compelling but incompatible values that have managed to survive on earth thus far, questions of political philosophy are most fertilely addressed by all ways of life in vigorous conversation with each other.

The main question in this context, as Cocks continues quite rightly, is how might a cultural conversation like this 'become genuinely reciprocal?' In answer to this, surely the first important gesture must be toward allowing and, in fact, facilitating alternative, equally modern, cultural voices not usually heard, or not usually heard in a positive way, to be heard as more equal partners in the fast becoming post-nation-state-international cultural conversation or dialogue and (global–local) praxis.

References

Anderson, B. (1983) *Imagined Communities* (London: Verso).

Appadurai, A. (1996) *Modernity at Large: Cultural Dimensions of Globalization* (Minneapolis, MN: University of Minnesota Press).

Appadurai, A. (2000a) The grounds of the nation-state: identity, violence and territory, in: K. Goldmann, U. Hannerz & C. Westin (Eds) *Nationalism and Internationalism in the Post-Cold War Era* (New York: Routledge).

Appadurai, A. (2000b) Grassroots globalization and the research imagination, *Public Culture*, 12, pp. 1–19.

Arthurs, A. (2003) Social imaginaries and global realities, *Public Culture*, 15, pp. 579–586.

Bartolovich, C. (2002) Introduction: Marxism, modernity, and postcolonial studies, in: C. Bartolovich & N. Lazarus (Eds) *Marxism, Modernity and Postcolonial Studies* (Cambridge: Cambridge University Press).

Bauman, G. (1999) *The Multicultural Riddle: Rethinking National, Ethnic, and Religious Ideas* (New York: Routledge)

Beck, U. (1997) *The Reinvention of Politics: Rethinking Modernity in the Global Social Order* (Oxford: Polity Press).

Beckert, J. (2002) *Beyond the Market: The Social Foundations of Economic Efficiency* (Princeton, NJ: Princeton University Press).

Berlin, I. (1992) *The Crooked Timber of Humanity* (New York: Vintage).

Bhabha, H. K. (2005) *The Location of Culture* (New York: Routledge).

Bobbit, P. (2002) *The Shield of Achilles: War, Peace, and the Course of History* (New York: Alfred A. Knopf).

Boyer, R. (1986) *La Theorie de la Regulation: Une analyse critique* (Paris: La Decouverte).

Boyer, R. & Y. Saillard (Eds) (1995) *Theorie de la régulation: L'état des saviors* (Paris: La Decouverte).

Brenner, N., Jessop, B., Jones, M. & Macleod, G. (Eds) (2003) *State/Space: A Reader* (Malden, MA: Blackwell Publishing).

Castells, M. (1996) *The Rise of Network Society* (Oxford: Blackwell).

Castoriadis, C. (1987) *The Imaginary Institution of Society* (Cambridge, MA: MIT Press).

Chorev, N. (2005) The institutional project of neo-liberal globalism: the case of the WTO, *Theory and Society*, 34, pp. 317–355.

Cocks, J. (2002) *Passion and Paradox: Intellectuals Confront the National Question* (Princeton, NJ: Princeton University Press).

Delanty, G. & O'Mahony, P. (2002) *Nationalism and Social Theory* (London: Sage).

Eagleton, T. (1991) *The Ideology of the Aesthetic* (Oxford: Blackwell).

Eagleton, T. (2000) *The Idea of Culture* (Oxford: Blackwell).

Fanon, F. (1963) *The Wretched of the Earth* (New York: Grove).

Friedman, J. (2002) From roots to routes: tropes for trippers, *Anthropological Theory*, 2, pp. 21–36.

Fukuyama, F. (Ed.) (2006) *Nation-Building: Beyond Afghanistan and Iraq* (Baltimore, MD: Johns Hopkins University Press).

Gaonkar, D. P. (2002) Toward new imaginaries: an introduction, *Public Culture*, 14, pp. 1–19.

Grillo, R. D. (2003) Cultural essentialism and cultural anxiety, *Anthropological Theory*, 3, pp. 157–173.

Harrison, L. E. (2006) *The Central Liberal Truth: How Politics Can Change a Culture and Save it from Itself* (New York: Oxford University Press).

Harrison, L. E. & Berger, P. L. (Eds) (2006) *Developing Cultures: Case Studies* (New York: Routledge).

Harrison, L. E. & Huntington, S. P. (Eds) (2000) *Culture Matters: How Values Shape Human Progress* (New York: Basic Books).

Harrison, L. E. & Kagan, J. (Eds) (2006) *Developing Cultures: Essays on Cultural Change* (New York: Routledge).

Harvey, D. (2006) Neo-liberalism as creative destruction, *Geografishe Annaler*, 88b, pp. 145–158.

Hedetoft, U. (2003) *The Global Turn: National Encounters with the World* (Copenhagen: Aalborg University Press).

Held, D. & McGrew, A. (Eds) (2002) *Governing Globalization: Power, Authority, and Global Governance* (Cambridge: Polity Press).

Held, D., McGrew, A. Goldblatt, D. & Perraton, J. (Eds) (1999) *Global Transformations* (Cambridge: Polity Press).

Herder, J. G. (1969) *Herder and Social and Political Culture: A Selection of Texts* (Cambridge: Cambridge University Press).

Hobsbawm, E. (1990) *Nations and Nationalism since 1780* (Cambridge: Cambridge University Press).

Hobsbawm, E. & Ranger, T. (1983) *The Invention of Tradition* (Cambridge: Cambridge University Press).

Jessop, B. (2002) *The Future of the Capitalist State* (Cambridge: Polity Press).

Kedourie, E. (1993) *Nationalism* (Oxford: Blackwell).

King, A. D. (1997) Introduction: spaces of culture, spaces of knowledge, in: A. D. King (Ed.) *Culture, Globalization and the World System* (Minneapolis, MN: University of Minnesota Press).

Melucci, A. (1989) *Nomads of the Present* (London: Hutchinson Radius).

Mittelman, J. H. (2004) *Whither Globalization? The Vortex of Knowledge and Ideology* (London: Routledge).

Nederveen Pieterse, J. (2004) *Globalization and Culture: Global Melange* (Lanham, MD: Rowman & Littlefield).

Polanyi, K. (1944) *The Great Transformation: The Political and Economic Origins of Our Time* (Boston: Beacon Press).

Scholte, J. A. (2000) *Globalization* (New York: St. Martin's Press).

Soederberg, S., Menz, G. & Cerny, P. G. (Eds) (2005) *Internalizing Globalization: The Rise of Neoliberalism and the Decline of National Varieties of Capitalism* (Basingstoke: Palgrave MacMillan).

Smith, A. D. (1986) *The Ethnic Origins of Nationalism* (Oxford: Blackwell).

Smith, A. D. (2001) *Nationalism: Theory, Ideology, History* (Cambridge: Polity Press).

Swyngedouw, E. (1997) Excluding the other: the production of scale and scaled politics, in: R. Lee & J. Wills (Eds) *Geographies of Economies* (London: Arnold).

Thompson, E. P. (1997) *The Romantics: England in a Revolutionary Age* (New York: New Press).

Weiler, J. H. H. (2000) To be a European citizen: Eros and civilization, in: K. Goldmann, U. Hannerz & C. Westin (Eds) *Nationalism and Internationalism in the Post-Cold War Era* (New York: Routledge), pp. 170–194.

Kevin Archer is former chair of the Department of Geography at the University of South Florida. He received his Ph.D. degree from The Johns Hopkins University. His research interests include globalizing cities and socio-spatial polarization as well as the production of post-industrial nature. Archer is co-editor of and contributor in *Relocating Global Cities: From the Center to the Margins* (Rowman & Littlefield, 2006).

M. Martin Bosman is Associate Professor in the Department of Geography at the University of South Florida. He received his MA (Geography) from the University of Natal in the Republic of South Africa and his Ph.D. (Geography) from the University of Kentucky in 1999. He has published widely on the geography of the digital divide and his current research is on globalization and newly emerging city regions. Bosman is assistant editor of *Globalizations* and co-editor of and contributor to *Relocating Global Cities: From the Center to the Margins* (Rowman & Littlefield, 2006).

M. Mark Amen is Academic Programs Director for the Kiran C. Patel Center for Global Solutions at the University of South Florida and has been a member of the faculty in the Department of Government and International Affairs since 1982. He received his doctorate in Political Science from the Graduate Institute of International Studies (Geneva, Switzerland) in 1978 and his research interests are in global political economy, theories of the state, and globalizing cities. Amen is deputy editor of *Globalizations* and co-editor of and contributor to *Relocating Global Cities: From the Center to the Margins* (Rowman & Littlefield, 2006).

Ella Schmidt is Assistant Professor in the Interdisciplinary Social Sciences Program at USF St. Petersburg. She received her MA in Cultural Anthropology from the Université Paris VII-Jussieu and her Ph.D. from the University of California at Davis. She has done research on Mexican farmworkers in West Central Florida and changes in their construction of identity. Currently her research focuses on transnational Mexican migrants in Clearwater and Valle del Mezquital, Hidalgo, Mexico and the creation of new social formations in both home and host communities.

Index

For Product Safety Concerns and Information please contact our EU
representative GPSR@taylorandfrancis.com
Taylor & Francis Verlag GmbH, Kaufingerstraße 24, 80331 München, Germany

* 9 7 8 0 4 1 5 4 9 5 6 8 4 *